# Microsoft® SQL Server 2005™ For Dummies®

Cheat Sheet

KT-512-305

| Datatype | Description |
|---|---|
| bigint | Stores whole numbers in the range –9,223,372,036,854,775,808 to +9,223,372,036,854,775, 807. Each `bigint` stored requires 8 bytes. |
| binary(n) | Stores binary data of specified length. The length is from 1 to 8,000 bytes. |
| bit | Stores 0 and 1. The string values TRUE are converted to 1, and FALSE to 0. If there are 1 to 8 bit columns in a table, they are stored in 1 byte. If there are 9 to 16 bit columns in a table, they are stored as 2 bytes. |
| char(n) | Stores non-Unicode character data of a specified length. The length is in the range from 1 to 8,000. |
| cursor | Stores variables or stored procedure output parameters that contain a reference to a cursor. |
| datetime | Stores values representing a date and time of day. This datatype stores values representing January 1, 1753 to December 31, 9999. Accuracy is to 3.33 milliseconds. |
| decimal(p,s) | Stores numeric values with fixed precision and scale. Precision is 1 to 38, with a default of 18. Scale is the maximum number of decimal digits that can be stored to the right of the decimal point. Storage is between 5 and 17 bytes. |
| float(n) | Stores floating point numeric values in the range of –1.79E+308 to –2.23E-308, 0 and 2.23E-308 to 1.79E+308. Each float value stored requires 8 bytes. |
| image | Stored variable length binary data. Now deprecated. Use `varbinary(max)` in new development work. |
| int | Stores whole numbers in the range –2,147,483,648 to +2,147,483,647. Each `int` stored requires 4 bytes. |
| money | Stores values that represent money in the range of –922,337,203,685,477.5808 to +922,337,203,685,477.5807 |
| nchar(n) | Stores Unicode strings of specified length. Each character takes 2 bytes. The length of the string is 1 to 4,000 characters. |
| ntext | Stores variable length Unicode data. Now deprecated. Use `nvarchar(max)` in new development work. |
| numeric | Same as the decimal type. Stores numeric values with fixed precision and scale. Precision is 1 to 38, with a default of 18. Scale is the maximum number of decimal digits that can be stored to the right of the decimal point. Storage is between 5 and 17 bytes. |
| nvarchar(n) | Stores variable length Unicode strings. Each character is stored in 2 bytes. The length is 1 to 4,000 characters. |

*(continued)*

## For Dummies: Bestselling Book Series for Beginners

# Microsoft® SQL Server 2005™ For Dummies®

Cheat Sheet

*(continued)*

| Datatype | Description |
|---|---|
| nvarchar(max) | New in SQL Server 2005. Each Unicode character is stored in 2 bytes. Stores variable length Unicode strings up to 2^31–1 bytes. |
| real(n) | Stores floating point numeric values in the range of –3.4E+38 to –1.18E-38, 0, and 1.18E-38 to 3.40E+38. |
| smalldatetime | Stores values representing a date and time of day. This datatype stores values representing January 1, 1900 to June 6, 2079. Accuracy is to 1 minute. |
| smallint | Stores whole numbers in the range –32,768 to +32,767. Each smallint stored requires 2 bytes. |
| smallmoney | Stores values that represent money in the range –214,748.3648 to +214,748.3647. |
| sql_variant | Stores values of any SQL Server 2005 datatype except text, ntext, image, timestamp, and sql_variant. |
| table | Stores the results of queries temporarily for later processing. |
| text | Stores variable length non-unicode data. Now deprecated. Use varchar(max) in new development work. |
| timestamp | Stores automatically generated unique binary values. Typically, this datatype is used to version table rows. |
| tinyint | Stores whole numbers in the range 0 to 255. Each tinyint stored requires 1 byte. |
| uniqueidentifier | Stores 16 byte values that are GUIDs (globally unique identifiers). |
| varbinary(n) | Stores variable length binary data. The length is in the range 1 to 8,000 bytes. |
| varbinary(max) | New in SQL Server 2005. Stores variable length binary data be up to 2^31–1 bytes. |
| varchar(n) | Stores variable length character data. The length is from 1 to 8,000. |
| varchar(max) | New in SQL Server 2005. Stores variable length character data of length up to 2^31–1 bytes. |
| xml | New in SQL Server 2005. Stores XML data. |

Copyright © 2006 Wiley Publishing, Inc. All rights reserved.

Item 7755-7.

For more information about Wiley Publishing, call 1-800-762-2974.

## For Dummies: Bestselling Book Series for Beginners

*Microsoft*®

## *SQL Server*™ *2005*

### FOR

# DUMMIES®

## ONE WEEK LOAN

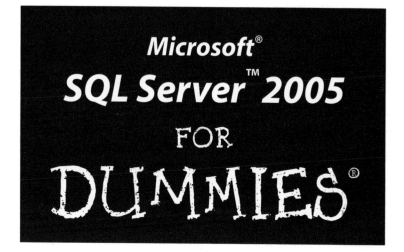

# Microsoft® SQL Server™ 2005 FOR DUMMIES®

by Andrew Watt

WILEY

Wiley Publishing, Inc.

**Microsoft® SQL Server™ 2005 For Dummies®**

Published by
**Wiley Publishing, Inc.**
111 River Street
Hoboken, NJ 07030-5774

www.wiley.com

Copyright © 2006 by Wiley Publishing, Inc., Indianapolis, Indiana

Published by Wiley Publishing, Inc., Indianapolis, Indiana

Published simultaneously in Canada

For general information on our other products and services, please contact our Customer Care Department within the U.S. at 800-762-2974, outside the U.S. at 317-572-3993, or fax 317-572-4002.

For technical support, please visit www.wiley.com/techsupport.

Wiley also publishes its books in a variety of electronic formats. Some content that appears in print may not be available in electronic books.

Library of Congress Control Number: 2005935163

ISBN-13: 978-0-7645-7755-0

ISBN-10: 0-7645-7755-7

Manufactured in the United States of America

10 9 8 7 6 5 4 3 2

1O/RT/QR/QW/IN

WILEY

# About the Author

**Andrew Watt** wrote his first computer programs in 1985. He is an independent consultant, experienced author, and Microsoft MVP (Most Valuable Professional). His areas of interest and expertise include XML, Microsoft InfoPath 2003, and SQL Server 2005.

Andrew first used SQL Server in version 7.0 and has been an active participant in the SQL Server 2005 beta program since August 2003.

Among the books Andrew has written, or co-written, are *Beginning Regular Expressions*, *Beginning XML*, 3rd Edition, *Beginning RSS & Atom Programming*, *Professional XML*, 2nd Edition and *Designing SVG Web Graphics*.

Andrew is often to be seen answering questions in Microsoft's SQL Server newsgroups and other newsgroups. Feel free to get involved in the community there. He can be contacted at `SVGDeveloper@aol.com`. Due to the volume of e-mail he receives, he can't guarantee a response to every e-mail.

# Dedication

To Jonathan, Stephen, Hannah, Jeremy, Peter, and Naomi. Each a very special human being to me.

# Author's Acknowledgments

Every technical book is the product of teamwork and this book is no exception. I particularly want to thank the technical editor, Stephen Giles. Stephen came up with many good suggestions for additional material but, unfortunately, there wasn't space to accept more than a few of them. It would be nice if somebody invented elastic paper. Until then, books are limited to being of a fixed size.

I would also like to thank my two acquisition editors on this book: Terri Varveris and Tiffany Franklin. Terri had the most productive summer of the whole team, ending it with a loveable new son. Thanks to Tiffany for her patience as time slipped. Isn't that supposed to happen only in science fiction books?

It's been great working with Nicole Sholly, my project editor, who has done so much to move the project forward to a successful conclusion. I would also like to thank Rebecca Senninger, copy editor, whose attention to detail picked up a few of those little errors that the rest of us had missed.

Thanks to all the team. It has been a good experience for me working with you all.

## Publisher's Acknowledgments

We're proud of this book; please send us your comments through our online registration form located at www.dummies.com/register/.

Some of the people who helped bring this book to market include the following:

### Acquisitions, Editorial, and Media Development

**Project Editor:** Nicole Sholly

**Acquisitions Editors:** Tiffany Franklin, Terri Varveris

**Copy Editor:** Rebecca Senninger

**Technical Editor:** Stephen Giles

**Editorial Manager:** Kevin Kirschner

**Media Development Specialists:** Angela Denny, Kate Jenkins, Steven Kudirka, Kit Malone, Travis Silvers

**Media Development Coordinator:** Laura Atkinson

**Media Project Supervisor:** Laura Moss

**Media Development Manager:** Laura VanWinkle

**Editorial Assistant:** Amanda Foxworth

**Cartoons:** Rich Tennant (www.the5thwave.com)

### Composition Services

**Project Coordinator:** Kathryn Shanks

**Layout and Graphics:** Carl Byers, Andrea Dahl, Joyce Haughey, Barbara Moore

**Proofreaders:** Leeann Harney, Jessica Kramer, Joe Niesen, TECHBOOKS Production Services

**Indexer:** TECHBOOKS Production Services

---

**Publishing and Editorial for Technology Dummies**

**Richard Swadley,** Vice President and Executive Group Publisher

**Andy Cummings,** Vice President and Publisher

**Mary Bednarek,** Executive Acquisitions Director

**Mary C. Corder,** Editorial Director

**Publishing for Consumer Dummies**

**Diane Graves Steele,** Vice President and Publisher

**Joyce Pepple,** Acquisitions Director

**Composition Services**

**Gerry Fahey,** Vice President of Production Services

**Debbie Stailey,** Director of Composition Services

# Contents at a Glance

# Table of Contents

# Introduction

$W$elcome to the world of SQL Server 2005. I am excited by the many new capabilities of SQL Server 2005 and I hope that you are too.

SQL Server 2005 is the new edition of Microsoft's SQL Server client-server relational database. It's a major release; the first in five years. SQL Server 2005 has many new features that help you manage a relational database and, in many editions, adds important new business intelligence functionality.

SQL Server 2005, quite simply, is bigger and better than SQL Server 2000. It offers functionality and pricing to help businesses of many sizes handle their crucial business data more effectively and more efficiently. No, I am not a Microsoft marketing person. It's quite simply true that a lot of new features and tools in SQL Server 2005 can help you look after your data.

SQL Server 2005 comes in several different editions:

- ✔ **Enterprise:** Has the full functionality to support scalability and availability needed by large enterprises. It supports an unlimited number of CPUs. In addition, it has the full suite of Business Intelligence functionality.

- ✔ **Standard:** Supports up to 4 CPUs. Has only some Business Intelligence functionality; for example, it includes only basic Integration Services transforms.

- ✔ **Workgroup:** It has limited Business Intelligence support. No Analysis Services or Integration Services support. No Web services support.

- ✔ **Developer:** Has all the functionality included in Enterprise Edition, but it is not licensed for production use.

- ✔ **Mobile:** Microsoft's mobile database solution. The successor to SQL Server CE.

- ✔ **Express:** A low-end free database with maximum 4GB database size. The successor to MSDE. No full-text search. This edition is not covered in this book, but another book — *Microsoft SQL Server 2005 Express For Dummies,* by Robert Schneider (Wiley) — is dedicated to it.

At the time of writing a full feature comparison of the editions of SQL Server 2005 is at www.microsoft.com/sql/prodinfo/features/compare-features.mspx.

# *About This Book*

SQL Server 2005 is huge. No book of this size can hope to cover it all. I have had to make choices about the topics to include in this book to help you understand how SQL Server works and how to use a range of its functionality.

Here are some of the things you can do with this book:

- ✔ Find out how to use SQL Server Management Studio, the new management tool in SQL Server 2005 that replaces Enterprise Manager and Query Analyzer.
- ✔ Create databases and tables.
- ✔ Retrieve data from a SQL Server database.
- ✔ Create maintenance plans.
- ✔ Create an Integration Services project.
- ✔ Create a simple Analysis Services project.
- ✔ Use Reporting Services.

# *Foolish Assumptions*

I make a few assumptions about what you already know. I assume that you know how to read. Without that skill, this book won't be much use to you.

I assume you know how to turn your computer on and off, and how to use a mouse and a keyboard.

More important, I also assume that you have installed SQL Server 2005 in a way that suits your circumstances. SQL Server 2005 has so many ways that you can install it that I could have used half the book to cover all the possibilities.

If you haven't installed SQL Server 2005 yet, you can access SQL Server Books Online, the official documentation set, on the Microsoft Web site. As I write this they haven't been released but it looks likely they will be at `www.microsoft.com/technet/prodtechnol/sql/2005/downloads/books.mspx`. If not, a Google search for **SQL Server 2005 Books Online site:microsoft.com** finds the online documents for the final release build.

The setup utility for SQL Server 2005 is pretty self-explanatory. If you choose the correct operating system to install on and read the hardware requirements, then you're in good shape.

If you've installed all components of the Developer Edition, you have the components to work through every step-by-step example in this book.

# Conventions Used in This Book

By conventions, I simply mean I've implemented certain formatting to convey that whatever text is treated in a special way means something to you. For instance, anything **bolded** denotes user entry — that is, it's for you to type somewhere. Anything formatted in `monofont` is a URL, an e-mail address, or lines of code. *Italics* highlight a new term that I've defined in the context of SQL Server 2005.

# How This Book Is Organized

*Microsoft SQL Server 2005 For Dummies* is split into seven parts. You don't have to read it sequentially, and you don't even have to read all the sections in any particular chapter. You can use the Table of Contents and the Index to find the information you need and quickly get your answer. In this section, I briefly describe what you find in each part.

## Part I: SQL Server 2005: An Overview

In Chapters 1 and 2, I give you a high-level view of what SQL Server 2005 does and cover the new features that Microsoft has added in this version.

In Chapter 3, I show you how to find your way around the new management tool, SQL Server Management Studio.

## Part II: Basic Operations

You find out how to create databases and tables and how to retrieve information from SQL Server 2005 databases.

You also find out how to create a simple Visual Studio 2005 application to retrieve information from SQL Server 2005.

## Part III: Working with SQL Server

This part covers XML in SQL Server 2005 and the new CLR (Common Language Runtime) functionality.

I also show you how to create stored procedures and handle errors in your code.

# Part IV: Protecting Your Data

Turn to this part to do the following tasks:

- ✔ Secure your data
- ✔ Prevent data loss
- ✔ Maintain your installation
- ✔ Create triggers

# Part V: Administering a SQL Server System

In this part, I cover the following topics:

- ✔ Configure your SQL Server installation
- ✔ Use SQL Server Agent
- ✔ Set up Notification Services
- ✔ Replication
- ✔ Use SQL Server Service Broker

# Part VI: Using SQL Server Business Intelligence (BI) Services

I explain the new Integrate, Analyze, Report paradigm in Business Intelligence. You can create solutions by using SQL Server Integration Services, Analysis Services, and Reporting Services.

# Part VII: The Part of Tens

In this part, I point you towards other resources and tools that you can use with SQL Server 2005.

## About the Web site

Because I wanted to make code samples available to you, this book has an accompanying Web site — located at www.dummies.com/go/sqlserver — where you can find all the code I use in the book.

# Icons Used in This Book

What's a *For Dummies* book without icons pointing you in the direction of really great information that's sure to help you along your way? In this section, I briefly describe each icon I use in this book.

The Tip icon points out helpful information that is likely to make your job easier.

This icon marks a general interesting and useful fact — something that you might want to remember for later use.

The Warning icon highlights lurking danger. With this icon, I'm telling you to pay attention and proceed with caution.

When you see this icon, you know that there's techie stuff nearby. If you're not feeling very techie, you can skip this info.

This icon highlights the new features you'll find in this latest version of SQL Server 2005.

# Where to Go from Here

If you are new to SQL Server and want to get a handle on what SQL Server 2005 is about, go to Chapter 1. If you are new to SQL Server 2005 and want to know about its new features, take a look at Chapter 2.

One chapter that you might want to spend time with early on, though, is the chapter on SQL Server Management Studio (Chapter 3). When you work with SQL Server 2005, you spend a lot of your time there and the SQL Server Management Studio is relevant to several later chapters.

# Part I

# SQL Server 2005: An Overview

The 5th Wave                    By Rich Tennant

SNOW GLOBE DATA STORAGE

Okay let's shake this thing and see what we come up with.

## *In this part . . .*

*I* introduce you to the characteristics of SQL Server 2005 and tell you about many of the features that are new in SQL Server 2005.

I also introduce you to the SQL Server Management Studio, the main administrative tool for SQL Server 2005. SQL Server Management Studio replaces Enterprise Manager and Query Analyzer that you may know from SQL Server 2000. It allows you to manage SQL Server 2005 servers whether they are Database Engine, Analysis Services, Integration Services, or Reporting Services server instances.

# Chapter 1

# Introducing SQL Server 2005

*I*n this chapter, I introduce you to SQL Server 2005. SQL Server 2005 is a multi-component relational database management system centered around a high-performance, highly available database engine.

The quality of the database engine in SQL Server is crucial to the reliability of SQL Server 2005 in handling large quantities of data. However, SQL Server 2005 is much more than a database engine and consists of a suite of tools and components that support you in designing, managing, maintaining, and programming a SQL Server 2005 installation and its associated data. In addition, there are powerful new or improved tools for business intelligence.

I introduce you to many of the important features and tools that you can find in SQL Server 2005. SQL Server 2005 is such an extensive suite of programs that I can only touch briefly on each of these many features. I show you how to put many of these features and tools to work in later chapters.

## Getting to Know SQL Server 2005

You can use SQL Server 2005 to store information for personal use, for departmental use, for mid-size company use, or for enterprise use. SQL Server 2005 has editions (Microsoft provides a full comparison of the editions online at www.microsoft.com/sql/2005/productinfo/sql2005features.mspx) to meet the needs in each of those scenarios:

> ✔ **Enterprise:** Provides a relational database to meet the exacting needs of the largest enterprises and busiest online databases. The Enterprise Edition includes high-end business intelligence support and clustering. I introduce you to business intelligence in Chapters 20 through 22. This book does not cover clustering.

 ✔ **Standard:** Meets the needs of medium-sized companies or large departments in larger companies.

 ✔ **Workgroup:** Meets the needs of small- to medium-sized businesses that don't require the features of Standard Edition.

 ✔ **Mobile:** Formerly called SQL Server CE. This book does not cover Mobile Edition.

 ✔ **Express:** A lightweight edition intended for use by application programmers. To find out more about Express Edition, see *Microsoft SQL Server 2005 Express For Dummies,* by Robert D. Schneider (Wiley).

# A Client-Server Database

SQL Server 2005 is a client-server database. Typically, the SQL Server 2005 database engine is installed on a server machine to which you connect anything from a few machines to many hundreds or thousands of client machines.

A client-server architecture can handle large amounts of data better than a desktop database such as Microsoft Access. The SQL Server instance provides security, availability, and reliability features that are absent from databases such as Access. A client-server architecture also can reduce network traffic.

The server side of a SQL Server installation is used for two broad categories of data processing: Online Transaction Processing (OLTP) and Online Analytical Processing (OLAP).

## OLTP

*Online Transaction Processing* is the kind of processing that the databases of Amazon.com or any other large online retailer needs to do. A large number of orders come in every minute and the information from each of those orders needs to be written to the database quickly and reliably.

With OLTP, you can group certain actions together. For example, the different aspects of a bank transfer between accounts would be carried out together, so that if money is moved out of one account, it is also moved into another account. Actions such as these that must be done together are called a *transaction*. In the account transfer, either both the transfers take place or neither do. The all or nothing characteristic of a transaction ensures that the data remains in a consistent state. An OLTP database is tuned to support high volumes of transactions that frequently change the data in the database. SQL Server 2005 performs well as an OLTP database management system.

The *transaction log* stores information about transactions and the data changes made in transactions, which are not rolled back. The transaction log is an important container for information about recent changes made to a database.

## OLAP

An *Online Analytical Processing* database is intended to process large amounts of data that doesn't change often. For example, an online retailer might want to store summary data about sales by month, by region, by product category, and so on. In SQL Server 2005, the OLAP functionality is carried out in Analysis Services. In Analysis Services, you create *cubes* that allow you to examine *dimensions* of a cube. I describe Analysis Services in more detail in Chapter 21.

OLAP often takes place in a *data warehouse*. Getting large amounts of data into good shape before putting it into a data warehouse is a major task, an important aspect of which is to maximize data quality.

After all the data is aggregated, it is unlikely to change in the future. However, you can query it in complex ways, so an OLAP database is typically optimized to support fast querying.

# A Secure Database

If the data on which your business depends is stored in SQL Server, you need to keep the wrong people from accessing the data or, worse, changing or deleting the data. Imagine if a hacker could change the price for certain goods and then buy a huge quantity for a nominal amount — your business could soon be a former business. Similarly, you don't want your competitors to be able to access information about the performance of your business.

SQL Server 2005 implements Microsoft's recent emphasis on security. Unlike its predecessor (SQL Server 2000), SQL Server 2005 is much more secure by default. Many potential attack points are turned off until you explicitly turn them on, so reducing the exposed risk of a default installation. The Surface Area Configuration tool is one way to configure this.

SQL Server 2005 builds on the authentication and authorization features present in SQL Sever 2000. If you want to allow users to use SQL Server 2005 in particular ways, you — as the administrator for SQL Server — can allow them access.

Table 1-1 summarizes some key security features in SQL Server 2005.

| Table 1-1 | Key Security Features of SQL Server 2005 | | | |
|---|---|---|---|---|
| **Feature** | **Express Edition** | **Workgroup Edition** | **Standard Edition** | **Enterprise Edition** |
| Authentication and authorization | Yes | Yes | Yes | Yes |
| Data encryption and key management | Yes | Yes | Yes | Yes |
| Best Practices Analyzer | Yes | Yes | Yes | Yes |
| Integration with Microsoft Baseline Security Analyzer | Yes | Yes | Yes | Yes |
| Integration with Microsoft Update | Yes | Yes | Yes | Yes |

As you can see from the table, all editions of SQL Server 2005 support an extensive range of important security features. I discuss security issues in Part IV.

# A Programmable Database

SQL Server 2005 is a great environment for programmers. If you're a developer, you might even find that your DBA (database administrator) is afraid of the programmability of SQL Server 2005 because it offers so many options. The good thing is that the increased programmability is accompanied by a detailed system of security permissions that greatly reduces the chances of rogue code doing harm to SQL Server itself.

Table 1-2 summarizes some key programmability support features in SQL Server 2005.

| Table 1-2 | Key Programmability Support Features | | | |
|---|---|---|---|---|
| *Feature* | *Express Edition* | *Workgroup Edition* | *Standard Edition* | *Enterprise Edition* |
| Stored procedures and triggers | Yes | Yes | Yes | Yes |
| New enhancements to T-SQL | Yes | Yes | Yes | Yes |
| Integration of the Common Language Runtime and .NET support | Yes | Yes | Yes | Yes |
| User-defined types | Yes | Yes | Yes | Yes |
| XML datatype | Yes | Yes | Yes | Yes |
| XQuery support | Yes | Yes | Yes | Yes |

I introduce stored procedures in Chapter 9 and triggers in Chapter 14. I introduce the Common Language Runtime in Chapter 8, and I describe use of the XML datatype in Chapter 7.

# Transact-SQL

SQL Server 2005 supports the *Structured Query Language* (SQL). In fact SQL is the main language that SQL Server uses. Like many other databases, SQL Server satisfies some standard SQL syntax and adds its own extensions to SQL, allowing you to easily write code.

The Microsoft flavor of SQL is called *Transact-SQL* (T-SQL). T-SQL allows you to add, modify, or query relational or XML data held in SQL Server 2005. In Chapter 5, I introduce you to using T-SQL to retrieve desired data. I introduce the manipulation of XML in Chapter 7.

# SQL Server Management Studio

Transact-SQL programming is commonly done in the query pane of SQL Server Management Studio. I cover SQL Server Management Studio in Chapter 3.

You can also use the SQLCMD utility to issue T-SQL commands interactively or to run T-SQL script files. In applications you create, you can use T-SQL to retrieve or manipulate data. I don't describe these uses of T-SQL in this book.

## Business Intelligence Development Studio

You can use Business Intelligence Development Studio (BIDS), which is based on Visual Studio components, to create business intelligence applications. BIDS is used to create SQL Server Integration Services, Analysis Services, and Reporting Services projects.

I cover business intelligence (BI) in Part VI. In Chapter 20, I show you how to use BIDS to create Integration Services projects. In Chapter 21, I introduce Analysis Services. And in Chapter 22, I introduce you to using BIDS with Reporting Services.

## A Scalable Database

A database management system, such as SQL Server 2005, must grow as your business grows. Table 1-3 summarizes some key features of the various editions of SQL Server 2005 and lists the limitations of each. I do not cover in detail in this book how to make decisions on the most appropriate scalability decisions for your business.

| Table 1-3 | SQL Server 2005 Editions and Their Limitations | | | |
|---|---|---|---|---|
| **Feature** | **Express Edition** | **Workgroup Edition** | **Standard Edition** | **Enterprise Edition** |
| CPU | 1 | 2 | 4 | No limit |
| RAM | 1GB | 3GB | No limit | No limit |
| Database size | 4GB | No limit | No limit | No limit |
| Partitioning | No | No | No | Yes |

Commercial decisions regarding which functionality is in which edition are subject to change up to the time of product release. Therefore, functionality may differ slightly from the information I give in this chapter.

# An Available Database

If your business uses the World Wide Web to sell goods or provide information to customers, your customers may be located around the world. In that case, your SQL Server 2005-based applications need to be available 24 hours a day, 7 days a week. This need for continuous availability has stimulated many availability features in SQL Server 2005. Table 1-4 summarizes availability features in different editions of SQL Server 2005.

**Table 1-4    The Availability Features of SQL Server 2005 Editions**

| Feature | Express Edition | Workgroup Edition | Standard Edition | Enterprise Edition |
|---|---|---|---|---|
| Database mirroring | No | No | Partial | Yes |
| Failover clustering | No | No | Limited to 2 nodes | Yes |
| Backup log shipping | No | Yes | Yes | Yes |
| Online system changes | Yes | Yes | Yes | Yes |
| Online indexing | No | No | No | Yes |
| Online page and file restore | No | No | No | Yes |

If you cluster multiple server machines, they can operate together to give availability that would either be unavailable or very expensive with a single server. Each machine in a cluster is called a *node*. If a node fails, then another node in the cluster picks up the work of the failed machine. This significantly reduces downtime, at a cost of increased hardware.

## Miscellaneous changes

You can add memory to the SQL Server machine if you have the relevant hardware. This allows you to add memory to a machine while it is available to users, so reducing downtime.

The Dedicated Administrator Connection (DAC) allows a database administrator to take control of the server even if an operation is using virtually all the CPU cycles. If a server process fails to complete, it can use virtually 100 percent of CPU time, making a server almost unusable or very slow. The DAC allows a server administrator to connect to the server and stop the runaway process without having to restart the server.

## Online indexing

Online indexing is available only in the Enterprise Edition. Online indexing improves the availability of a database by avoiding the need to take a table or database offline while, for example, an index is rebuilt. I do not cover online indexing further in this book.

## Online page and file restore

This feature is available only in Enterprise Edition. If you have to restore data from backups, the database becomes available for use more quickly than was possible in SQL Server 2000. I do not cover this feature further in this book.

# A Reliable Database

Disasters, small and large, can happen. If the hard drive crashes on your SQL Server machine, your business doesn't need to crash with it.

## Backing up data

You can back up your data with SQL Server Management Studio (see Chapter 3). You need to back up all your data regularly, especially the following system databases, with the exception of `tempdb`:

- ✔ **Master:** The `master` database contains system level information for a SQL Server 2005 system.

- ✔ **Model:** The `model` database is the template that is used when you create a new database.

- ✔ **Msdb:** The `msdb` database is used by SQL Server Agent to record information for scheduling alerts and jobs.

- ✔ **Resource:** The `resource` database is new in SQL Server 2005 and contains the system objects for SQL Server 2005. When you update SQL Server 2005 — for example a service pack — the new version replaces the `resource` database. Be careful not to restore an out-of-date version after applying a service pack.

✔ **Distribution:** The `distribution` database exists only if the SQL Server machine is a distributor for replication. The database contains metadata about replication.

✔ **Temp:** The `temp` database is deleted when you close down SQL Server 2005. Although `tempdb` is a system database, you cannot back it up.

## Replication

SQL Server 2005 supports replication of data by using a publish/subscribe metaphor. I describe replication in more detail in Chapter 19.

# A Manageable Database

You need to manage many aspects of a SQL Server 2005 installation. Table 1-5 summarizes some features of manageability in SQL Server 2005. I cover SQL Server Management Studio in Chapter 3. I don't describe the Database Engine Tuning Advisor or Full Text Search in detail in this book.

| Table 1-5 | SQL Server 2005 Manageability Features | | | |
|---|---|---|---|---|
| *Feature* | *Express Edition* | *Workgroup Edition* | *Standard Edition* | *Enterprise Edition* |
| Automatic performance tuning | Yes | Yes | Yes | Yes |
| SQL Server Management Studio | No | Yes | Yes | Yes |
| Database Engine Tuning Advisor | No | Yes | Yes | Yes |
| Full text search | No | Yes | Yes | Yes |
| SQL Agent job scheduling | No | Yes | Yes | Yes |

## Command-line tools

In SQL Server 2005, the main command-line tool is SQLCMD. The SQLCMD utility allows you to manage a SQL Server 2005 installation by using the T-SQL language. You can use T-SQL interactively from the command line or can use SQLCMD to run T-SQL scripts. I do not cover the SQLCMD in detail in this book.

## Graphical tools

The main graphical tool for administering SQL Server 2005 is SQL Server Management Studio. Management Studio allows you to administer many SQL Server 2005 database engine instances, Analysis Services instances, Integration Services instances, and Reporting Services instances from a single interface. I describe SQL Server Management Studio in more detail in Chapter 3.

## SQL Server Agent

Any database administrator has tasks that need to be carried out repeatedly and, often, these tasks take place at set times. SQL Server Agent (or simply *SQL Agent*) is the software component that allows you to carry out such tasks automatically. For example, you may need to back up data at 2 a.m. every day. It is much more convenient for you to be at home asleep and let SQL Server Agent take the strain. See Chapter 16 for more about SQL Server Agent.

## Performance tools

SQL Server Profiler allows you to monitor and analyze performance of a SQL Server instance. New in SQL Server 2005 is the ability to monitor and analyze the performance of Analysis Services. I do not cover SQL Server Profiler in detail in this book.

# A Database That Supports Business Intelligence

SQL Server 2005 supports many pieces of business intelligence functionality, grouped under the headings of Integration Services, Analysis Services, and

Reporting Services. Table 1-6 summarizes the availability of business intelligence functionality by SQL Server 2005 edition.

| Table 1-6 | Business Intelligence Functionality | | | |
|---|---|---|---|---|
| *Feature* | *Express Edition* | *Workgroup Edition* | *Standard Edition* | *Enterprise Edition* |
| Data can be used by Report Server | Yes | Yes | Yes | Yes |
| Report Builder | No | Yes | Yes | Yes |
| Scale out of Report Servers | No | No | No | Yes |
| Data warehousing | No | No | Yes | Yes |
| Business Intelligence Development Studio | Not included but is compatible | Not included but is compatible | Yes | Yes |
| Analysis Services | No | No | Yes | Yes |
| Advanced analytic functions | No | No | Yes | Yes |
| Data mining | No | No | Yes | Yes |
| Integration Services | No | No | No | Yes |

Chapter 20 describes SQL Server Integration Services. Chapter 21 has more on Analysis Services. And Chapter 22 includes information on Reporting Services.

# Chapter 2

# New Features in SQL Server 2005

*In This Chapter*

▶ Checking out SQL Server's improved security features

▶ Finding out about other SQL Server 2005 enhancements

SQL Server 2005 is the most exciting release of SQL Server for years. It may be the only release in the last five years, but it's genuinely an exciting release full of new and useful features. In addition to new features, SQL Server 2005 also includes many features that are big improvements on their counterparts in SQL Server 2000.

In this chapter, I briefly describe many of SQL Server 2005's new and improved features.

To get a good feel for the range of new and improved features in SQL Server 2005, be sure to read all sections of the chapter.

To describe all these features in detail and explain how to use them would need a book maybe ten times as long as this one. I had to make choices about which tools or features to cover in detail later in the book. I often assume that you have some familiarity with SQL Server 2000, but you should be able to follow along even if you are new to SQL Server 2005. For many topics I tell you where I describe the functionality in more detail.

Because one of the most important aspects of any database is security (a topic I explore further in Part IV), I start there.

## Security Enhancements

Security is a major focus for new features in SQL Server 2005. In part, this focus reflects a response to issues such as the Slammer worm that hit SQL Server 2000. In part, it reflects a world where more business data is potentially exposed on the Internet. SQL Server has to give you the tools to keep your data safe in order to allow the right people to access data that you want them to access and to stop other people from accessing data that you don't want them to access.

I describe security in SQL Server 2005 in more detail in Chapter 11.

## System catalog security

The system catalog in SQL Server 2005 consists of views of the underlying system data structures. Users do not see any underlying tables, so unskilled or malicious users can't change or otherwise corrupt them. This stops you or anyone else from damaging the core structures on which your SQL Server installation depends.

## Password policy enforcement

When installed on Windows 2003 Server, you can apply to SQL Server 2005 any Windows password policy that you have in effect. You can enforce policies for password expiration and strength on SQL Server 2005 in exactly the same way as for Windows logins. Windows 2000 Server does not support this.

You can turn off (or on, in some cases) password policy enforcement for individual logins. For example, you can turn off password policy enforcement when you're using an application with built-in authentication information that you can't change.

I show you how to alter password enforcement in Chapter 11.

## Schema and user separation

SQL Server 2000 had no concept of a schema: A user owned a database object. So if a user User1 created an object called myTable, then the object's qualified name was User1.myTable. If User1 is deleted — for example, when the individual leaves the company — you needed to change the name of the object, which caused problems for applications that depended on the name of the object for data access. In SQL Server 2005, a user can create a schema, which in turn contains database objects, which has a different name from the user. User1 can create a schema called HR. and create an object called myTable. You refer to that object as HR.myTable. So if User1 leaves the company, you can leave the schema name unchanged, which means you can leave your application code unchanged because the object is still called HR.myTable.

## *Automated certificate creation for SSL*

In SQL Server 2000, when using *Secure Sockets Layer* (SSL) to log in to a SQL Server instance, you had to manually create a certificate to underpin the use of SSL. SQL Server 2005 creates a certificate automatically. That allows you to use SSL without manually creating a certificate.

# *Transact-SQL Enhancements*

SQL Server 2005 has added several new features to Transact-SQL.

Transact-SQL is the version of the Structured Query Language (SQL) used by SQL Server 2005. Transact-SQL is often abbreviated to *T-SQL*. T-SQL has many features, which are not included in ANSI SQL.

## *Improved XML support*

SQL Server 2000 allowed you to retrieve relational data as XML with the FOR XML clause or store XML as relational data in SQL Server, using the OPEN XML clause. SQL Server 2005 has a new xml datatype that allows you to write code to retrieve XML data as XML, avoiding the transformation from XML to relational data that occurred when using OPEN XML. You can also use a schema document expressed in the W3C XML Schema Definition language (sometimes called XSD schema) to specify allowed structures in the XML.

*Note:* Strictly speaking, the xml datatype stores data in a proprietary binary format. For practical purposes, you can retrieve and manipulate the data as XML.

The xml datatype supports several keywords in T-SQL. I show you how to use these keywords in Chapter 7.

## *Error handling*

SQL Server 2005 allows you to use TRY ... CATCH blocks in your T-SQL code. So, if your code causes an error, the code in the CATCH block allows you to specify what to do when an error occurs. I show you how to use TRY ... CATCH blocks in Chapter 10.

## Transact-SQL templates

In SQL Server Management Studio, you can find many templates to help you carry out common tasks with Transact-SQL. To view the range of T-SQL templates, choose View➪Template Explorer in SQL Server Management Studio. The Template Explorer displays. View the nodes to see the range of templates available. Check out Chapter 5 for more on templates.

# Other Developer-Orientated Enhancements

SQL Server 2005 has several new developer-orientated enhancements. I describe those in the following sections.

## Support for the Common Language Runtime

The Common Language Runtime (CLR), which is used by .NET code, is embedded in the SQL Server 2005 database engine. You can write stored procedures, triggers, functions, aggregates, and user-defined datatypes by using languages such as Visual Basic .NET or C#. Stored procedures written in a .NET language are a good replacement for SQL Server 2000 extended stored procedures, because you can specify a security level for the .NET code.

You find three security levels for .NET code:

- ✔ **Safe:** This level allows no access outside SQL Server. For example, your code cannot access the file system, registry, environment variables, or the network. This security level is the most secure.

- ✔ **External Access:** This security level allows limited external access by your code. Specifically, you can access the registry, the file system, environment variables, and the network.

- ✔ **UnSafe:** You can access any desired functionality outside SQL Server 2005 with the UnSafe security level. You should use the UnSafe security level only if you are certain that the code is well written and you trust the author of the code.

# New datatypes

SQL Server 2005 supports several new datatypes:

- ✔ **varchar(max):** This allows you to use sequences of characters greater than 8000 bytes (8000 characters). The maximum size is 2GB.

- ✔ **nvarchar(max):** This allows you to use sequences of Unicode characters greater than 8000 bytes (4000 characters). The maximum size is 2GB.

- ✔ **varbinary(max):** This allows you to use binary data greater than 8000 bytes.

Each of the preceding datatypes can be up to 2GB in size. This allows major size increases in size compared to varchar(8000) and nvarchar(8000), which were each limited to 8K.

# SQL Management Objects (SMO)

SQL Management Objects (SMO) replaces Distributed Management Objects (DMO), which were used in SQL Server 2000. SQL DMO applications run on SQL Server 2005 but no updating of DMO objects took place for SQL Server 2005. Developers use SMO. However, applications created with SMO often provide custom management tools for administrators.

SMO is faster than SQL Server 2000 DMO in many settings because each object is only partially instantiated. For example, if you want to enumerate what might be thousands of databases on a powerful server, you don't need fully instantiated objects to populate a tree view. You need only the object's name. Having partially instantiated objects saves a lot of time for commonly used, simple tasks because you probably need a fully instantiated object for only a small number of the total number of objects.

# Scripting actions

If you have used Microsoft programs such as Access and Excel you'll know that you can create macros to allow you to automate certain tasks. SQL Server 2005 now has a feature that automatically creates Transact-SQL scripts from actions you take using the graphical user interface in SQL Server Management Studio. You can use these scripts exactly as SQL Server Management Studio creates them or you can modify them in ways to exactly suit your intentions.

## HTTP endpoints

HTTP access to SQL Server 2005 is a new feature that allows programmers to access SQL Server without depending on an IIS server running on the same machine. SQL Server can coexist with IIS but unlike with SQL Server 2000, IIS is no longer required for SQL Server 2005. HTTP endpoints allow developers to use XML Web services with SQL Server 2005. The HTTP endpoint can execute T-SQL batch statements or stored procedures.

For security reasons, HTTP endpoints are disabled by default. To use HTTP endpoints you need to specify which users, stored procedures, and databases are enabled to support it.

# Manageability Enhancements

The management tools in SQL Server 2005 have changed greatly from SQL Server 2000. The main change is the arrival of SQL Server Management Studio, which I describe in more detail in Chapter 3.

## New management tools

SQL Server 2005 has new management tools. SQL Server Management Studio replaces Enterprise Manager and Query Analyzer that you may be familiar with from SQL Server 2000. SQL Server Management Studio also allows you to manage Analysis Services instances and, therefore, also replaces Analysis Manager.

SQL Server Management Studio allows you to manage multiple SQL Server instances more easily. From one interface you can manage multiple instances of the SQL Server database engine, Analysis Services, Integration Services, and Reporting Services. I describe SQL Server Management Studio in detail in Chapter 3.

SQL Server Configuration Manager is a new tool that allows you to control services associated with SQL Server 2005. SQL Server Configuration Manager replaces Service Manager and the server and client networking tools. You can use SQL Server Configuration Manager to control the following:

✔ SQL Server

✔ SQL Agent

✔ SQL Server Analysis Services

✔ DTS Server (for SQL Server Integration Services)

✔ Full-text Search

✔ SQL Browser

## Profiler

Profiler has many features that allow you to analyze performance problems in SQL Server 2005. For example, Profiler opens trace files that you store in the file system, which allows you to replay and analyze interesting SQL Server processes. Profiler can display a graphical representation of a trace so you can easily see what is happening.

Profiler can import data recorded by using the Windows Performance Monitor. You can display the data graphically, letting you see performance over a selected period of time. From the graph, you can enter the trace at the point where a problem lies — for example, where CPU usage spikes. You can then closely examine what is causing a performance problem.

I don't cover Profiler in detail in this book.

## SQL Server Agent

The capabilities of SQL Server Agent, the component that supports scheduled jobs, have been enhanced. For example, the number of concurrent jobs that SQL Server Agent can run has increased. SQL Server 2000 used SQL Agent only in relation to jobs for the database engine. SQL Server 2005 also uses SQL Server Agent to run jobs for Analysis Services and Integration Services. I discuss SQL Server Agent jobs further in Chapter 16.

SQL Server Agent uses Windows Management Instrumentation (WMI). WMI support allows you to write code to avoid running a job, such as when the disk space is insufficient to let the job run successfully.

## Dynamic configuration

In SQL Server 2005, you can make many configuration changes without having to restart SQL Server (if you're running on the Windows Server 2003 operating system). This is a big improvement over SQL Server 2000 when you often had to restart SQL Server after making configuration changes. In SQL Server 2005, you can change CPU affinity or I/O affinity if you need to. If you have the necessary hardware you can hot-add extra memory to your server.

## Full-text search

You can back up and restore Full-text Search catalogs (the databases where the metadata is stored) in the same way as you back up and restore any other SQL Server 2005 databases.

## SQL Server Service Broker

SQL Server Service Broker allows you to create asynchronous message-based applications. The asynchronous nature of Server Broker messages means that processing tasks needn't be done all at the same time, which can slow the server down. Instead, messages are queued for processing when the server load is lighter, improving overall performance.

Turn to Chapter 19 for more info on Service Broker.

## Dedicated Administrator connection

This is not a connection only for dedicated administrators but a connection that only administrators can use. The connection is used when a runaway process is on the server and you need access to the database engine to kill the process. Even if the runaway process is using close to 100 percent of the CPU cycles, the Dedicated Administrator connection allows administrators to get a share of CPU cycles and so kill the runaway process. This capability allows you to kill a runaway process without having to restart the server.

## SQLCMD

The SQLCMD command-line utility is the recommended command-line tool in SQL Server 2005. You can write SQLCMD commands individually or use SQLCMD to execute T-SQL scripts.

The SQLCMD utility allows you to use command-line parameters to replace variables in a T-SQL script. For example, suppose you had a simple backup script

```
BACKUP DATABASE $(db) TO DISK = "$(path)\$(db).bak"
```

called backup.sql. It backs up a specified database to a specific location. You can run that script from the command line, replacing the $db and $path variables with the relevant database name and file path. For example, to back up AdventureWorks into the C:\Backups folder, you write:

```
sqlcmd -E -i Backup.sql -v db="AdventureWorks"
          path="C:\Backups"
```

## Easier updates

System objects are in the `resource` database in SQL Server 2005. When a service pack or other update is applied to a SQL Server instance, replacing the `resource` database updates all the system objects. This gives a more easily manageable upgrade path.

## Replication

The setup and administration of replication has been improved in SQL Server 2005. This is carried out from SQL Server Management Studio. There is a new system health monitor to allow you to check on replication settings and performance. For example, it can tell you how long replicated data takes to reach subscribers.

## WMI configuration

*Windows Management Instrumentation* (WMI) allows you to carry out a range of configuration tasks such as specifying client and network settings. You can also use WMI to determine whether you can safely and effectively carry out a task at a particular time. For example, you can test whether a target drive has enough disk space to carry out a backup.

## Database Mail

Database Mail is a new feature. It replaces SQLMail, which was present in SQL Server 2000. Database Mail uses Simple Mail Transfer Protocol (SMTP). There is no longer any dependency on the Messaging Application Programming Interface (MAPI), and Outlook is no longer required. The removal of these dependencies avoids many of the availability problems that SQL Server 2000 users had with SQLMail. In addition, Database Mail is cluster aware, unlike SQLMail. Database Mail supports logging and auditing.

# Availability Enhancements

SQL Server 2005 supports three broad types of enhanced availability:

- ✔ Concurrent data access
- ✔ Availability after server failure or other disaster
- ✔ Availability during database maintenance and repair

## Concurrent data access

Concurrent data access is about getting to data when others are also accessing it:

- **Database snapshots:** Creates a logical copy of a database at a specific point in time. You can use snapshots as the basis for Reporting Services reports without putting a load on the live copy of the database.

- **Snapshot isolation:** This is a new transaction isolation level that improves availability for read applications, because writes do not block reads. Write applications are subject to mandatory conflict detection.

- **Online Indexing:** During the time that an index is being rebuilt, it remains possible to use the index for accessing data. This is likely to improve performance during that period.

## Availability after server failure

SQL Server 2005 provides better availability in scenarios relating to server failure or some other catastrophic situation. The following features are additional to server failover clustering that was supported in SQL Server 2000 Enterprise edition:

- **Faster Recovery:** After a server failure, databases are made available to users more quickly during the recovery process, which improves availability.

- **Database Mirroring:** Using standard hardware, a mirror server always maintains an up-to-date copy of the database. On failure of the principal server, the mirror server is available within three seconds, making the server failure invisible to users.

- **Transparent Client Redirect:** Under the covers, Database Mirroring uses Transparent Client Redirect. The MDAC (Microsoft Data Access Components) layer notes the mirror server when connecting to a principal server. If the principal server fails, MDAC redirects the connection to the mirror server.

## Availability during database maintenance

The backup and restore process must be reliable if you are to restore a database effectively, such as after a hardware failure. Here are the relevant features of SQL Server 2005:

✔ **Finer Grained Online Repairs:** You can restore data filegroup by filegroup with the database being available after the primary filegroup is restored.

✔ **Enhanced Backup Verification:** The verifying of backups is more complete than in previous versions of SQL Server. The RESTORE VERIFY ONLY syntax checks everything that can be checked, short of writing the backup to the server.

✔ **Backup Media Mirroring:** This allows you to make extra copies of backups to minimize the chance of a failed restore or to make an archival copy for offsite storage, for example.

✔ **Database Page Checksums:** Checksums are added to individual pages in the database to detect errors that otherwise might go undetected.

✔ **Backup Checksums:** Adds an additional error detection mechanism during backup. It is possible to proceed past errors and fix them later.

✔ **Backup Data and Logs:** The former problems with log backups at the same time as data backups have been remedied. It is now possible to carry out a data backup at the same time as the corresponding log backup.

# Scalability Enhancements

One of the key aims of SQL Server 2005 is to improve the scalability of databases and the applications that depend on them.

## Installing in a cluster

You can install SQL Server 2005 in a cluster of up to eight nodes with status reporting of install progress on each node. SQL Server 2005 setup has the ability to install Analysis Services in a cluster. New in SQL Server 2005 is the ability to carry out unattended installation to a cluster.

## Partitioning data

Some database objects are very large. Partitioning splits large database objects into multiple more manageable pieces. Suppose you have a huge table that contains many months of data. You could improve performance by partitioning the table into several smaller partitions with each partition containing the data for a single month.

You can also partition indexes. If the partitions for data and for indexes are aligned, you can move partitions into or out of a table. This is useful if you have data for the last 12 months, partitioned by month. You can move the data for 12 months ago out and create a new partition for the current month.

## Database Engine Tuning Advisor

The Database Engine Tuning Advisor (DTA) is the SQL Server 2005 replacement for the SQL Server 2000 Index Tuning Wizard. The Database Tuning Advisor can help you tune performance for the whole database, not just for indexes, as previously.

The DTA can handle partitions and can assist in tuning some operations that involve using multiple databases. It has a high availability recommendation mode that recommends creation of indexes only if those indexes can be built online, which improves availability of a database during creation of indexes. You can specify a maximum time for DTA to reach its recommendations to avoid very long running scenarios. You can also explore what if analyses in the Database Tuning Advisor to allow you to explore the effects of possible approaches.

## Hot-add memory support

If the demands on your SQL Server increase markedly and you have the appropriate hardware and are running SQL Server on Windows Server 2003, you can take advantage of hot-add memory support. This allows you to improve performance under high load and also allows you to avoid downtime.

## Replication

Replication performance has been improved in SQL Server 2005. The number of subscribers supported in replication is increased.

# Business Intelligence Enhancements

Business Intelligence is a prominent strength of SQL Server 2005. Features have been added to Analysis Services, Integration Services has replaced Data

Transformation Services, and Reporting Services builds on the features of Reporting Services 2000 that was first released early in 2004.

Business Intelligence in SQL Server 2005 uses an Integrate, Analyze, and Report paradigm. You can use Integration Services to bring data together from various sources. Use Analysis Services to provide insight into the data. You can create reports to present the analyses to business users with Reporting Services.

## Integration Services

SQL Server Integration Services replaces SQL Server 2000 Data Transformation Services. You can use Integration Services to import and restructure data. You can also load data into a data warehouse with Integration Services. I describe Integration Services in detail in Chapter 20.

## Analysis Services

SQL Server 2005 extends Analysis Services functionality. You use Analysis Services to extract information that is meaningful in a business context. Analysis Services contains two major parts: OnLine Analytical Processing (OLAP) and Data Mining. I describe Analysis Services in more detail in Chapter 21.

## Reporting Services

You can use SQL Server Reporting Services to create customized reports for end users. Reporting Services for SQL Server 2000 was introduced in January 2004, but was originally intended as a new feature in SQL Server 2005. If you are a developer, you create report projects in the Business Intelligence Development Studio. If you have the Enterprise Edition of SQL Server 2005, you can create a report model project in the Business Intelligence Development Studio, and your end users can use report model projects to create ad hoc reports with the new Report Builder design tool. I describe Reporting Services in more detail in Chapter 22.

# Chapter 3

# Introducing and Configuring Management Studio

• • • • • • • • • • • • • • • • • • • • • • • • • • • • • • • • • • • • • • •

## In This Chapter

▶ Running Management Studio

▶ Registering a SQL Server instance

▶ Exploring the Object Explorer

▶ Looking over the Summary tab

▶ Querying with the query pane

▶ Applying templates in Management Studio

• • • • • • • • • • • • • • • • • • • • • • • • • • • • • • • • • • • • • • •

SQL Server Management Studio is the main tool that you're likely to use to administer SQL Server 2005 databases. You can also use it to administer SQL Server 2000 databases.

You cannot use SQL Server Management Studio to administer SQL Server 7.0 databases.

*Note:* SQL Server Management Studio has replaced familiar tools such as Enterprise Manager and Query Analyzer in SQL Server 2000. If you go looking for Enterprise Manager and Query Analyzer, you won't find them in a SQL Server 20005 installation.

SQL Server Management Studio allows you to administer SQL Server instances, Analysis Services instances, Integration Services instances, and Reporting Services instances.

# *Starting Management Studio and Connecting to SQL Server*

To run SQL Server Management Studio, you must choose to install Client Tools in the Setup utility when you install SQL Server 2005.

To start SQL Server Management Studio, choose Start➪All Programs➪ Microsoft SQL Server 2005➪SQL Server Management Studio.

When SQL Server Management Studio starts, the Connect to Server dialog box opens (see Figure 3-1). You can choose to connect to an instance of SQL Server or start SQL Server Management Studio without connecting to a SQL Server instance.

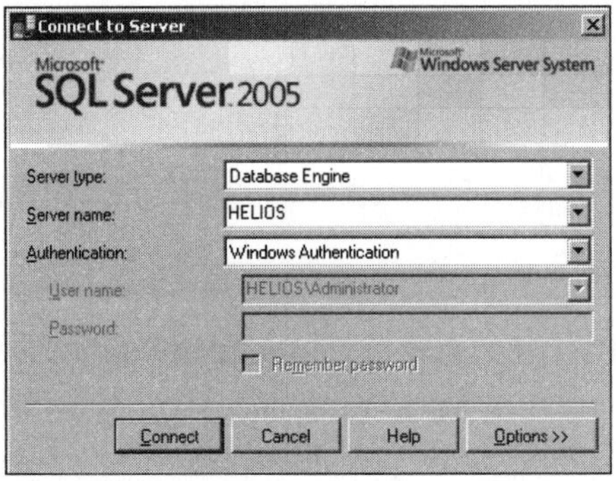

**Figure 3-1:** The Connect to Server dialog box.

To connect to a local instance of the SQL Server Database Engine, select Database Engine from the Server Type drop-down menu and select (or enter) a period character or type **(local)** in the Server Name drop-down menu. Select the authentication method that you prefer and then click the Connect button. The Object Explorer displays containing a tree of nodes, which represents the local default instance of the SQL Server database engine. I describe how to use the Object Explorer in the "Exploring Database Objects Using the Object Explorer" section, later in this chapter.

# *Using Registered Servers*

The Registered Servers pane in Management Studio allows you to specify instances of the SQL Server 2005 database engine, Analysis Services,

Reporting Services, SQL Server Mobile, and Integration Services. Each of these five categories has its own view in the Registered Servers pane. You can see only one of those views at any one time.

The dialog boxes for the Registered Servers pane (and the name of the pane itself) refer to *servers*. In fact, you connect to a SQL Server *instance* — not a server. You connect to one instance. On some servers, multiple instances may be displayed that you can connect to.

If the Registered Servers pane is not visible, choose View➪Registered Servers. The Registered Servers pane opens on the left side of Management Studio, unless you have altered its position previously.

Use the Registered Servers pane for the following tasks:

✔ Save connection information for SQL Server instances on the network

✔ Display whether or not an instance is running

✔ Connect to an instance in the Object Explorer or the Query Editor

✔ Edit the information about a registered server

✔ Group your servers

To register a SQL Server instance, follow these steps:

1. **On the Registered Servers toolbar, click the icon for the type of the instance you want to connect to.**

   The available options are Database Engine, Analysis Services, Reporting Services, SQL Server Mobile, and SQL Server Integration Services.

2. **If the instance you want to connect to isn't displayed, right-click a blank part of the Registered Servers pane and choose New➪Server Registration from the context menu.**

   The New Server Registration dialog box appears.

3. **Enter or select the name of the instance you want to connect to.**

   In the Server Name drop-down menu, enter the name in the form *machineName\instanceName*. To connect to an instance named Test on a server machine named OnlineStore, enter **OnlineStore\Test**.

4. **Click the Test button to confirm that the connection is working correctly.**

5. **If the test of the connection is successful, click the Save button. If testing the connection is unsuccessful, carefully check and correct the information you entered in Step 3.**

   The newly registered server displays in the Registered Servers pane.

To connect to a SQL Server instance and display its node tree in the Object Explorer, follow these steps:

1. **Click the relevant icon on the Registered Servers toolbar to select the type of instance to connect to.**

   The available options are Database Engine, Analysis Services, Reporting Services, SQL Server Mobile, and Integration Services. The instances of the selected type are displayed.

2. **Right-click the SQL Server instance that you want to connect to.**

3. **From the context menu, choose Connect⇨Object Explorer.**

To connect to a SQL Server instance and create a new query connected to that instance, follow these steps:

1. **Click the relevant icon on the Registered Servers toolbar to select the type of instance to connect to.**

2. **Right-click the SQL Server instance that you want to connect to.**

3. **From the context menu, choose Connect⇨New Query.**

   The query pane opens or (if you already have the query pane open) a new tab is created in the query pane.

# Exploring Database Objects Using the Object Explorer

When SQL Server Management Studio starts, you are presented with the Connect to Server dialog box (refer to Figure 3-1). You can choose to connect to an instance of SQL Server (database engine, Analysis Services, Reporting Services or Integration Services) or to start SQL Server Management Studio without connecting to a SQL Server instance. To explore and manage a SQL Server instance, specify the server name and the type of instance to connect to.

The left pane in SQL Server Management Studio typically displays the Object Explorer (and the Registered Servers pane). If the Object Explorer is not visible at startup of SQL Server Management Studio, choose View⇨Object Explorer. The Object Explorer opens.

The Object Explorer allows you to carry out several management tasks in Management Studio, depending which instance type you chose:

✔ Create and manage databases

✔ View and modify database properties

✔ Create and manage database objects such as tables and views

✔ Grant and revoke privileges and permissions

✔ Configure replications

✔ Manage SQL Server Integration Services packages (Integration Services packages are created in Business Intelligence Development Studio.)

✔ View SQL Server and Windows log files

✔ Manage SQL Server Agent

Chapter 4 describes the steps to create databases and database objects.

Figure 3-2 shows the top-level nodes in the Object Explorer.

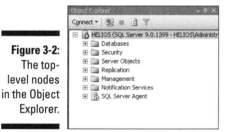

**Figure 3-2:**
The top-
level nodes
in the Object
Explorer.

# View and modify database properties

To view and modify the properties of a database, follow these steps:

1. **Click the + sign to the left of the Databases node.**

   The System Databases node and the individual user database nodes display.

2. **If you want to view the properties of a system database, click the System Databases node to display the individual system database nodes.**

3. **Right-click the name of the database.**

   I selected `AdventureWorks` in Figure 3-3.

4. **From the context menu, click the Properties option.**

   The Database Properties dialog box opens (see Figure 3-3).

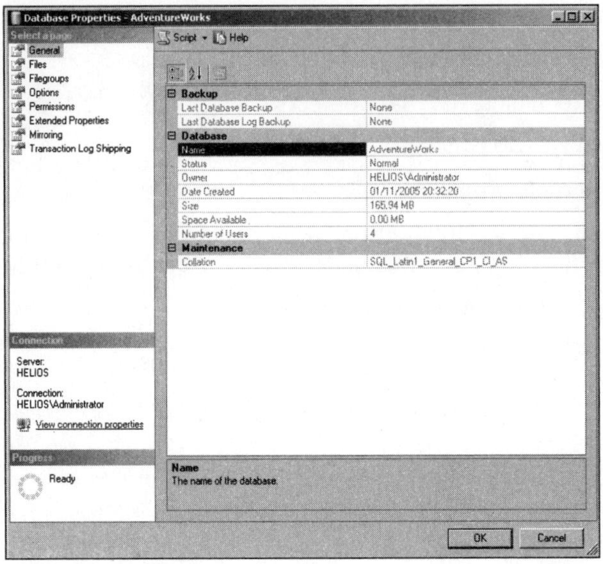

Figure 3-3:
The
Database
Properties
dialog box.

**5. Select each of the tabs in the left pane to inspect the available properties.**

The options available in database properties are grouped under the following tabs:

- General

- Files

- Filegroups

- Options

- Permissions

- Extended Properties

- Mirroring

- Transaction Log Shipping

You can alter properties of the database, as appropriate.

To view the system databases (or more precisely views of the hidden system databases), follow these steps:

**1. Click the + sign to the left of the System Databases node.**

The nodes for the system databases display. On a minimum install the system databases are `master`, `model`, `msdb`, and `tempdb`.

2. **Click the + sign to the left of the master database node.**

   The nodes for the master database display. The nodes displayed are Tables, Views, Synonyms, Programmability, Service Broker, Storage, and Security.

3. **Explore the nodes displayed in the previous step by clicking the + sign to the left of each node.**

# Security

There are Security nodes at two levels: SQL Server instance level and database level.

The Security node you see when the Object Explorer opens contains information about the SQL Server instance. You use this Security node to view or manage security settings that are relevant at the SQL Server instance level.

To add a new login for the SQL Server instance, follow these steps:

1. **Right-click the Security node and choose New⇨Login from the context menu.**

   The Login - New dialog box displays.

2. **On the General tab, give the new login a name.**

   Assuming that you want to grant access to the instance, leave the Grant Server Access radio button checked.

3. **If you want to add the new login to an existing built-in role, click the Server Roles tab and check one or more check boxes.**

4. **If you want to grant permissions on specific databases, click the Database Access tab and check the check box(es) for the database(s) that you want to grant access to.**

To work at the database level, you create a user (not a login). Follow these steps to create a new user for the AdventureWorks database (or another database):

1. **If the Databases node is not expanded, click the + sign to the left of the Databases node.**

   The subsidiary nodes display.

2. **Click the + sign to the left of the AdventureWorks node.**

   The subsidiary nodes for the AdventureWorks database display. Select a different database node if you don't have the AdventureWorks database installed.

3. **Right-click the Security node (which is a subsidiary node to the AdventureWorks node) and choose New➪User.**

   The Database User - New dialog box opens (see Figure 3-4).

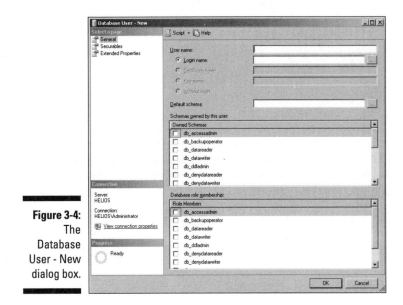

**Figure 3-4:**
The
Database
User - New
dialog box.

4. **Supply a name for the new user.**

5. **As appropriate, associate the new user with an existing login and/or a default schema.**

6. **If you want to make the new user the owner of an existing schema, check one or more relevant check boxes on the General tab.**

7. **If you want to add the new user to an existing role (or roles), check one or more check boxes.**

I tell you more about how to work with security settings in Chapter 11.

# Replication

You can define the participation of a SQL Server instance in replication from the Replication node. In SQL Server 2005, replication uses the metaphor of publication and subscription. SQL Server Management Studio allows you to create both publications and subscriptions.

Click the + sign to the left of the Replication node to see the subsidiary nodes —
Local Publications and Local Subscriptions, by default. The context menus
for those nodes allow you to create new publications and subscriptions.

I describe replication in more detail in Chapter 19.

# Getting an Overview on the Summary Tab

When you first open SQL Server Management Studio, you see the Summary
tab to the right of the Registered Servers pane and the Object Explorer. The
Summary tab provides information that summarizes some characteristics of
the SQL Server instance to which you have most recently connected.

Figure 3-5 shows the appearance of the Summary tab when the SQL Server
instance is selected.

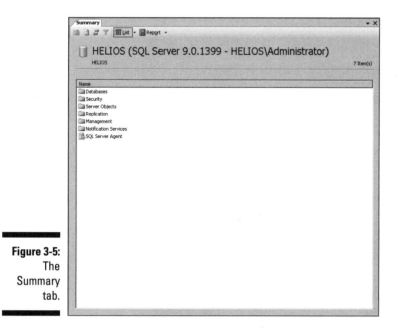

**Figure 3-5:**
The
Summary
tab.

Notice the navigation icons near the top of the Summary tab. The List icon
contains an extensive menu, as shown in Figure 3-6.

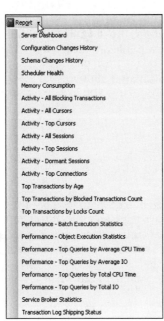

**Figure 3-6:**
The options
on the
List icon.

Figure 3-7 shows the Server Dashboard for a default database engine instance.

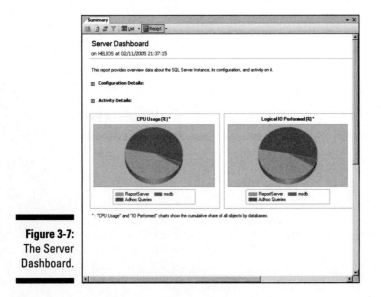

**Figure 3-7:**
The Server
Dashboard.

Explore the other options shown on the List icon's menu to fully understand the information available to you on the Summary tab.

# Asking Questions in the Query Pane

To create a new query, click the New Query button on the Standard toolbar. In the default layout, the New Query button is positioned at the top-left of Management Studio. In addition, five icons allow you to select the type of query you want to create (see Figure 3-8).

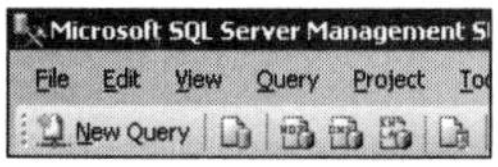

**Figure 3-8:**
These icons
allow you
to choose
query type.

The five types of query supported in Management Studio are

- ✔ **Transact-SQL:** Runs against the relational database engine
- ✔ **MDX (Multi-Dimensional Expressions):** Runs against Analysis Services
- ✔ **DMX (Data Mining Extensions):** Runs against Analysis Services
- ✔ **XMLA (XML for Analysis):** Runs against Analysis Services
- ✔ **SQL Server Mobile Query:** Runs against an instance of SQL Server 2005 Mobile Edition

To create a simple query, using the AdventureWorks sample database, follow these steps:

1. **Click the Database Engine Query icon.**

   The Query Pane opens or a new tab is added to the query pane.

2. **On the new query tab, type the following Transact-SQL code:**

   ```
   USE AdventureWorks
   SELECT LastName, FirstName, Title FROM Person.Contact
   ORDER BY LastName
   ```

   The first line of the code specifies that the AdventureWorks database is used. The second line of the code is a SELECT statement that selects three columns, LastName, FirstName, and Title from the Contact table in the Person schema. The third line, which isn't strictly necessary, ensures that the returned rows are ordered by the content of the LastName column.

3. **Click the Execute button on the toolbar.**

   If you prefer, you can use the F5 keyboard shortcut to execute the T-SQL code.

Depending on whether you have customized how results of queries display you see the results in a grid (see Figure 3-9) or as text.

Notice that the specified three columns are displayed in the grid and they are ordered by last name.

In Chapter 5, I describe querying SQL Server by using T-SQL in more detail.

# Customizing the Environment

SQL Server 2005 gives you many options to adjust how SQL Server Management Studio works.

To see the available options, choose Tools⇨Options. Figure 3-10 shows some of the options. Expand the nodes in the left part of the Options dialog box to see all the options available.

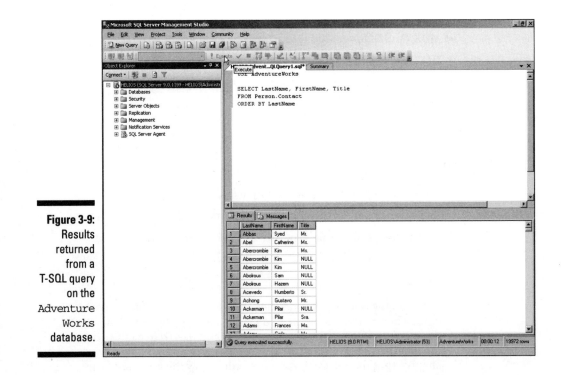

**Figure 3-9:**
Results
returned
from a
T-SQL query
on the
Adventure
Works
database.

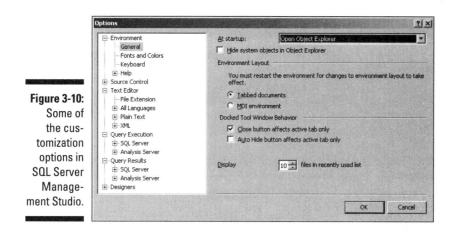

**Figure 3-10:**
Some of
the cus-
tomization
options in
SQL Server
Manage-
ment Studio.

## Setting Startup options

On the Environment, General tab you can specify what displays when you
open SQL Server Management Studio (see Figure 3-11).

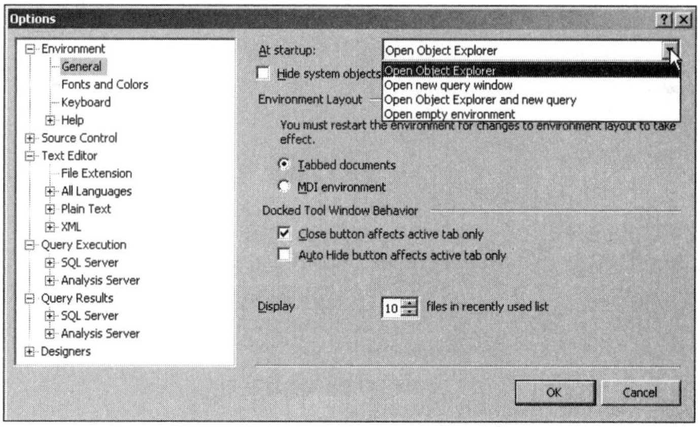

**Figure 3-11:**
Adjust
startup
options for
SQL Server
Manage-
ment Studio.

## Displaying results

To alter the display of query results, select the Query Results, SQL Server
tab. You can display the results in a grid or as text or send the results to a
file. Figure 3-12 shows how you choose the option.

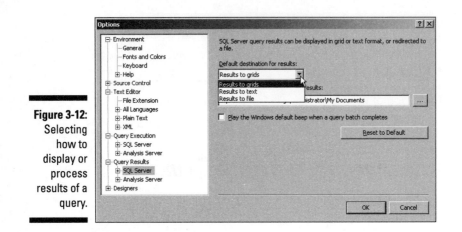

**Figure 3-12:**
Selecting
how to
display or
process
results of a
query.

## *Keyboard shortcuts*

SQL Server Management Studio supports two options for using keyboard shortcuts. One option follows the Visual Studio conventions for keyboard shortcuts. The other closely follows shortcuts available in SQL Server 2000 Query Analyzer.

To select a keyboard scheme, choose Tools➪Options. In the Options dialog box, choose General➪Keyboard. You can select the keyboard scheme from a drop-down menu, as shown in Figure 3-13.

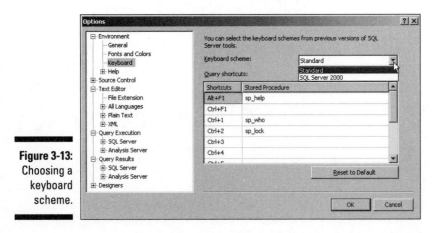

**Figure 3-13:**
Choosing a
keyboard
scheme.

## Restoring the default configuration

SQL Server Management Studio allows you to modify many aspects of the appearance. It is possible that you can create a configuration that you don't like so that you want to restore the original settings. To restore the default configuration of windows in SQL Server Management Studio, choose Window⇨Reset Window Layout.

## Using templates in Management Studio

When you are creating a Transact-SQL query, it can be useful to have a template that you tweak to get the effect that you want. In SQL Server 2005, Microsoft has provided a large number of templates that you can adapt to your specific needs.

To view the available templates, choose View⇨Template Explorer.

# Part II
# Basic Operations

The 5th Wave                    By Rich Tennant

"Look, I've already launched a search for 'reanimated babe cadavers' three times and nothing came up!"

## In this part . . .

I show you how to use Transact-SQL (T-SQL) to create SQL Server databases and tables. I introduce you to how to use T-SQL to retrieve data from a SQL Server database.

I also show you how easily you can create basic Windows applications based on SQL Server 2005 data.

# Chapter 4

# Creating Databases, Tables, and Relationships with T-SQL

SQL Server 2005 is a relational database management system that can have multiple instances on one server. Each instance of SQL Server 2005 can manage multiple relational databases. Relational databases consist of tables. Most relational databases contain multiple tables with logical relationships between data in different tables expressed with keys.

SQL Server Management Studio allows you to have access to database objects, such as tables, controlled by SQL Server 2005. It replaces the Enterprise Manager and Query Analyzer from SQL Server 2000.

In this chapter, I show you how to navigate database objects with the Object Explorer in SQL Server Management Studio and how to use SQL Server Management Studio to create database objects, which are essential in typical business databases that you use in SQL Server 2005.

Each thing in a database, including the database itself, can be thought of as a database *object*. Examples of database objects include tables, views, indexes, and stored procedures.

To carry out the tasks of creating databases and tables, you need to have SQL Server 2005 installed.

# *Firing Up SQL Server 2005*

To carry out the tasks that I describe in this chapter, you must have SQL Server 2005 running. Typically, with Windows 2003 or Windows XP, you can run SQL Server 2005 as a service. When you install SQL Server 2005, you can set the SQL Server service to run automatically when Windows starts; if not, you must start SQL Server manually.

Opening the Services window differs slightly depending on the operating system you're using. To check that the SQL Server 2005 service is running, and to start the service if necessary, follow these steps:

1. **With Windows XP, choose Start➪Control Panel➪Administrative Tools➪ Services. With Windows 2003, choose Start➪Administrative Tools➪ Services.**

   The Services window lists the available services, as shown in Figure 4-1.

2. **Scroll down to the SQL Server (MSSQLSERVER) option, which is high- lighted in Figure 4-1.**

   If you installed SQL Server as a named instance, the name of the service is displayed as SQL Server (*instancename*).

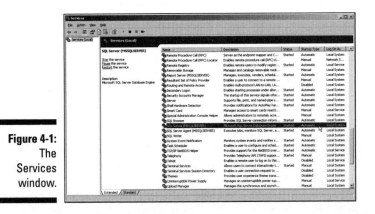

**Figure 4-1:** The Services window.

3. **Check the values in the Status column and the Startup Type column. If SQL Server is not already started, select the Start option or icon in the upper-left corner of the Services window.**

You can also set SQL Server to start automatically by following these steps:

1. **Right-click the Startup Type column and choose Properties to start SQL Server automatically upon startup.**

   The SQL Server (MSSQLSERVER) Properties dialog box appears.

2. **Select Automatic from the Startup Type drop-down menu on the General tab.**

To carry out the tasks that I describe later in this chapter, you must also start SQL Server Management Studio (Start⇨All Programs⇨Microsoft SQL Server 2005⇨SQL Server Management Studio).

When SQL Server Management Studio starts, you must connect to a SQL Server database engine instance if you want to create a database or add database objects to an existing database. The Connect To Server dialog box appears automatically when SQL Server Management Studio starts. Follow these steps to connect to a server:

1. **Select Database Engine in the Server Type drop-down menu.**

2. **Select an appropriate server name in the Server Name drop-down menu.**

   If you installed a default instance you can type . (a period) or **(local)**. If you installed a named instance, type **.\\*instancename*** (a period followed by a backslash and then the instance name). If you're connecting to a remote server, type ***servername*\\*instancename*** (server name followed by a backslash followed by the instance name).

3. **Select the appropriate authentication mode.**

   The choices offered depend on how you installed SQL Server 2005.

You can have several copies of SQL Server 2005 installed on one physical server. Each copy of SQL Server is called an *instance*. One instance is the default instance and is not named. All other instances must be named. If you have multiple instances running, each instance has its own entry in the Services window.

# *Exploring the Object Explorer*

The Object Explorer in SQL Server Management Studio allows you to access objects in any of possibly several databases in an instance controlled by SQL Server 2005. To access the Object Explorer, you need to have SQL Server Management Studio open. The Object Explorer in SQL Server Management Studio displays by default and its default position is to the left of the SQL Server Management Studio window.

If the Object Explorer is not visible, choose View⇨Object Explorer. The Object Explorer is empty until you connect successfully to a SQL Server instance by using the Connect To Server dialog box. After you connect to a server, a hierarchy of database objects displays in the Object Explorer, as shown in Figure 4-2.

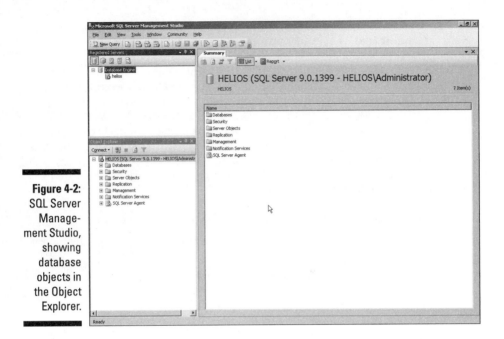

**Figure 4-2:**
SQL Server
Manage-
ment Studio,
showing
database
objects in
the Object
Explorer.

The Registered Servers pane resides above the Object Explorer. In that pane, you can see multiple instances of SQL Server if you have installed and registered more than one SQL server instance. To access a server in the Object Explorer, you must register it in Registered Servers.

To register a Database Engine instance, follow these steps:

1. **Click the Database Engine icon on the Registered Servers toolbar.**

2. **Right-click the Database Engine registration group that appears, and choose New.**

3. **Select New Server Registration.**

   The New Server Registration dialog box opens.

4. **Type the name of the server.**

5. **Click the Test button to test whether or not you can connect to the chosen server by using the default connection settings.**

6. **If the test connection succeeds, click Save.**

   The server displays below the Database Engine registration group in the Registered Servers pane.

To display objects in a registered server, right-click it and choose Connect⇨ Object Explorer. The selected server displays in the Object Explorer with its highest-level folders visible.

The objects in the Object Explorer are arranged in a hierarchy. Each part of the hierarchy that you can expand is called a *folder* or *node*. The terms are used interchangeably.

In Figure 4-2, the single registered server is called Helios. The first line of the Object Explorer shows the Helios server is open and that it is a SQL Server 2005 instance, and it is version 9.0. By default, all the nodes in the Object Explorer are unexpanded.

# Creating Databases

To store your business data, you need to design and create databases that match your business needs. To create a new database with the Object Explorer, right-click the Databases node in the Object Explorer and choose New Database from the context menu. The New Database dialog box opens (see Figure 4-3).

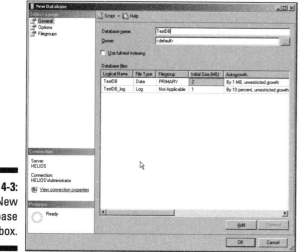

**Figure 4-3:** The New Database dialog box.

Back up the master database before you create a new database. The master database contains information about all databases managed by an instance of SQL Server 2005. Backing up the master database protects you from the effects of inappropriate choices and allows you to restore the situation before you created the database.

You must supply a name for the new database on the General tab of the New Database dialog box. You also need to specify who is the owner of the database that you are about to create. The default owner is the login `sa`.

All instances of SQL Server 2005 have several *system databases*. System databases contain information that SQL Server 2005 uses to correctly manage databases that you create. To see the system databases, click the Databases node, and then choose System Databases. Among the system databases are the master and model databases.

Do not alter or delete system databases unless you fully understand the effects of the action you are about to take.

The default properties of the database you create are inherited from the model database, which is one of the databases visible when you click the System Databases node under the Databases node in the Object Explorer.

If you want the databases you create to share custom properties, customizing the model database before creating other databases is efficient.

When you finish adding the name of the database and selecting the options that you want, click the OK button in the New Database dialog box. A file with a `.mdf` extension is created that holds the data and a file with a `.ldf` extension is created that holds log information for the database that you create.

To confirm that you just created a new database, click the Databases node in the Object Explorer to expand it. Databases that are not system databases are listed in their individual folder below the System Databases node. Your new database displays there.

The content of the Object Explorer doesn't always refresh automatically when you add or delete database objects. To refresh the object hierarchy, if necessary, right-click and choose Refresh.

# Creating Tables

After you create a new database, you need to design and create tables to hold your data.

In a relational database, data is held in tables. A *table* is a two-dimensional grid consisting of columns and rows.

Each *column* in the grid contains information about a particular characteristic. The data in each column is of a specified datatype. For example, in a table holding information about an order, an `ItemCost` column might contain the cost of an item and might be of the money data type.

The Cheat Sheet lists all the SQL Server 2005 datatypes.

A *row* contains all the information about a particular entry. For example, a row that contains information about an order might contain values in columns for `ItemPrice`, `NumberOfItems`, and `TotalPrice`. Each row in a table contains information about one item; for example, an orders table row usually contains information about one order. Typically, each row contains a column (or combination of columns) that allows SQL Server to uniquely identify the row.

To store data, you must add tables to a database. To add a table to a database, follow these steps:

1. **Click the node that contains the database name.**

2. **Right-click the Tables node and choose New Table from the context menu.**

   A new tab, called the *Table Designer,* displays in the right pane of SQL Server Management Studio (see Figure 4-4).

   The Table Designer contains columns for Column Name, Data Type, and Allow Nulls. Each row in the Table Designer contains the specification for a column in the database table that you are about to create.

3. **In the Table Designer, add the name of each column in the new table, specify its datatype, and indicate whether or not to allow NULL values. You can also add indexes by using the context menu (see Figure 4-5) and specify full-text indexing.**

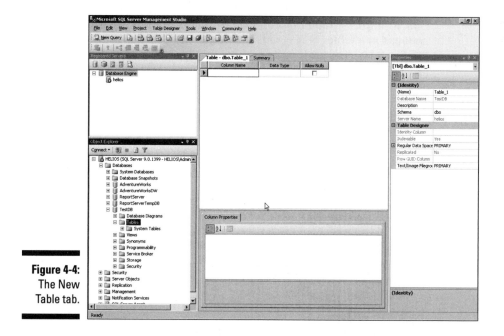

**Figure 4-4:**
The New
Table tab.

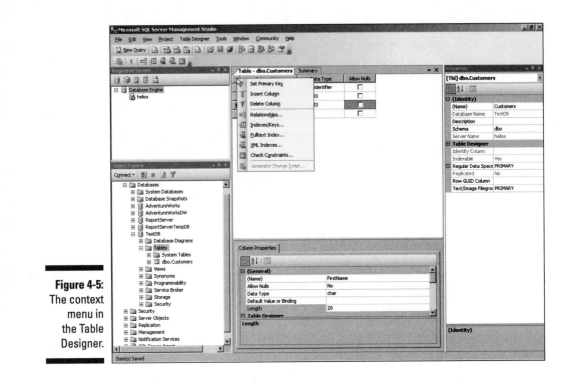

**Figure 4-5:**
The context
menu in
the Table
Designer.

An *index* provides a quick way for SQL Server to retrieve information from a database. An index contains keys corresponding to one or more columns in a table (or a view). A table can have these types of index: clustered and nonclustered.

SQL Server automatically updates indexes when you modify a table or view.

4. **When you're done specifying the column names and datatypes and making any other choices, press Ctrl+S to save the definition of the table columns.**

The Choose Name dialog box displays (see Figure 4-6).

*Note:* Names of tables and columns must follow specified rules. The first character of the name must be a letter, @, underscore, or #. In English, the first character can be a through z or A through Z. Names beginning with @ or # are used for specific purposes, and I recommend that you don't use those characters for the first character of the name of a table or column. Subsequent characters of a name can also include numbers and the dollar sign, $. Names for tables and columns must not be Transact-SQL reserved words.

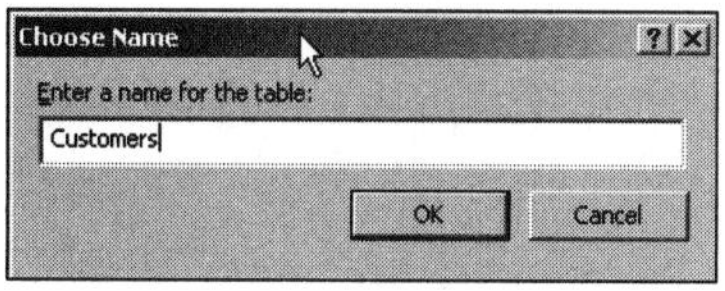

**Figure 4-6:**
The Choose
Name
dialog box.

| Choose Name | ? × |
| --- | --- |

Enter a name for the table:

Customers

OK     Cancel

**5. Specify an appropriate name for the newly created table and click OK.**

Test whether you created the table and columns correctly by clicking the node for your new database in the Object Explorer:

**1. Click the Tables node.**

The new table has its own node.

**2. Click that node to expand it.**

The columns you created display.

Your table has no data yet, but you can run a Transact-SQL query against the table.

**3. In Management Studio, click the New Query button on the toolbar, select Database Engine Query, and type the following code in the Query Editor:**

```
USE TestDB
SELECT * FROM Customers
```

**4. Click the Results to Grid button on the toolbar.**

**5. Click the Execute button on the toolbar.**

A grid displays the column names you created in the table.

# Defining Relationships

Relational databases operate by using relationships that are defined between tables contained in each database. Relationships help avoid duplication of information. Avoiding duplicate data reduces the chance of inconsistent data. You specify relationships by using primary and foreign keys in related tables.

A *primary key* is a unique identifier for each row in a table. The primary key is often contained in one column of the row, although in some situations two or more columns are used together as a primary key. If a relationship is with another table, then another column of the row contains a key that matches a primary key unique identifier column in another table. That key is called a *foreign key*. The column that is the foreign key in one table is also present as the primary key in another table.

To add a relationship, follow these steps:

1. **If the Table Designer is not open, right-click the table in the Object Explorer and choose Modify Table from the context menu.**

2. **Right-click the Table Designer for the table that contains the foreign key.**

3. **Select Relationships from the context menu.**

   The Foreign Keys dialog box opens.

4. **Click Add in the Foreign Keys dialog box to create a new foreign key relationship.**

   A default name is provided in the left pane for the new relationship and its default properties display in the right pane.

5. **In the right pane, click the ellipsis (shown in Figure 4-7) to open the Tables and Columns dialog box.**

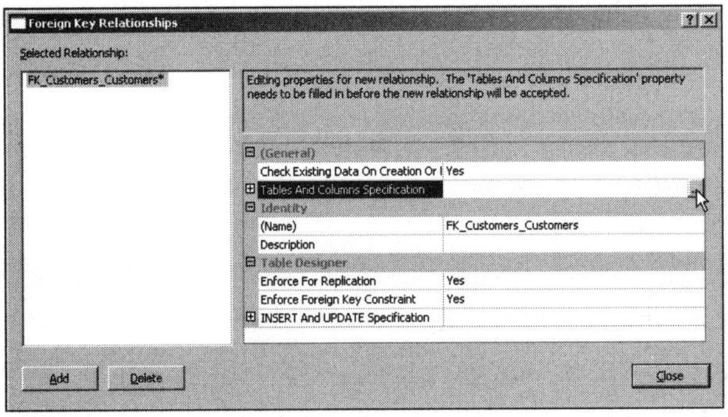

**Figure 4-7:** Expand the Tables and Columns Specifications node.

6. **In the Tables and Columns dialog box (see Figure 4-8), choose an appropriate name for the relationship.**

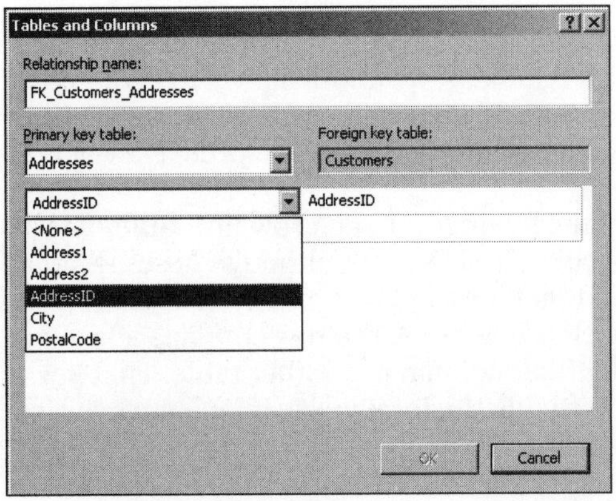

**Figure 4-8:** The Tables and Columns dialog box.

7. Specify the table and column that contain the primary key that the foreign key relates to.

8. Specify the appropriate column that contains the primary key in the other table.

9. Specify the column in the current table that contains the foreign key.

10. Click OK to accept the changes you have made.

11. Click Close to close the Foreign Keys dialog box and confirm the new relationship.

# Adding Constraints

SQL Server 2005 allows you to constrain the values allowed in a particular column so that inappropriate data is not permitted. The datatype in the Table Designer also constrains the values allowed in a column but is not considered to be a constraint.

SQL Server 2005 supports five types of constraint:

- ✔ **NOT NULL:** When this constraint is specified, you are not allowed to have a field in a column with no data in it.

- ✔ **CHECK:** This constraint specifies allowed values. For example, you might want age of employees to be between 16 and 65.

- ✔ **UNIQUE:** This constraint specifies that you can't repeat the value in a field in any other field in the same column.

- ✔ **PRIMARY KEY:** This constraint specifies a unique identifier for the value in a field, which uniquely identifies a row.

- ✔ **FOREIGN KEY:** This constraint references a unique identifier in another table in the database.

When you create a table, you typically add a primary key to the table. A table may have only one primary key.

If you do not designate a column (or combination of columns) as the primary key when you create the table you can specify a primary key later, provided certain conditions are met. A column intended as a primary key can't have NULL values and each value in the column must be unique. If the table has data and those conditions are not met, your attempt to create a primary key on that column causes an error and no primary key is created.

Choose a primary key when you first create a table. By doing so, you avoid possible time-consuming changes to a table after it contains data.

If you want to change the column (or combination of columns) that is the primary key, you need to delete the primary key constraint on the original column(s) and add a primary key constraint. If the original primary key is referenced by a foreign key constraint, you must delete the foreign key constraint first, and then delete the original primary key constraint.

To add a CHECK constraint, follow these steps:

1. **Right-click the row that specifies the relevant column.**

2. **Choose Check Constraints from the context menu.**

3. **In the Check Constraints dialog box, click the Add button to add a new constraint.**

4. **Click the ellipsis in the Expression row of the right pane of the Check Constraints window (see Figure 4-9).**

   The Check Constraints dialog box opens.

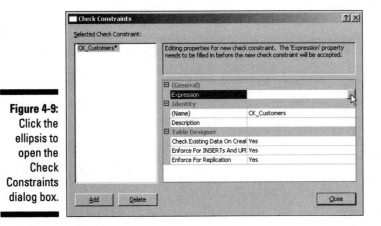

**Figure 4-9:** Click the ellipsis to open the Check Constraints dialog box.

5. **Enter an expression that specifies the constraint.**

The allowed expressions depend on the datatype of the column. For example, in an Age column, you can specify that allowed ages are between 16 and 70 by using the following expression:

```
Age >= 16 AND Age <= 70
```

# Adding Data to the Database

When you design and create a database and its tables, you must add data to it. To add data to a database, follow these steps:

1. **In the Object Explorer, select the database that you want to add data to.**

2. **Expand the database node and then expand the Tables node.**

3. **Right-click the node for the table you want to add data to and choose Open Table.**

   The table opens in the right pane of SQL Server Management Studio. You can then add data directly to the table.

4. **Enter data a row at a time.**

   Make sure that you provide a value for each field, if you have specified that the field cannot contain a NULL value.

   Figure 4-10 shows data being added to a Customers table.

If you try to add data to a table that has a foreign key, you can't add data if no corresponding primary key is in the table with which it has a relationship.

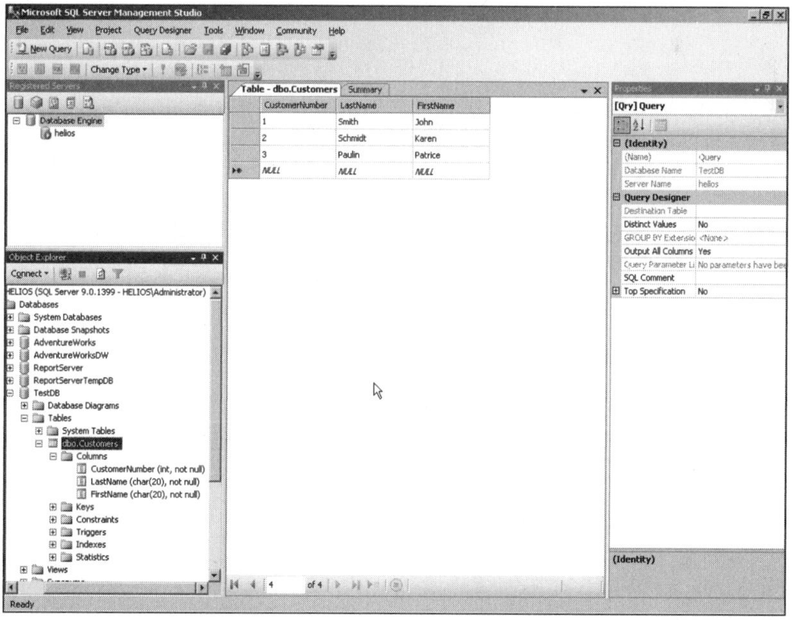

**Figure 4-10:**
Adding data to a table.

# Chapter 5

# Asking Questions and Getting Answers

● ● ● ● ● ● ● ● ● ● ● ● ● ● ● ● ● ● ● ● ● ● ● ● ● ● ● ● ● ● ● ● ● ● ● ● ● ● ● ● ● ● ● ● ●

## In This Chapter

▶ Querying with the Query Editor

▶ Retrieving data with the SELECT statement

▶ Specifying what data to return

▶ Sorting with ORDER BY

▶ Retrieving data from multiple tables through querying and joins

▶ Modifying a template

● ● ● ● ● ● ● ● ● ● ● ● ● ● ● ● ● ● ● ● ● ● ● ● ● ● ● ● ● ● ● ● ● ● ● ● ● ● ● ● ● ● ● ● ●

*O*ne of the commonest things you do with a database is ask questions about the data that it contains. The Query Editor in SQL Server Management Studio allows you to easily query SQL Server.

In this chapter, I show you how to ask questions of a SQL Server database by using the Query Editor in SQL Server Management Studio.

## Using the Query Editor

To open the Query Editor in SQL Server Management Studio, click the New Query button on the toolbar. A Connect to Server dialog box displays (see Figure 5-1). This allows you to specify whether you connect to a database engine instance (the default) or to an instance of Analysis Services or SQL Server Mobile. You also specify the name of the instance of the selected type that you want to connect to. Finally, you specify whether you want to use Windows Authentication or SQL Server Authentication.

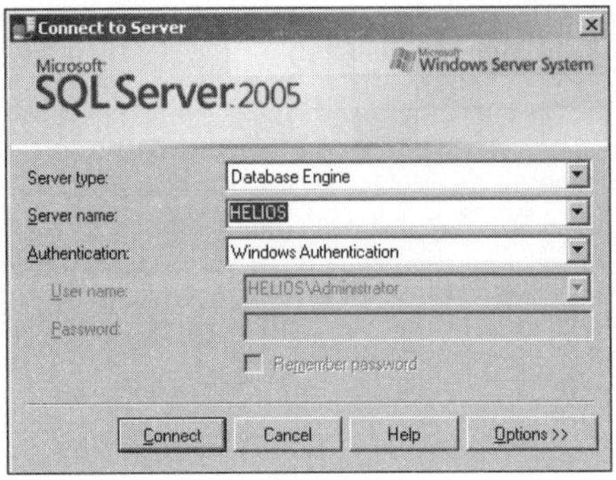

**Figure 5-1:**
The
Connect
to Server
dialog box.

A new tab opens in the right pane of SQL Server Management Studio with a surface on which you type T-SQL code.

If you want to run a second query against the same instance, simply click the New Query button again. If you want to change the instance, click the Database Engine Query, Analysis Services MDX Query, Analysis Services DMX Query, Analysis Services XMLA Query, or SQL Server Mobile Query button on the toolbar. The buttons for the preceding queries are shown in Figure 5-2.

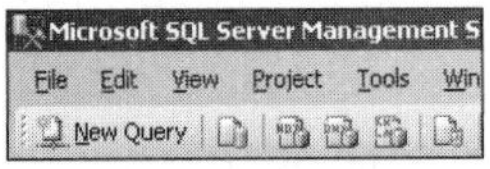

**Figure 5-2:**
The buttons
to run
queries in
the query
pane.

You can have multiple tabs open in the query pane at one time. Each tab has its own connection. For example, you can connect to a database engine instance in one tab and an Analysis Services instance in another.

When running a T-SQL query, clicking the Execute button on the toolbar (or pressing F5) runs the whole query. Highlighting some T-SQL code and then clicking the Execute button runs only the highlighted code. This is a convenient way to step through T-SQL scripts.

By default, the output goes to a results grid. If you want to output to text, choose Query➪Results To➪Results to Text. If you want the output of a query to be sent to a file, choose Query➪Results To➪Results to File.

# Using the SELECT Statement

Much of the T-SQL programming that you do involves retrieving data by using one of the many syntax variants of the SELECT statement.

The examples I show you use the sample databases that Microsoft has distributed for some time: AdventureWorks (which is not the same as the AdventureWorks2000 database that Microsoft distributed with SQL Server 2000) and pubs. At the time of writing, AdventureWorks is available as installation options with SQL Server 2005 editions. You can download the pubs (and Northwind) databases from here:

```
www.microsoft.com/downloads/details.aspx?FamilyId=06616212
        -0356-46A0-8DA2-EEBC53A68034&displaylang=en
```

To install the pubs database, follow these steps:

1. **Choose Start⇨All Programs⇨Microsoft SQL Server 2000 Sample Database Scripts.**

   The folder containing the T-SQL installation scripts opens.

2. **Double-click instpubs.sql.**

   The instpubs.sql T-SQL script opens in a tab in the query pane in SQL Server Management Studio.

3. **Click the Execute button on the toolbar in SQL Server Management Studio (or use the F5 keyboard shortcut).**

4. **To confirm successful installation of the pubs database, create a new Database Engine query:**

   ```
   USE pubs
   SELECT *
   FROM authors
   ```

5. **Click the Execute button.**

   The results grid displays rows of data returned from the Authors table of the pubs database.

If the URLs for download have changed from those given in the preceding paragraph, I suggest you find the AdventureWorks database by going to Google and entering **AdventureWorks site:microsoft.com** in its Search box. To find the pubs database, enter **pubs download site:microsoft.com** in Google's Search box.

To retrieve data from a SQL Server database, you use the SELECT statement. In SQL Server 2005, you can specify the table that you want to retrieve data from with the database drop-down menu on the toolbar of SQL Server Management Studio (see Figure 5-3).

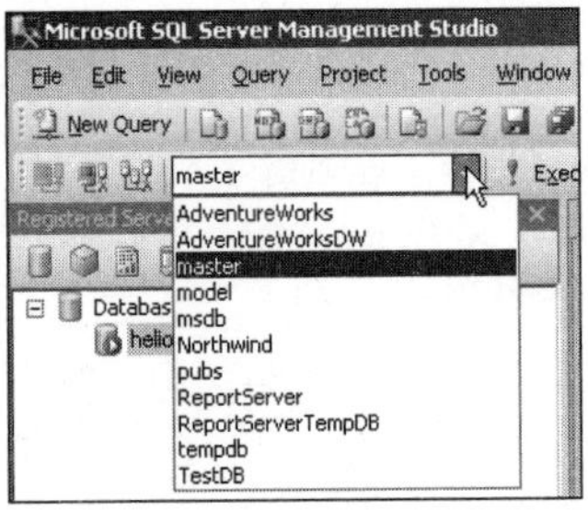

**Figure 5-3:**
**The**
**database**
**drop-down**
**menu in SQL**
**Server**
**Management**
**Studio.**

I sometimes forget which database I have selected. I often use the USE statement to specify the database. The following T-SQL code specifies that you want to retrieve data from the pubs database:

```
USE pubs
```

To retrieve a list of the last names and first names of the authors in the pubs database, follow these steps:

1. **Open SQL Server Management Studio and connect to the instance of SQL Server where you installed the pubs database.**

2. **Click the New Query button on the toolbar and select the Database Engine Query option.**

   A new tab opens in the query pane.

3. **In the query pane, enter the following T-SQL code:**

   ```
   USE pubs
   SELECT au_lname, au_fname
   FROM dbo.authors
   ```

4. **Click the Execute button on the toolbar.**

   Depending on how you set the results to display (see Chapter 3 for how to set SQL Server Management Studio options), you see an appearance similar to that in Figure 5-4.

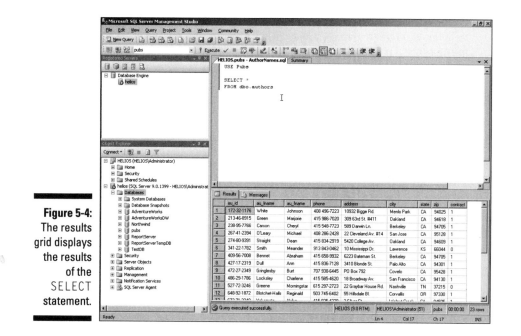

The second line of the T-SQL code specifies that the pubs database contains the data you want to retrieve. The line

```
SELECT au_lname, au_fname
```

contains a SELECT statement. The SELECT statement is often used to retrieve data from columns in a table but can also be used with string literals or the result of an expression. The names listed after the SELECT keyword specify a list of one or more column names (in this case two) from which data is to be retrieved.

The From clause

```
FROM dbo.authors
```

specifies the table in the pubs database from which you're retrieving data. The name of the table (dbo.authors) is in two parts: The first is the schema, dbo, and the second is the name of the table, authors.

A *schema* is a way to avoid naming collisions in SQL Server 2005. If a company holds data on people who are customers and who are employees, that data may be held in Person tables. If there is a Person table in the Employees schema and a Person table in the Customers schema, there is no chance of the two Person tables being confused, provided that the schema name is used when retrieving data from a Person table.

You may often want to retrieve data from a table with which you are not fully familiar. But to retrieve data, you need to know the names of all the columns in the table. To do so, use the * wildcard character, as follows:

```
SELECT *
FROM dbo.authors
```

An alternative way to explore the columns contained in a table is to navigate down the folder hierarchy in the Object Explorer in SQL Server Management Studio. When you click the Columns node, a list of the columns displays (see Figure 5-5). One advantage of using the Object Explorer is that the datatype of the column displays with an indication of whether or not NULL values are allowed for each column.

A NULL value indicates the absence of a value. It is not the same as a space character, an empty string, or a zero. If a column does not allow NULL values then, before you can add a row to the table, you must provide a value in that column.

**Figure 5-5:**
Examining
columns in
the Object
Explorer.

```
⊟ 🗊 pubs
  ⊞ 📁 Database Diagrams
  ⊟ 📁 Tables
    ⊞ 📁 System Tables
    ⊟ 🔲 dbo.authors
      ⊟ 📁 Columns
          🔑 au_id (PK, id(varchar(11)), not null)
          📄 au_lname (varchar(40), not null)
          📄 au_fname (varchar(20), not null)
          📄 phone (char(12), not null)
          📄 address (varchar(40), null)
          📄 city (varchar(20), null)
          📄 state (char(2), null)
          📄 zip (char(5), null)
          📄 contract (bit, not null)
```

Simple SELECT statements like these allow you to specify which columns you want to retrieve data from. Often you want to filter the data so that only some of the rows in the table are returned. Filtering the returned data is where the WHERE clause comes in.

# Filtering with the WHERE Clause

The WHERE clause is part of the SELECT statement. The WHERE clause allows you to specify which rows of data to return. For example, you may want to retrieve data for a specific sales year or authors with a specific surname.

You can easily filter authors returned from the pubs database. To retrieve information on authors whose surname is Ringer, follow these steps:

1. **Open SQL Server Management Studio. Click the Database Engine Query button.**

2. **Type the following code (or you can add the WHERE clause to the previous T-SQL query):**

```
USE pubs
SELECT au_lname, au_fname
FROM dbo.authors
WHERE au_lname = 'Ringer'
```

3. **Click the Execute button on the toolbar.**

The WHERE clause means that it returns only rows where the last name of the author exactly matches the name Ringer in the au_lname column. In the pubs database, it returns only two rows. Notice that the value you want to match is enclosed in paired single quotes.

In the WHERE clause, you can also use other operators to select a range of values in the au_lname column. To retrieve all rows where the author last name is Ringer or comes later than Ringer in the alphabet, modify the T-SQL code as follows:

```
USE pubs
SELECT au_lname, au_fname
FROM dbo.authors
WHERE au_lname >= 'Ringer'
```

By simply changing the = sign in the WHERE clause to >= (greater than or equal to), you can select a range of surnames. Table 5-1 summarizes some of the operators that you can use in a WHERE clause.

| Table 5-1 | Operators with the WHERE Clause |
|-----------|--------------------------------|
| *Operator* | *Description* |
| = | The value in the row is equal to the specified value. |
| <> | The value in the row is not equal to the specified value. |
| != | The value in the row is not equal to the specified value. |
| >= | The value in the row is equal to or greater than the specified value. |
| <= | The value in the row is equal to or less than the specified value. |
| NOT | Can be used with other operators. Negates the normal sense of any other operators. |
| BETWEEN | Returns rows where the value is between two specified values. |

*(continued)*

| Table 5-1 *(continued)* | |
|---|---|
| **Operator** | **Description** |
| IN | Returns rows where the value is in a specified list of values. |
| LIKE | Returns rows where the value in a column has a pattern similar to a specified value. |

In the WHERE clause, you can also retrieve rows where the values in a column are similar to a particular value, using the LIKE keyword. You can use the LIKE keyword to retrieve matches that begin with a particular sequence of characters or contain a specified sequence of characters.

The LIKE keyword uses two wildcard characters. The underscore ( _ ) wildcard character matches any single character. The % character matches zero or more characters.

To retrieve authors whose surname begins with the characters green, follow these steps:

1. **Open SQL Server Management Studio and click the Database Engine Query button.**

2. **In the query pane, type the following T-SQL code:**

```
USE pubs
SELECT au_lname, au_fname
FROM dbo.authors
WHERE au_lname LIKE 'Green%'
```

3. **Click the Execute button on the toolbar.**

The sequence of characters in the last line of the T-SQL matches literal characters, Green, plus the % wildcard character (which matches zero or more characters). So, in the data in the authors table, the WHERE clause limits returned rows to those where the value in the au_lname column is Green or Greene, as shown in Figure 5-6. If the authors table had contained books by Greening and Greenberg, those would also be returned.

To retrieve all authors whose surnames begin with B, C, or D, follow these steps:

1. **Modify the last line of the T-SQL code:**

```
USE pubs
SELECT au_lname, au_fname
FROM dbo.authors
WHERE au_lname BETWEEN 'B' AND 'E'
```

2. **Click the Execute button on the toolbar.**

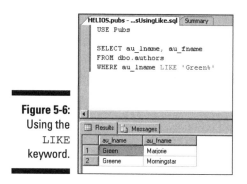

**Figure 5-6:**
Using the
LIKE
keyword.

As you can see in Figure 5-7, authors whose surname begins with B, C, or D are retrieved from the pubs database.

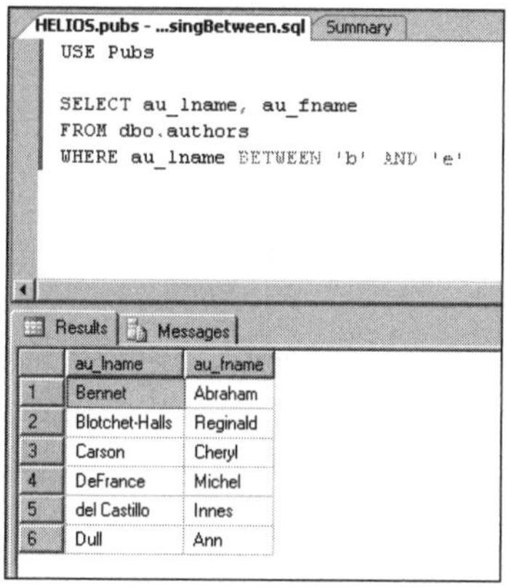

**Figure 5-7:**
Using the
BETWEEN
keyword in
a WHERE
clause.

# Sorting with ORDER BY

You can use the ORDER BY clause to sort the results from a SELECT statement in any way you want. If you don't use the ORDER BY clause, you cannot rely on data being returned in any specific order.

To specify the sort order, follow these steps:

1. **Create a new query in SQL Server Management Studio and click the Database Engine Query button.**

2. **In the query pane, type the following T-SQL code:**

```
USE pubs
SELECT au_lname, au_fname
FROM dbo.authors
ORDER BY au_lname ASC
```

The ASC keyword specifies that rows are sorted by last name in ascending order.

3. **Click the Execute button on the toolbar.**

   The data displays in the grid in ascending order (refer to Figure 5-2).

4. **To display the data in descending order by the author's last name, modify the code as follows:**

```
USE pubs
SELECT au_lname, au_fname
FROM dbo.authors
ORDER BY au_lname DESC
```

   The DESC keyword specifies that the rows returned are sorted in descending order.

5. **Click the Execute button.**

   The data displays with the last names in the alphabet first, as shown in Figure 5-8.

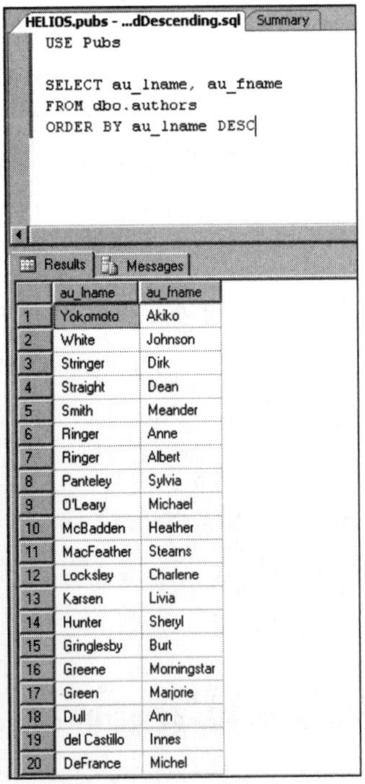

**Figure 5-8:**
Author
names
sorted in
descending
order by
last name.

# *Retrieving Data from Multiple Tables*

In the previous section, I show you how to retrieve data from a single table. In real life, you're more likely to retrieve data from at least two tables — and sometimes from more than two tables. In this section, I show you how to retrieve data from multiple tables.

First, I show you how to retrieve data from the pubs database to find any titles written by authors with the last name of Green. Follow these steps to do so:

1. **Open SQL Server Management Studio and create a new database engine query by clicking the Database Engine Query button.**

2. **In the query pane, type the following T-SQL code:**

```
USE pubs
SELECT authors.au_lname, authors.au_fname,
        titleauthor.au_id, titles.title
FROM dbo.authors, dbo.titleauthor, dbo.titles
WHERE authors.au_lname = 'Green'
AND titleauthor.au_id = authors.au_id
AND titles.title_id = titleauthor.title_id
```

The preceding code constructs a join by using the WHERE clause. Alternatively, you can use the FROM clause to construct the same join with the following code:

```
USE Pubs
SELECT authors.au_lname, authors.au_fname,
        titleauthor.au_id, titles.title
FROM dbo.authors
JOIN dbo.titleauthor
ON (authors.au_id = titleauthor.au_id)
JOIN dbo.titles
ON (titleauthor.title_id = titles.title_id)
WHERE authors.au_lname = 'Green'
```

The syntax using the FROM clause is the recommended approach, but both forms work in T-SQL. I discuss the JOIN syntax later in the chapter.

3. **Click the Execute button to run the code.**

The results appear (see Figure 5-9). You can see that two titles are by Marjorie Green.

```
HELIOS.pubs - ...NamesJoin1.sql   Summary
  USE Pubs

  SELECT authors.au_lname, authors.au_fname, titleauthor.au_id, titles.title
  FROM dbo.authors
  JOIN dbo.titleauthor
  ON (authors.au_id = titleauthor.au_id)
  JOIN dbo.titles
  ON (titleauthor.title_id = titles.title_id)
  WHERE authors.au_lname = 'Green'
```

| | au_lname | au_fname | au_id | title |
|---|---|---|---|---|
| 1 | Green | Marjorie | 213-46-8915 | The Busy Executive's Database Guide |
| 2 | Green | Marjorie | 213-46-8915 | You Can Combat Computer Stress! |

**Figure 5-9:** Retrieving titles written by anybody called Green.

To understand how querying multiple tables works, first take a step back and take a look at the way the tables in the pubs database are structured.

I suggest you follow these steps with SQL Server Management Studio open.

To explore the tables in the pubs database, follow these steps:

1. **Open SQL Server Management Studio.**

2. **In the Registered Servers, select the SQL Server instance that contains the pubs database. Right-click and choose Connect⇨Object Explorer.**

3. **Expand the Databases node. Expand the pubs node, and then expand the Tables node.**

   You now see an appearance similar to Figure 5-10.

```
☐ 📒 pubs
   ☐ 📁 Database Diagrams
   ☐ 📁 Tables
      ☐ 📁 System Tables
      ☐ 📄 dbo.authors
      ☐ 📄 dbo.discounts
      ☐ 📄 dbo.employee
      ☐ 📄 dbo.jobs
      ☐ 📄 dbo.pub_info
      ☐ 📄 dbo.publishers
      ☐ 📄 dbo.roysched
      ☐ 📄 dbo.sales
      ☐ 📄 dbo.stores
      ☐ 📄 dbo.titleauthor
      ☐ 📄 dbo.titles
   ☐ 📁 Views
   ☐ 📁 Synonyms
   ☐ 📁 Programmability
   ☐ 📁 Service Broker
   ☐ 📁 Storage
   ☐ 📁 Security
```

**Figure 5-10:** The Tables node in the pubs database.

The three tables that I queried in the previous steps are the dbo.authors, dbo.titleauthor, and dbo.titles tables. Expand the nodes for each of these tables and look at the columns they contain.

The dbo.authors table has the following columns:

- ✔ **au_id:** The primary key for the table
- ✔ **au_lname:** The author's last name
- ✔ **au_fname:** The author's first name

The table has several other columns, but I use these three columns in the current query.

If you look at all the columns in the dbo.authors table, you can see that no column shows the titles each author has written. This is a typical situation in a relational database. The design of a relational database means that each piece of information is recorded only once. If the table contained author and title information, then the author information would have to be duplicated. In a relational database, the author information is contained in one table and the title information is stored in another table. In the pubs database, the title information is stored in the dbo.titles table.

If you use the Object Explorer to examine the columns in the dbo.titles table, you see that it includes these columns:

- ✔ **title_id:** The primary key for the table
- ✔ **title:** The title of the book
- ✔ **price:** The price of the book

So you can find the title information in the title column of the dbo.titles table. But how do you connect a title to its author(s)?

Here you need to think about the relationship between an author (or authors) and a book or books. One author can write many books. Similarly, a single title can have multiple authors. This is called a *many-to-many relationship*.

A typical way to represent a many-to-many relationship is to have an extra table containing two columns that correspond to the primary key columns of two other tables.

In this example, the table that contains this information is the dbo.titleauthor table. It contains the following columns that I use in the query:

- ✔ **au_id:** The au_id column in the dbo.titleauthor table allows you to make a logical connection to the au_id column in the dbo.authors table.
- ✔ **title_id:** The title_id column in the dbo.titleauthor table allows you to make a logical connection to the title_id column in the dbo.titles table.

This is how the many-to-many relationship between authors and titles is expressed in the pubs database.

With that background, you're now ready to look in more detail at the T-SQL code.

First, I describe how the WHERE clause syntax works, which I show again here for convenience:

```
USE pubs
SELECT authors.au_lname, authors.au_fname,
          titleauthor.au_id, titles.title
FROM dbo.authors, dbo.titleauthor, dbo.titles
WHERE authors.au_lname = 'Green'
AND titleauthor.au_id = authors.au_id
AND titles.title_id = titleauthor.title_id
```

The first line specifies to query the pubs database.

The next line retrieves data from four columns: the au_lname and au_fname columns from the dbo.authors table, plus the au_id column from the dbo. titleauthor table plus the title column from the dbo.titles table.

The FROM clause specifies that you're can retrieve data from three different tables: dbo.authors, dbo.titleauthor, and dbo.titles.

The first line in the WHERE clause specifies that you retrieve data where the author's last name is Green.

Click the Comment Out the Selected Lines button on the toolbar to comment out the last two lines of the code. Click the Execute button to run the query.

The query results in 450 rows. But, as you can probably guess if you examine the results, Marjorie Green hasn't written 25 different books called *But Is It User Friendly?*

So what is happening? Without the last two rows of the code, you're making this query: "Create a new table that has an au_lname column containing the string Green plus the au_fname, au_id, title, and royaltyper columns created by retrieving data from the relevant tables."

You want a query equivalent to "Create a new table where content of the au_lname column is Green and find rows in the dbo.titles table where the author is somebody with the last name of Green."

If you uncomment the second last line the number of returned rows decreases to 35. There is a row for each value in the title column in the dbo.titles table. You still need to specify that only titles written by Green are to be returned. After you uncomment the last line only two titles return both written by Marjorie Green.

The technique I have showed you uses the WHERE clause to specify how to retrieve columns from multiple tables. You can do the same thing by using *joins*, which I describe next.

# *Joins*

You can use the WHERE clause, as described in the preceding section to construct *inner joins*, which is the most commonly used type of join. For anything other than fairly simple joins, the WHERE syntax becomes unwieldy. In more complex queries, the JOIN syntax is recommended.

SQL Server 2005 supports several types of joins. I describe only the INNER JOIN in this chapter. The types of join are listed here:

- ✔ **INNER JOIN:** Matches rows on common columns and returns rows where there are matches for the columns used in the join.

- ✔ **OUTER JOIN:** There are two types — RIGHT OUTER JOIN and LEFT OUTER JOIN.

- ✔ **FULL JOIN.**

- ✔ **SELF JOIN.**

A *join* allows you to retrieve data from multiple tables. Using the JOIN syntax to write complex queries is usually easier than using the WHERE clause.

I show you how to achieve the same result as in the previous example by using an inner join. Follow these steps:

1. **Open SQL Server Management Studio and open a new database engine query by clicking on the Database Engine Query button.**

2. **Type the following T-SQL code:**

```
USE pubs
SELECT authors.au_lname, authors.au_fname,
       titleauthor.au_id, titles.title
FROM dbo.authors INNER JOIN dbo.titleauthor
ON titleauthor.au_id = authors.au_id
INNER JOIN dbo.titles
ON titles.title_id = titleauthor.title_id
WHERE authors.au_lname = 'Green'
```

3. **Click the Execute button to run the code.**

   Figure 5-11 shows the results.

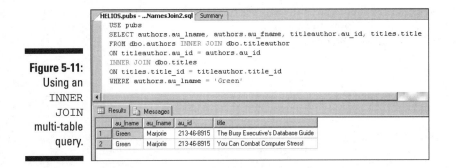

**Figure 5-11:**
Using an
INNER
JOIN
multi-table
query.

The SELECT clause specifies that you want to retrieve four columns:
authors.au_lname, authors.au_fname, titleauthor.au_id, and
titles.title.

The first two lines in the FROM clause

```
FROM dbo.authors INNER JOIN dbo.titleauthor
ON titleauthor.au_id = authors.au_id
```

specify that you want an inner join on two tables, dbo.authors and
dbo.titleauthor, where the value of titleauthor.au_id and
authors.au_id are equal.

Because the relationship between the authors and titles is many-to-many, you
need a second inner join:

```
INNER JOIN dbo.titles
ON titles.title_id = titleauthor.title_id
```

so that you correctly associate an author's name with the title(s) that he/she
has written.

The final WHERE clause

```
WHERE authors.au_lname = 'Green'
```

filters the results so that only rows containing results where the author last
name is Green are returned.

You can use the full range of the WHERE clause with such queries. To return all authors from Carson to Panteley, modify the WHERE clause to the following:

```
WHERE authors.au_lname BETWEEN 'C' AND 'R'
```

You can also use the ORDER BY clause with such queries. Add the following code:

```
ORDER BY titles.title
```

to display the results sorted alphabetically by title.

The inner join is the most commonly used join. Other types of join that I don't describe here are LEFT JOIN, RIGHT JOIN, and CROSS JOIN.

# Modifying a Template

SQL Server 2005 provides a large number of templates containing T-SQL code. You access the Template Explorer from SQL Server Management Studio. If the Template Explorer is not visible, choose View➪Template Explorer. The Template Explorer displays, as shown in Figure 5-12.

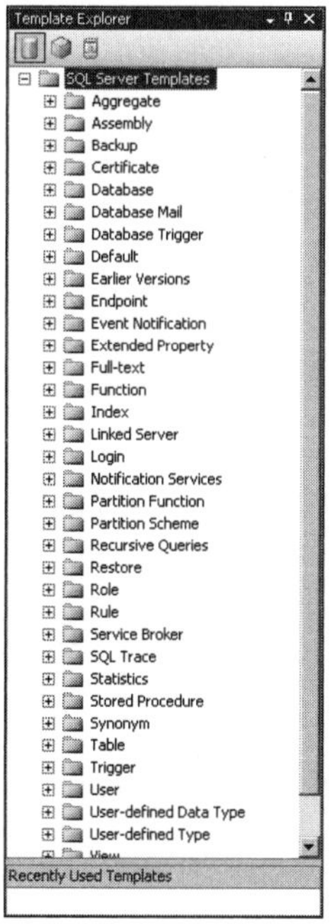

**Figure 5-12:** The Template Explorer.

I suggest you explore the huge range of templates by navigating through the hierarchy of nodes.

One of many uses for a template is when creating a database. Follow these steps to create a new database with T-SQL:

1. **Click the Databases node in Template Explorer to expand it.**

2. **Double-click the Create Database node.**

   A new query window opens and, depending on which panes you have visible, looks something similar to Figure 5-13.

   Notice that some of the code is contained between angled brackets (< and >).

3. **Choose Query⇨Specify Values for Template Parameters.**

   The Specify Values for Template Parameters dialog box opens, as shown in Figure 5-14.

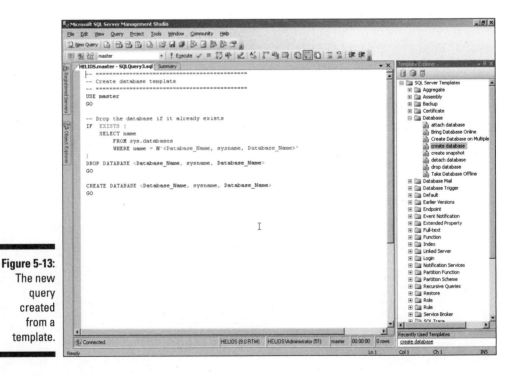

**Figure 5-13:**
The new query created from a template.

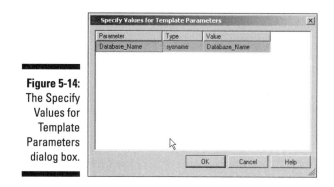

**Figure 5-14:**
The Specify
Values for
Template
Parameters
dialog box.

If you compare the columns in the Specify Values for Template
Parameters dialog box with the values inside the angled brackets in the
query pane you see that they are the same. The Specify Values for
Template Parameters dialog box allows you to enter a value once for a
parameter. SQL Server 2005 adds that value at each appropriate place in
the T-SQL code.

4. **Double-click in the Value column of the Specify Values for Template
   Parameters dialog box and enter** FromTemplate.

5. **Click OK. Examine the code in the query pane and note that the parameter has been replaced by the name FromTemplate.**

   The angled brackets are no longer there because they are no longer
   needed as placeholders.

6. **Click the Execute button on the toolbar to run the code.**

7. **In the Object Explorer, right-click the Databases node and choose
   Refresh from the context menu.**

   The FromTemplate database displays.

# Chapter 6

# Building a Simple Application

· · · · · · · · · · · · · · · · · · · · · · · · · · · · · · · · · · · · · · · · · · · · · ·

## In This Chapter

▶ Customizing the development environment

▶ Adding a connection

▶ Creating the user interface

▶ Diagnosing problems

· · · · · · · · · · · · · · · · · · · · · · · · · · · · · · · · · · · · · · · · · · · · · ·

*Y*ou can use SQL Server 2005 in many ways. If you are a database administrator, you can use the management tools such as SQL Server Management Studio to help you administer one or more instances of SQL Server. If you are a database developer, you can create custom applications based on SQL Server 2005. Typically, to create such custom applications you use one of the several editions of Visual Studio 2005 as the tool to create an application that uses SQL Server 2005 as the database layer.

You can use the Business Intelligence Development Studio that is part of SQL Server 2005 to create specialized applications for SQL Server Integration Services, Analysis Services, and Reporting Services. I describe using the Business Intelligence Development Studio to create such applications in Chapters 20, 21, and 22.

In this chapter, I show you basic techniques to create a simple application that uses SQL Server 2005 as the back end database. I use Visual Studio 2005 to create the front end of the application. To create the sample application shown in this chapter you need some edition of Visual Studio installed. Because Visual Studio has multiple editions, I do not describe installation here.

The editions of Visual Studio or related products are listed here:

✔ Visual Basic 2005 Express Edition

✔ Visual C# 2005 Express Edition

✔ Visual C++ 2005 Express Edition

✔ Visual Web Developer 2005 Express Edition

✔ Visual Studio 2005 Standard Edition

✔ Visual Studio 2005 Professional Edition

✔ Visual Studio 2005 Team Suite

✔ Visual Studio 2005 Team Foundation Server

✔ Visual Basic 2005 Standard Edition

✔ Visual C# 2005 Standard Edition

*Note:* Throughout this chapter, I use the term "Visual Studio" to refer to any of the preceding products. Where I refer to Visual Studio, you can use any product you have from the preceding list.

For fuller information on Visual Studio 2005, see *Visual Basic 2005 For Dummies,* by Bill Sempf (Wiley).

# Designing the Application

Visual Studio 2005 has a complex user interface with numerous options that you can adapt to customize the development environment. In this section, I haven't changed the default settings. If you have an edition of Visual Studio 2005 and have changed options through Tools⇨Options, then you may have to take slightly different actions and/or you may see a slightly different appearance than the one you see in the figures. The example application that I create in this chapter uses basic functionality of Visual Studio so you can create a similar application with any version of Visual Studio.

When designing an application, you must ensure that you have stored all the relevant data in SQL Server 2005. To correctly design the database, you need to consider a range of business needs — both current and future. In practical applications, you need to spend significant amounts of time deciding what data to store and how to store it.

When creating an application, consider points such as the following:

✔ Will users access the application through your company network or through the Internet?

✔ How many people need to access the data? What are peak user numbers at any one time?

✔ Will users view data only or will they have the capability to add or update data?

✔ How can you best present the information to users? For example, you need to consider whether different groups of users need different interfaces to meet their business needs.

Depending on the answers to some of the preceding points you want to choose an appropriate edition of SQL Server 2005 to ensure good availability of the data to the anticipated users of the application. I describe the available editions of SQL Server 2005 in Chapter 1.

In Chapter 11, I describe the security functionality that is available in SQL Server 2005 and show you how to use that functionality to take control of your SQL Server 2005 data. When designing an application, you need to give careful thought about how to secure your data and how to allow access to legitimate users.

For simplicity, in this example I use one of Microsoft's sample databases for SQL Server, the pubs database. In the example application I want to retrieve information about authors in the pubs database. The aim of this simple application is to display author names and phone numbers for users in alphabetical order.

Instructions for downloading and installing the pubs database are in Chapter 5.

When creating an application, it is useful to have a good understanding of the data and how it is stored. In practical applications, you can study the table and column structure of a database by following these steps:

1. **Open SQL Server Management Studio by choosing Start⇨All Programs⇨ Microsoft SQL Server 2005⇨SQL Server Management Studio.**

2. **Connect to the SQL Server instance you want to use while developing your application.**

   Typically that won't be a production server.

3. **In the Registered Servers pane of SQL Server Management Studio, right-click the server you want to use and choose Connect⇨Object Explorer.**

4. **In the Object Explorer, navigate down the tree of nodes for the server until you find the node for the database you plan to use for your application.**

   In this example, after expanding the node for the SQL Server instance, I expand the Databases node, and then the pubs node, and then the Tables node, the node for dbo.authors next, and finally, the Columns node for the dbo.authors table. You can then study the columns in the dbo.authors table, as shown in Figure 6-1. Notice that the Object Explorer displays information about the datatypes of the columns in the table.

**Figure 6-1:**
The
Columns
node of
the pubs
database
expanded.

```
☐ 📖 pubs
    ⊞ 📁 Database Diagrams
    ☐ 📁 Tables
        ⊞ 📁 System Tables
        ☐ 🗒 dbo.authors
            ☐ 📁 Columns
                🔑 au_id (PK, id(varchar(11)), not null)
                📰 au_lname (varchar(40), not null)
                📰 au_fname (varchar(20), not null)
                📰 phone (char(12), not null)
                📰 address (varchar(40), null)
                📰 city (varchar(20), null)
                📰 state (char(2), null)
                📰 zip (char(5), null)
                📰 contract (bit, not null)
```

For this example, I use the au_lname, au_fname, and phone columns.

In large databases, you may have two tables with the same table name. If so, you need to be careful to include the name of the schema that the table belongs to. In this example, the authors table belongs to the dbo schema so I select the dbo.authors table.

# Creating a New Project

In a production application you need to give careful consideration as to how you display information to users and whether you allow them to add new data to the database.

In this example, I create a very simple application that retrieves author name and phone number information and displays it in a simple on-screen tabular layout.

To create a basic Windows Forms application in Visual Studio, follow these steps:

1. **Choose Start⇨Microsoft Visual Studio 2005⇨Microsoft Visual Studio 2005.**

   If you're using one of the Express products the path is similar.

2. **To create a new project, choose File⇨New⇨Project.**

   A New Project dialog box, shown in Figure 6-2, displays.

   The selection of options offered to you in the Project Types pane of the New Project dialog box varies according to the edition of Visual Studio that you are using.

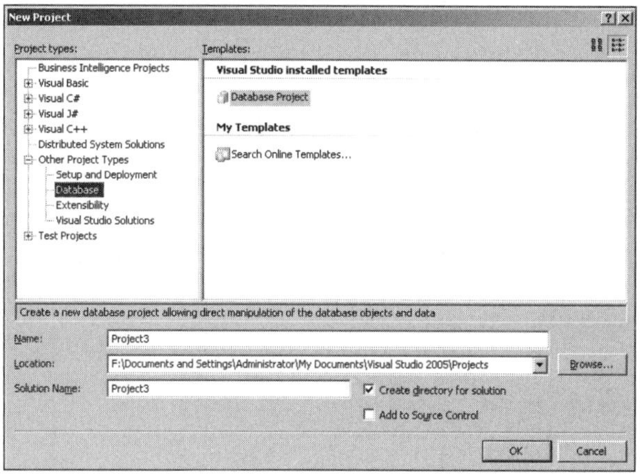

**Figure 6-2:**
The New
Project
dialog box.

3. **If available, select Visual Basic in the Project Types pane. Select Windows. In the Templates pane, select Windows Application.**

   If you're using Visual C# or Visual C# Express, select the options for a Windows Application.

4. **In the Name text box, enter** SimpleProject **as the name of the project. Ensure that the Create Directory for Solution check box is checked.**

   The appearance should be similar to Figure 6-3.

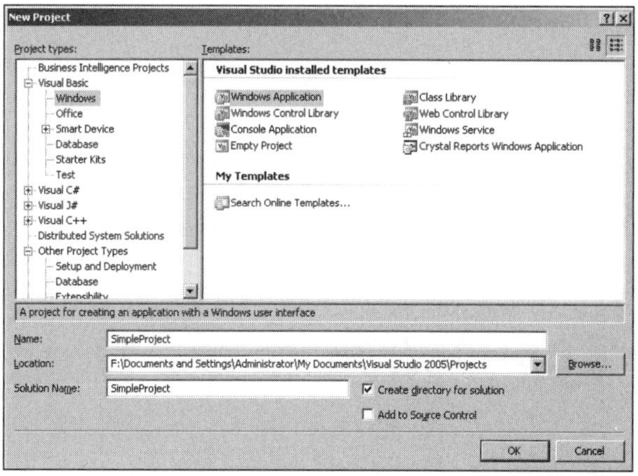

**Figure 6-3:**
Creating
and naming
a new
project.

5. **Check that a file location is displayed in the Location text box.**

   The path displayed depends on where you installed Visual Studio. Unless you want to customize the location where you create Visual Studio projects, you can simply accept the default location that Visual Studio provides.

6. **Click the OK button.**

   After a pause, usually of a few seconds, you see an appearance similar to that in Figure 6-4. The gray rectangle is the form that you can customize to provide the user interface.

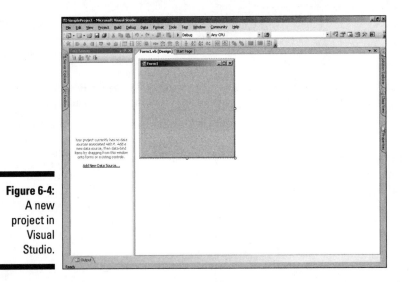

**Figure 6-4:**
A new project in Visual Studio.

Notice the information in the Data Sources pane of Visual Studio that no data source has been configured. So, next, you need to create a data source for the project, which I show you how to do in the next section.

# Building the Connection to the Data

To add a connection to the pubs database by using the Data Source Configuration Wizard, follow these steps:

1. **Click the Add New Data Source link in the Data Sources pane.**

   The Data Source Configuration Wizard displays, as shown in Figure 6-5.

2. **The default option is Database, which is what you want for this example. Click the Next button.**

   On the next screen you specify where the data is to come from.

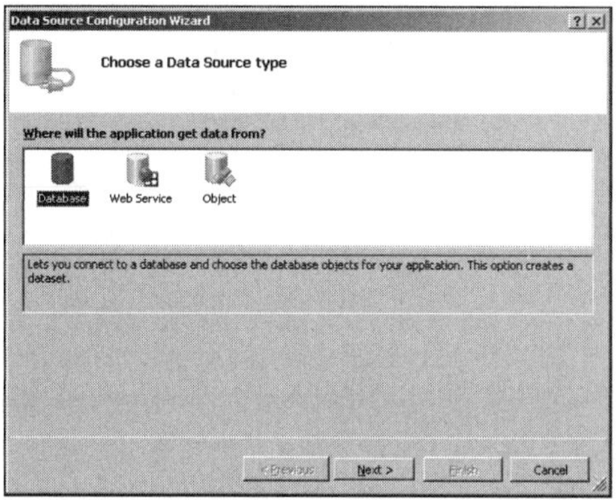

**Figure 6-5:**
The Data
Source Con-
figuration
Wizard.

3. **To create a new connection, click the New Connection button.**

   The Choose Data Source dialog box, shown in Figure 6-6, displays.

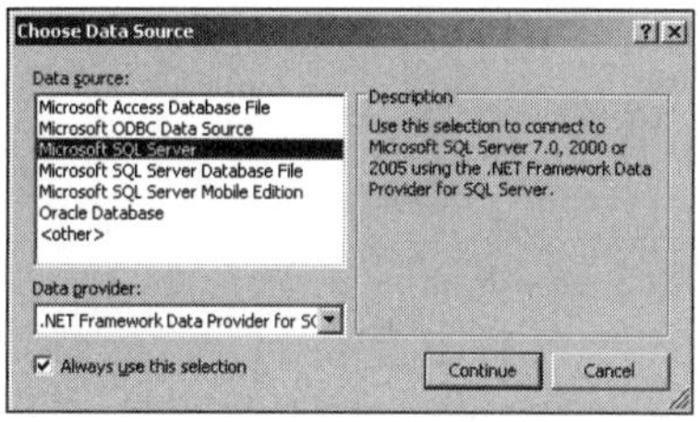

**Figure 6-6:**
The Choose
Data Source
dialog box.

4. **Select the Microsoft SQL Server option. Click Continue.**

   The Add Connection dialog box opens, as shown in Figure 6-7.

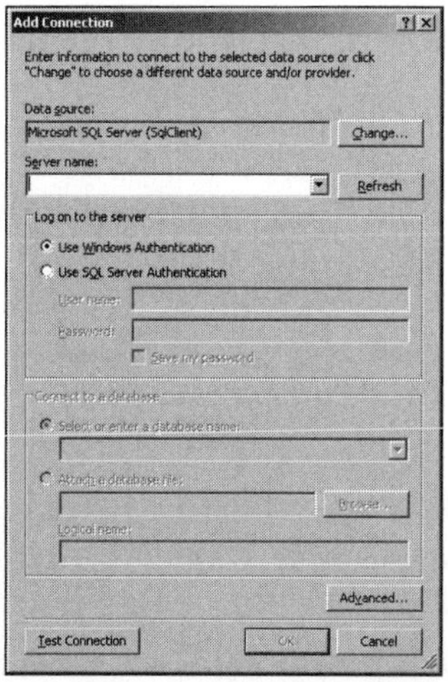

**Figure 6-7:**
The Add
Connection
dialog box.

5. **In the Server Name text box, enter a single period character (which means the connection is to the local development machine) or the server name and instance name (if you're using a named instance of SQL Server).**

6. **In the Select or Enter a database name drop-down menu, select the pubs database, as shown in Figure 6-8.**

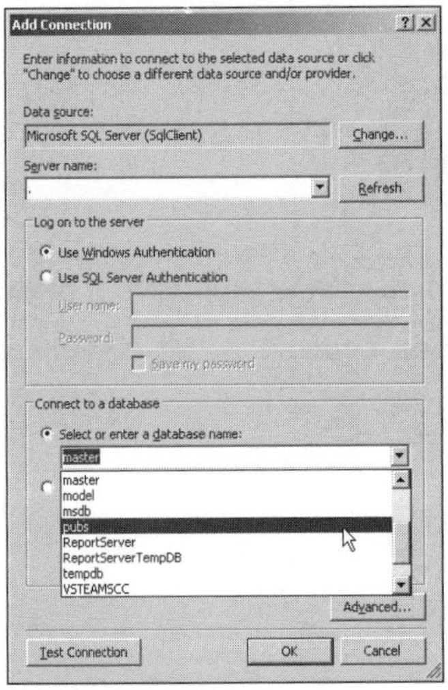

**Figure 6-8:**
Selecting a
connection
to the pubs
database as
data source.

If the pubs database isn't displayed in the drop-down menu, check that you are connecting to the desired SQL Server instance and that you have correctly installed the pubs database.

7. **Click the Test Connection button to test the connection.**

If everything is working correctly, the dialog box, shown in Figure 6-9, displays.

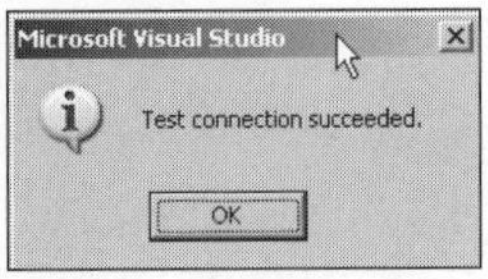

**Figure 6-9:**
The
confirmation
that you can
make a
connection
to the
desired data
source.

8. **Click OK in that dialog box and then click the OK button in the Add Connection dialog box.**

   If the connection fails, check the choices you made in the earlier steps. If you're connecting across a network, check that you can access the SQL Server instance by using SQL Server Management Studio.

   You return to the Data Source Configuration Wizard.

9. **Click the Next button in the Data Source Configuration Wizard.**

10. **The next screen that appears in the Data Source Configuration Wizard offers you a choice about storing the connection string; click Next.**

    The next screen displays, as shown in Figure 6-10.

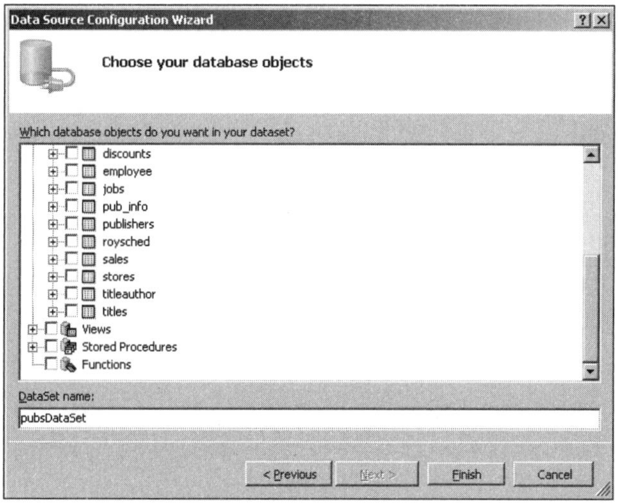

**Figure 6-10:**
Selecting the database objects.

You now need to select which database objects you want to connect to. For these steps, choose data from the au_lname, au_fname, and phone columns of the dbo.authors table.

11. **Expand the Tables node, expand the authors node, and check the check boxes for the au_lname, au_fname and phone columns.**

    Notice that in this dialog schema information is not displayed.

12. **Click the Finish button.**

    You return to the Visual Studio main window. Notice that the Data Sources pane now contains a data source called pubsDataSet (see Figure 6-11), assuming you didn't change the default name.

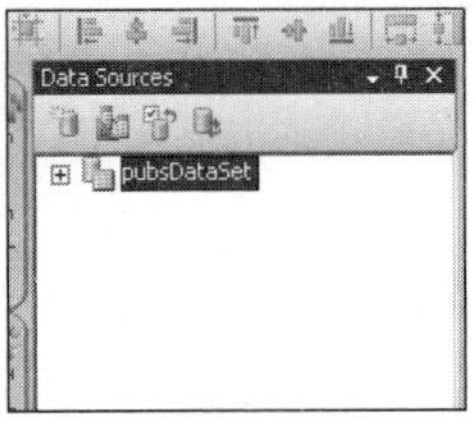

**Figure 6-11:**
A data
source
added to
the Data
Sources
pane.

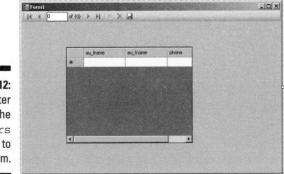

You now have successfully created a data source. The next step is to display data from that data source.

# Building the User Interface

To add a simple user interface to display the data, follow these steps:

1. **In the Data Sources pane, expand the pubsDataSet node.**

2. **Drag the `authors` table to the form.**

   After a few seconds the form looks similar to Figure 6-12. You may need to expand the gray area to get it to look exactly like Figure 6-12.

**Figure 6-12:**
After
dragging the
`authors`
table to
the form.

In the main area of the form a DataGridView control has been added. In the lower part of the window, notice the controls that enable access to the data have been added to the form. These four controls are not visible when you run your application but provide the functionality to retrieve the data you want to see.

3. **Choose File⇨Save All to save all the project files.**

4. **Press F5 to run the application in debug mode.**

   If all is working correctly, data displays in the form with an appearance similar to Figure 6-13.

Visual Studio offers many techniques to add more interesting visual appearances and more sophisticated functionality. Hopefully this simple example shows you how easy you can create a simple custom database application. Did you notice that although I told you to select a Visual Basic project that you didn't have to write a single line of code?

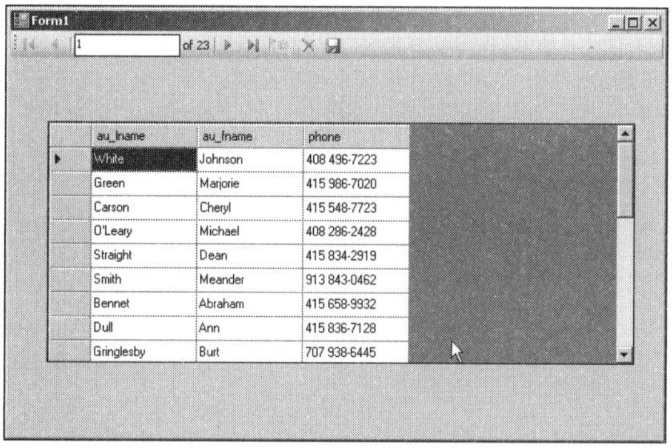

**Figure 6-13:**
Author
information
displayed in
a Windows
form.

# Debugging the Application

Visual Studio provides powerful debugging features to help you diagnose problems when you create applications. The drop-down menu beside the green arrow button on the toolbar allows you to specify to run code in debug mode. That code can be code that you have written or, as in the preceding example, code that Visual Studio generated automatically for you.

If your code has problems, helpful error messages are provided and Visual Studio displays multiple additional widows to help you diagnose the source of the problem.

# Part III
# Working with SQL Server

The 5th Wave · By Rich Tennant

AUTO SHOW FOR COMPUTER STORAGE EXECUTIVES

## In this part . . .

1 introduce you to working with the new xml datatype in SQL Server 2005 and using the Common Language Runtime (CLR) that is now part of SQL Server 2005.

I show you how to work with stored procedures and handle errors.

# Chapter 7

# Working with XML

● ● ● ● ● ● ● ● ● ● ● ● ● ● ● ● ● ● ● ● ● ● ● ● ● ● ● ● ● ● ● ● ● ● ● ● ● ● ● ● ● ● ● ● ● ● ● ● ● ● ●

## In This Chapter

▶ Introducing XML

▶ Creating XML documents and fragments

▶ Storing XML by using untyped and typed XML

▶ Querying XML

▶ Modifying data with XML Data Modification Language

▶ Converting data to and from XML

● ● ● ● ● ● ● ● ● ● ● ● ● ● ● ● ● ● ● ● ● ● ● ● ● ● ● ● ● ● ● ● ● ● ● ● ● ● ● ● ● ● ● ● ● ● ● ● ● ● ●

*N*ot all data is ideally suited to storage in relational tables, using relations to express logical associations between parts of the data. XML, e*X*tensible *M*arkup *L*anguage, is a very useful alternate way to represent certain types of data, particularly data that has a hierarchical structure. Hierarchical data is quite common in real-life business data. For example, an invoice contains various elements such as date, invoice number, and line items. You can envisage the invoice as the top of a hierarchy and the other elements as subsidiary elements in the hierarchy. The line items section may, in turn, contain several individual line items. You can easily represent this type of conceptual data structure as XML.

XML is also useful for storing or transmitting across a network information that can vary in structure from one document to another. XML was developed as a specification produced by the World Wide Web Consortium (W3C) and therefore is widely accepted internationally.

Sometimes the term *semi-structured* is used to refer to XML because it is not structured in the same way as relational data. In reality, XML data is always structured. It simply isn't structured in the same way as relational data.

SQL Server 2005 provides several tools to allow you to store XML and to retrieve selected parts of that XML for use in your applications. You can break XML data into a structure that can be stored in SQL Server and you can take the results of relational data queries and combine that data into an XML structure. SQL Server 2005 allows you, for the first time, to store your XML data in SQL Server and query it as if it was XML. Strictly speaking, SQL Server 2005 stores XML in a proprietary binary format, not as a sequence of characters.

The binary format allows you to search your XML data quicker, because the indexes you can create on the binary format allow you to navigate the logical structure of the XML quickly and efficiently.

# Introducing XML

XML is a markup language that is highly flexible. Unlike HTML, which has various specified element names, you can define your own element names in XML documents. This makes it very flexible but that flexibility can cause problems too. If you don't know how a business partner is going to structure a purchase order written in XML, you will likely have problems in creating a way to process the purchase order automatically. A common approach to ensuring that a class of XML documents are structured in a predictable way is to validate the structure of each document of that class, using a *schema*. A schema simply defines the allowed structure of that class of XML documents. You can use two schema languages to specify a schema for XML: Document Type Definition (DTD) and XSD (also called W3C XML Schema Definition language). SQL Server 2005 supports the XSD schema language. I describe it briefly later in this chapter, in the "Understanding the XML Schema Definition language" section.

An XML document has to conform to several rules, including

- ✔ An XML *document* must have a single document element and all other elements must be contained inside it. An XML *fragment* needn't meet this criterion.

- ✔ Each start tag of an element must have a matching end tag, unless the element is empty when you can use an empty element structure.

- ✔ Attributes are added to a start tag (or empty element).

You can express a simple purchase order like this in XML (`PurchaseOrder.xml`):

```xml
<?xml version="1.0"?>
<PurchaseOrder>
 <Date></Date>
 <From>Some Fictional Company</From>
 <Contact>Fred Smith</Contact>
 <ContactPhone>123-456-7890</ContactPhone>
 <LineItems>
  <LineItem Quantity="3">Some article</LineItem>
  <LineItem Quantity="12">Some other article</LineItem>
  <LineItem Quantity="300">Yet another kind of
          article</LineItem>
 </LineItems>
</PurchaseOrder>
```

The first line of the code is the *XML declaration*. It isn't compulsory but it can include information about the version of XML and the encoding of the characters in the document. By default XML parsers support Unicode UTF-8 and UTF-16. If you want to use other character encoding, you add an `encoding` attribute whose value specifies the encoding of the document.

The `PurchaseOrder` element is the *document element* (sometimes called the *root element*). It has a start tag, on the second line of the code, and an *end tag*, on the last line of the code. All other elements are contained between the start tag and the end tag of the `PurchaseOrder` element.

All other elements in the document must have matching start and end tags unless they are empty. Notice that the `Date` element is written as

```
<Date></Date>
```

Because it has no content — that is, it's empty — you can also use the special syntax for an empty element:

```
<Date/>
```

The order of elements is significant in an XML document. If an element has two or more attributes, the order of those attributes in the document is not significant.

# XML and SQL Server 2000

SQL Server 2000 was the first version of SQL Server that included support for XML. SQL Server 2000 provided two pieces of XML functionality. The first was the FOR XML clause that you use to query relational data to return that data as XML. The second was the OPENXML keyword that you use to split up XML into components that could be stored in the tables of a relational database.

# XML and SQL Server 2005

SQL Server 2005 builds on the XML support by adding several new pieces of functionality:

- ✔ A new datatype for XML, the xml datatype. I describe that datatype in the next section.
- ✔ Support for querying XML by using the XML Query Language, *XQuery*.
- ✔ An XML Data Manipulation Language (a proprietary extension to XQuery), which you can use to insert, update, or delete components of XML data held as the xml datatype.

✔ Enhancements to the T-SQL FOR XML clause.

✔ The ability to create indexes on the xml datatype.

✔ The ability to use XML Web services, using *HTTP Endpoints*.

## The xml datatype

SQL Server 2005 supports an xml datatype that wasn't supported in SQL Server 2000. SQL Server 2005 supports two flavors of XML: XML documents and XML fragments. I discuss these two entities and how to use them in the next section.

You can use the xml datatype in the following situations:

✔ Columns in a SQL Server 2005 table

✔ Variables

✔ Stored procedures

✔ Function parameters

You create a column of the xml datatype in a table to store purchase orders written in XML as follows:

```
CREATE TABLE xmlSample (ID int primary key, PurchaseOrder
        xml)
```

You create a variable of the xml datatype as follows:

```
DECLARE @myXMLVariable xml
```

You create a stored procedure with a parameter of the xml datatype as follows:

```
CREATE PROCEDURE myProcedure (myXMLDoc xml)
AS -- the rest of the stored procedure goes here
```

Later in the chapter, I show you how to store and retrieve XML data in and from a column that contains data of the xml datatype. I show you how to retrieve XML data in the "Querying XML" section.

## Creating XML Documents and Fragments

The XML specification has many rules that define how to construct XML documents and fragments. Detailed discussion of those rules is beyond the scope of this chapter. If you have access to one, I suggest that you use an XML editor such as XML Spy, XMLwriter, and Stylus Studio. These and other tools check that the XML is well-formed and typically even highlighted where any errors occur.

Many editors also provide automated element completion. As soon as you create a start tag, the editor automatically adds an end tag. If you use that functionality, you need to be careful to create the elements in the order where autocompletion is a help, not a hindrance.

Many XML editors also allow you to validate an XML document against an XSD schema document. Validation allows you to be sure that any XML you attempt to store in SQL Server is created correctly according to the constraints of the schema. You can use SQL Server to validate XML when you have a typed XML column, which I describe in the next section.

An XML document is often the most convenient flavor of XML to use. All XML parsers and editors recognize it as well-formed.

An XML fragment doesn't satisfy the requirement to have a single document element that contains every other element. However, the fragment must otherwise be well-formed so that you can successfully insert it in an XML document. If you use XML fragments, some editors and parsers may report inappropriate errors.

# Using Untyped and Typed XML

SQL Server 2005 allows you to store XML in two broad ways. *Untyped XML* is XML that is stored without having a schema specified for it. *Typed XML* is XML that has an associated schema document that defines which structure(s) are allowed in the XML that is stored.

Untyped XML is easier to use, because you don't need to create a schema document. It is also more flexible because you can change the structure of XML documents. A downside of untyped XML is that the data stored in that column can contain errors that you may avoid with typed XML instead.

If you use typed XML, then each XML document is checked to ensure that it has the correct structure — for example, before it is stored in a column in a SQL Server table.

Stored XML, whether it is untyped or typed, cannot exceed 2GB in size per instance. That means that the data in a column that has the xml datatype cannot exceed 2GB. For many purposes that size limit won't be a problem.

## Using untyped XML

To demonstrate how to use untyped XML, I use the Purchase order document from earlier in this chapter.

In the examples in this chapter, you can either type the code or you can use the T-SQL file that contains the code. To run the code in the file for each step, highlight the relevant part of the code and then press the F5 key.

To create a `PurchaseOrders` table and add a single purchase order to it, follow these steps:

1. **Open the SQL Server Management Studio and create a new database engine query.**

   The code is included in the `UntypedXML.sql` file.

2. **Create a database called `Chapter7` by using this code:**

   ```
   CREATE DATABASE Chapter7
   ```

3. **Elect to use the newly created `Chapter7` database by using this code:**

   ```
   USE Chapter7
   ```

4. **Create a table called `PurchaseOrders` with two columns.**

   The `PurchaseID` column contains an integer value and the `PurchaseOrder` column contains an XML document. Use the following code:

   ```
   CREATE TABLE PurchaseOrders (PurchaseID int primary
           key, PurchaseOrder xml)
   ```

5. **Add a purchase order to the `PurchaseOrders` table with the following code:**

   ```
   INSERT INTO PurchaseOrders VALUES(1, '<?xml
           version="1.0"?>
   <PurchaseOrder>
    <Date>2005/12/31</Date>
    <From>Some Fictional Company</From>
    <Contact>Fred Smith</Contact>
    <ContactPhone>123-456-7890</ContactPhone>
    <LineItems>
     <LineItem Quantity="3">Some article</LineItem>
     <LineItem Quantity="12">Some other
           article</LineItem>
     <LineItem Quantity="300">Yet another kind of
           article</LineItem>
    </LineItems>
   </PurchaseOrder>')
   ```

6. **Retrieve the purchase order that you added to the `PurchaseOrders` table in Step 5 using the following code:**

   ```
   SELECT PurchaseOrder FROM PurchaseOrders
   ```

   Figure 7-1 shows the results of the query.

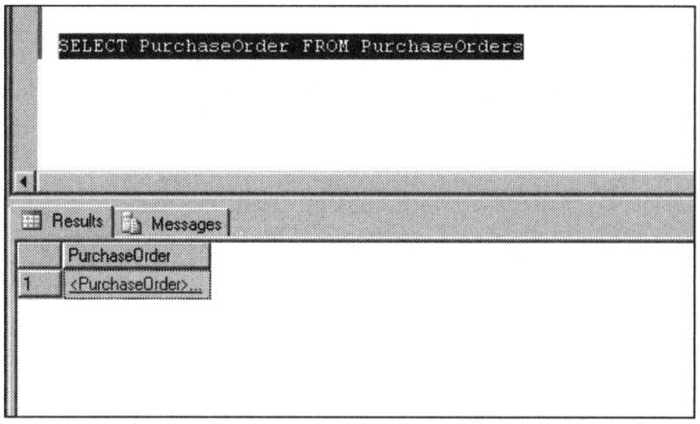

**Figure 7-1:**
The results
of query-
ing for
purchase
orders.

7. **To view the XML document that displays in the grid shown in Figure 7-1, drag the column separator to the right.**

8. **To view the entire XML document, displayed in a hierarchical way, click the XML.**

   A window opens similar to Figure 7-2.

**Figure 7-2:**
The
retrieved
XML
document
displays
in a new
window.

## Understanding the XML Schema Definition language

The W3C has defined a Schema Definition language, often called W3C XML Schema Definition language and abbreviated to XSD. In SQL Server 2005, the only schema definition language supported is XSD, which replaces the proprietary XML Data Reduced (XDR) schema language that Microsoft provided in SQL Server 2000.

An XSD schema can apply the following constraints to associated instance XML documents:

- The structure of elements in the document.

- The number of similar elements allowed in a place in the XML structure. For example, you can specify whether an element is optional (occurs zero or one time) or that it occurs a specified number of times.

- Whether or not a particular element has one or more attributes.

- The values allowed in a particular element or attribute. For example, in an element to store the date of an invoice, you can specify that the element stores only valid dates. Similarly, if an element is specified as containing string data, you won't be allowed to carry out arithmetic on data contained in it.

These constraints remove important classes of possible problems or variability in the data you store. This improves data quality at the cost of creating and applying an XSD schema document.

SQL Server validates the XML to be stored every time that you add or change data in a column.

W3C XML Schema is a complex topic that deserves a book of its own.

If you have a copy of Visual Studio 2005, you can create an XSD schema for the purchase order document used in the earlier example (in the "Using untyped XML" section) by following these steps:

1. **Open Visual Studio 2005.**

2. **Open the `PurchaseOrder.xml` file in Visual Studio by choosing File⇨Open and navigating to the directory that you stored `PurchaseOrder.xml` in.**

3. **To create an XSD schema, choose XML⇨Create Schema.**

   The XML menu displays in Visual Studio only when you have an XML file open.

   After a pause while Visual Studio creates the XSD schema, you see an appearance similar to Figure 7-3.

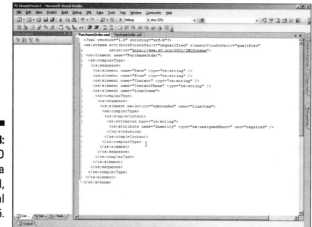

**Figure 7-3:**
An XSD
Schema
created,
using Visual
Studio 2005.

The schema that Visual Studio created is in the `PurchaseOrder.xsd` file. For convenience, I show the XSD schema here:

```xml
<?xml version="1.0" encoding="utf-8"?>
<xs:schema attributeFormDefault="unqualified"
           elementFormDefault="qualified"
 xmlns:xs="http://www.w3.org/2001/XMLSchema">
 <xs:element name="PurchaseOrder">
  <xs:complexType>
   <xs:sequence>
    <xs:element name="Date" type="xs:string" />
    <xs:element name="From" type="xs:string" />
    <xs:element name="Contact" type="xs:string" />
    <xs:element name="ContactPhone" type="xs:string" />
    <xs:element name="LineItems">
     <xs:complexType>
      <xs:sequence>
       <xs:element maxOccurs="unbounded" name="LineItem">
        <xs:complexType>
         <xs:simpleContent>
          <xs:extension base="xs:string">
           <xs:attribute name="Quantity"
           type="xs:unsignedShort" use="required" />
          </xs:extension>
         </xs:simpleContent>
        </xs:complexType>
       </xs:element>
      </xs:sequence>
     </xs:complexType>
    </xs:element>
   </xs:sequence>
  </xs:complexType>
 </xs:element>
</xs:schema>
```

Notice that the XSD schema is itself an XML document. The document element is an `xs:schema` element. The name of the `xs:schema` element defines it as being a W3C XML Schema element. The prefix, `xs`, is associated with a URL that is unique to W3C XML Schema in the start tag of the `xs:schema` element:

```
<xs:schema attributeFormDefault="unqualified"
  elementFormDefault="qualified"
  xmlns:xs="http://www.w3.org/2001/XMLSchema">
```

The association of a namespace prefix with a namespace URI is called a *namespace declaration*.

As is often the case, the XSD schema document is much longer than the XML instance document it describes. In this document, the first `xs:element`

```
<xs:element name="PurchaseOrder">
```

tells you that the name of the document element of `PurchaseOrder.xml` and other documents of the same class is `PurchaseOrder`. The rest of the schema defines the allowed structure of the purchase order.

Now you have an XSD schema that you can use to work with a typed XML column.

## Using typed XML

Typed XML is used in a similar way to untyped XML but you must specify the schema(s) to be associated with the typed XML before the XML is stored, if you want SQL Server to automatically validate XML data as you add it to the database.

You can associate an XSD schema with XML in the following situations:

- Column
- Function parameter
- Variable

The following steps show you how to create a table to hold a typed XML column. You can omit Steps 1 and 2 if you created the `Chapter7` database in the earlier example (in the "Using untyped XML" section) and left SQL Server Management Studio open.

1. **Open SQL Server Management Studio and click the Database Engine Query button to create a new database engine query.**

2. **Create the `Chapter7` database by using the following code:**

```
CREATE DATABASE Chapter7
```

3. **Elect to use the newly created `Chapter7` database using this code:**

```
USE Chapter7
```

4. **Create an XML schema collection called `PurchaseOrderCollection` in the `Chapter7` database using the following code:**

```
CREATE XML SCHEMA COLLECTION PurchaseOrderCollection
       AS
'<?xml version="1.0" encoding="utf-8"?>
<xs:schema attributeFormDefault="unqualified"
       elementFormDefault="qualified"
      xmlns:xs="http://www.w3.org/2001/XMLSchema">
 <xs:element name="PurchaseOrder">
  <xs:complexType>
   <xs:sequence>
    <xs:element name="Date" type="xs:string" />
    <xs:element name="From" type="xs:string" />
    <xs:element name="Contact" type="xs:string" />
    <xs:element name="ContactPhone" type="xs:string"
       />
    <xs:element name="LineItems">
     <xs:complexType>
      <xs:sequence>
       <xs:element maxOccurs="unbounded"
         name="LineItem">
        <xs:complexType>
         <xs:simpleContent>
          <xs:extension base="xs:string">
           <xs:attribute name="Quantity"
       type="xs:unsignedShort" use="required" />
          </xs:extension>
         </xs:simpleContent>
        </xs:complexType>
       </xs:element>
      </xs:sequence>
     </xs:complexType>
    </xs:element>
   </xs:sequence>
  </xs:complexType>
 </xs:element>
</xs:schema>'
```

The `CREATE SCHEMA COLLECTION` statement specifies the name for the schema collection and you supply a literal XSD schema document as the argument.

5. **Verify that the schema collection has been created by using the following code:**

```
SELECT name, create_date
FROM sys.xml_schema_collections
```

You see an appearance similar to Figure 7-4.

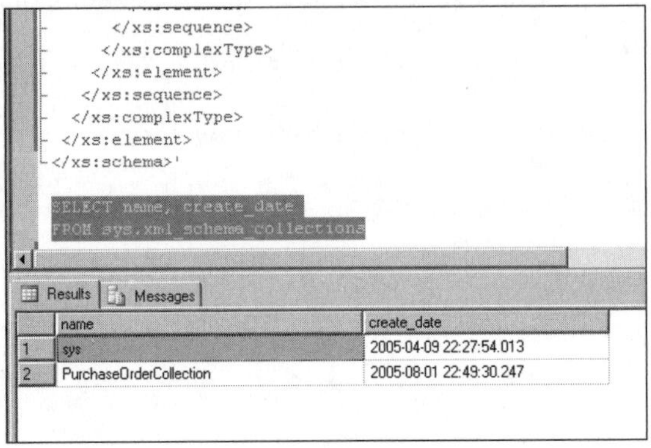

**Figure 7-4:**
Verifying
that the
Purchase
Orders
Collection
schema
collection
has been
created
successfully.

6. **Create the `TypedPurchaseOrders` table by using the following code:**

```
CREATE TABLE TypedPurchaseOrders (PurchaseID int
        primary key,
  PurchaseOrder xml (PurchaseOrderCollection))
```

Notice that after you specify the `PurchaseID` and `PurchaseOrder` columns in the normal way, you supply the name of an XML schema collection to specify which schema is to apply to the `PurchaseOrder` column.

7. **Add a valid purchase order to the `TypedPurchaseOrders` table using the following code:**

```
INSERT INTO TypedPurchaseOrders VALUES(1, '<?xml
        version="1.0"?>
<PurchaseOrder>
 <Date>2005/12/31</Date>
 <From>Some Fictional Company</From>
 <Contact>Fred Smith</Contact>
 <ContactPhone>123-456-7890</ContactPhone>
 <LineItems>
   <LineItem Quantity="3">Some article</LineItem>
   <LineItem Quantity="12">Some other
        article</LineItem>
   <LineItem Quantity="300">Yet another kind of
        article</LineItem>
 </LineItems>
</PurchaseOrder>')
```

Apart from the change in the name of the table, this syntax is the same as the untyped XML syntax. After you associate the schema with a column in Step 6, you simply add the XML to the column in the same way as with untyped XML.

8. **Check that the purchase order was added correctly, using the following code:**

```
SELECT PurchaseOrder FROM TypedPurchaseOrders
```

9. **Attempt to add an invalid purchase order to the TypedPurchaseOrders table by using the following code.**

   Notice that the XML contains two Contact elements, when the schema specifies that only one is allowed. You see an error.

```
INSERT INTO TypedPurchaseOrders VALUES(2, '<?xml
       version="1.0"?>
<PurchaseOrder>
 <Date>2005/12/31</Date>
 <From>Some Fictional Company</From>
 <Contact>Fred Smith</Contact>
 <Contact>Not allowed here.</Contact>
 <ContactPhone>123-456-7890</ContactPhone>
 <LineItems>
  <LineItem Quantity="3">Some article</LineItem>
  <LineItem Quantity="12">Some other
       article</LineItem>
  <LineItem Quantity="300">Yet another kind of
       article</LineItem>
 </LineItems>
</PurchaseOrder>')
```

I show you how to store both untyped and typed XML. You also need to retrieve XML data.

# Querying XML

You will have realized that XML is stored differently from traditional relational data. Not surprisingly, the way to query XML isn't quite the same as querying relational data. However, because you're retrieving data from a SQL Server column, you use T-SQL code as the framework.

## Understanding XQuery

The language used to retrieve data in columns that are of the xml datatype is called the *XML Query Language* (XQuery). Microsoft has chosen to use a subset of the XQuery specification and is aware that the specification is, at the time of writing, not yet finalized at the W3C. The hope is that the subset of XQuery that Microsoft used doesn't change between the draft that Microsoft used in SQL Server 2005 and the final release of XQuery but that is not guaranteed.

XQuery is based on an earlier XML specification called the *XML Path Language* (XPath). If you have worked with XML, you may have worked with XPath 1.0. XQuery is based on XPath 2.0.

Among the XQuery syntax you can use to retrieve XML data are

- ✔ XPath expressions
- ✔ FLWOR expressions

A FLWOR expression has the following components:

- ✔ FOR
- ✔ LET
- ✔ WHERE
- ✔ ORDER BY
- ✔ RETURN

The LET keyword is not supported in SQL Server 2005.

Both XPath expressions and FLWOR expressions in SQL Server 2005 use the query keyword. Broadly the syntax is as follows:

```
SELECT ColumnList
FROM ColumnName.query('XPathOrXQueryExpression')
```

To demonstrate how to use XPath expressions, I retrieved some data from the PurchaseOrders table from the earlier example. This is untyped XML but the same syntax is used for typed XML.

To retrieve selected parts of the PurchaseOrder column, follow these steps:

1. **Open SQL Server Management Studio and click the Database Engine Query button to create a new query.**

2. **Ensure that you're using the Chapter7 database by using this code:**

   ```
   USE Chapter7
   ```

3. **Confirm that you can retrieve data from the PurchaseOrders table by using the following code:**

   ```
   SELECT * FROM PurchaseOrders
   ```

4. **Retrieve the PurchaseOrder element and its children using the following code:**

   ```
   SELECT PurchaseOrder.query('/PurchaseOrder')
   AS Result
   FROM dbo.PurchaseOrders
   ```

5. **Retrieve the `Date` element and its content by using the following code:**

```
SELECT PurchaseOrder.query('/PurchaseOrder/Date')
AS Result
FROM dbo.PurchaseOrders
```

The `Date` element and its content displays in the results grid.

6. **Retrieve the value contained in the `Date` element using the following code:**

```
SELECT
        PurchaseOrder.query('/PurchaseOrder/Date/text(
        )')
AS Result
FROM dbo.PurchaseOrders
```

The `text()` function is an `XPath` function that retrieves the value contained in an XML element.

7. **To test the use of `XPath` expressions in combination with the `WHERE` clause, add a new purchase order to the table by using the following code:**

```
INSERT INTO PurchaseOrders VALUES(2, '<?xml
        version="1.0"?>
<PurchaseOrder>
 <Date>2006/01/01</Date>
 <From>Some Other Fictional Company</From>
 <Contact>John Jones</Contact>
 <ContactPhone>234-567-8901</ContactPhone>
 <LineItems>
  <LineItem Quantity="3">Some article</LineItem>
  <LineItem Quantity="12">Some other
        article</LineItem>
  <LineItem Quantity="300">Yet another kind of
        article</LineItem>
 </LineItems>
</PurchaseOrder>')
```

8. **Confirm that the row has been successfully added using the following code:**

```
SELECT * FROM PurchaseOrders
```

Notice that two rows now display in the results grid.

9. **To retrieve the date of the purchase order that has a value of 2 for the `PurchaseID`, use the following code:**

```
SELECT PurchaseID,
        PurchaseOrder.query('/PurchaseOrder/Date')
AS Result
FROM dbo.PurchaseOrders
WHERE PurchaseID = 2
```

The result is similar to Figure 7-5.

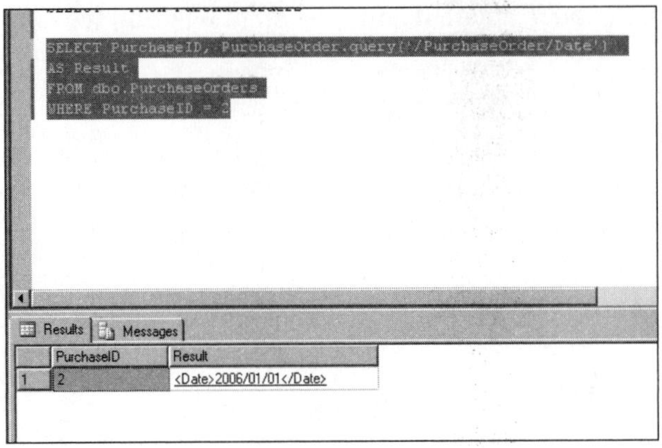

**Figure 7-5:**
Using the
WHERE
clause with
an XPath
expression.

## Creating indexes for the xml datatype

When you query for XML data as I did in the preceding examples, every row of the PurchaseOrders table is queried in turn. In production size databases, this way is very inefficient and is likely to produce poor performance. To improve performance, you can create one or more XML indexes.

There are two types of XML index:

✔ **Primary:** A primary XML index must exist before you can create a secondary XML index.

✔ **Secondary:** There are three types: PATH, VALUE, and PROPERTY.

A PATH secondary index can give improved performance when using XPath expressions, such as those demonstrated in the preceding section. A VALUE index can give improved performance when using value comparisons, for example in XPath predicates.

# Using the XML Data Modification Language

XQuery, which I briefly introduce in the previous section, is a W3C standard in development. Version 1.0 of XQuery doesn't include any syntax to support inserting, deleting, or updating of XML data. SQL Server 2005 contains a proprietary extension to XQuery that provides this data modification functionality. The XQuery Working Group at W3C are likely to adopt a syntax very similar to the one that Microsoft has added to SQL Server 2005, but it remains possible that there may be significant differences. As far as the initial release of SQL Server 2005 is concerned, three new keywords allow you to modify data:

- ✔ insert
- ✔ delete
- ✔ change value of

Each of the preceding keywords is case sensitive, so it's important that you get the case correct to avoid errors when running your code.

To insert XML, you use the insert keyword. You can specify where to insert the new piece of XML with the following keywords:

- ✔ **after:** Inserts after the specified point in the existing XML structure.
- ✔ **before:** Inserts before the specified point in the existing XML structure.
- ✔ **into:** Inserts into a position specified by using the as first or as last keywords.

In the following example, I create a variable that is of xml datatype, set its value to a Contact element, and then modify it to add a ContactName element. To run the example, follow these steps. I explain the code after the steps.

1. **Open the SQL Server Management Studio and click the Database Engine Query button to create a new database engine query.**

2. **Specify to use the Chapter7 database with the following code:**

```
USE Chapter7
```

3. **Enter the following code, highlight it all, and then press F5 to run it.**

   It is important that you run all the code in a single batch or you get errors about undeclared variables.

```
DECLARE @insertXML xml
SET @insertXML = '<Contact>This contact was
        inserted.</Contact>'
SELECT @insertXML


SET @insertXML.modify('
insert <ContactName>Jimmy Case</ContactName>

after
/Contact[1]
')
SELECT @insertXML
```

In the first line you declare an insertXML variable. The second line sets the value of the insertXML variable. The SELECT statement in the third line of code causes the value of the `insertXML` variable to display in the results grid. In Figure 7-6, that value displays in the upper part of the results grid.

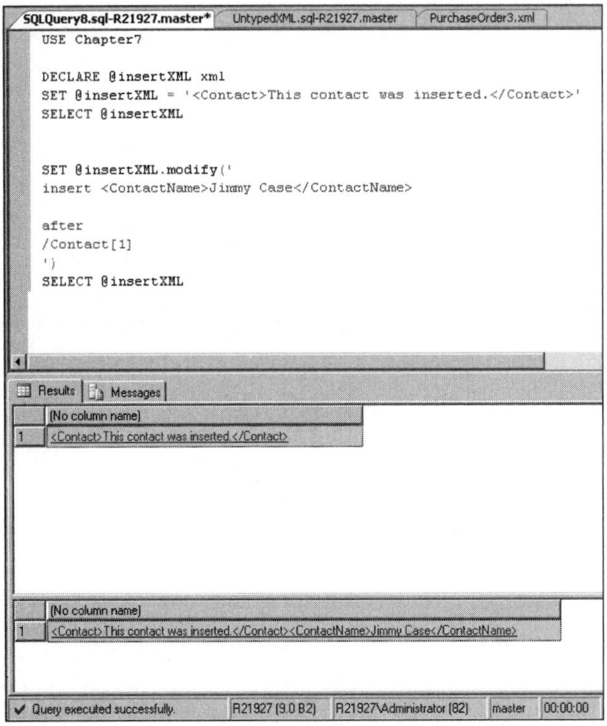

**Figure 7-6:**
The value of the `@insert XML` variable at two points in the sample code.

The next `SET` statement uses the `modify` keyword (it must be all lowercase) to modify the value of the `insertXML` variable. A `ContactName` element is added. Notice the `after` keyword that specifies that the new element is added after the `Contact` element.

The final `SELECT` statement retrieves the value of the `insertXML` variable after it has been modified.

# *Converting Data to and from XML*

The earlier parts of this chapter describe using the `xml` datatype. The SQL Server 2000 functionality to retrieve relational data using the `FOR XML` statement has been extended in SQL Server 2005. Also, the `OPENXML` keyword functionality is used to shred XML into relational data, if that fits with your storage needs.

# Using the FOR XML statement

A T-SQL SELECT statement retrieves relational data as a rowset. The FOR XML clause of a SELECT statement lets you optionally convert a retrieved rowset as XML.

In SQL Server 2005, the FOR XML clause has the following options:

- ✔ **AUTO:** The AUTO option automatically creates an XML hierarchy that, for the most part, is outside your control. You can use nested FOR XML queries to take some control of the XML structure. The document element is created automatically using the table name.

- ✔ **EXPLICIT:** The EXPLICIT option gives you enormous control over the structure of returned XML, but at a cost of very complex syntax that's not easy to understand nor to modify or debug.

- ✔ **PATH:** The PATH option is new to SQL Server 2005 and gives the full control that the EXPLICIT option gives but with less complex syntax.

- ✔ **RAW:** The RAW option creates a single row element for each row returned in the rowset. To create a hierarchy of XML elements, you can nest FOR XML queries.

To retrieve some relational data from the AdventureWorks database and display it by using the AUTO option, follow these steps:

1. **Open SQL Server Management Studio and click the Database Engine Query button to create a new database engine query.**

2. **Type the following code (also available as ForXML.sql in the code download):**

   ```
   USE AdventureWorks

   SELECT *
   FROM Person.Contact
   WHERE ContactID = 1
   FOR XML AUTO
   ```

   The first line of the code specifies to use the AdventureWorks database. The SELECT statement retrieves all columns from the Person.Contact table. The WHERE clause specifies to filter the data so that only data where ContactID = 1 displays. The FOR XML AUTO specifies to transform the filtered data into XML.

3. **Click the data that returns and you see an appearance similar to Figure 7-7.**

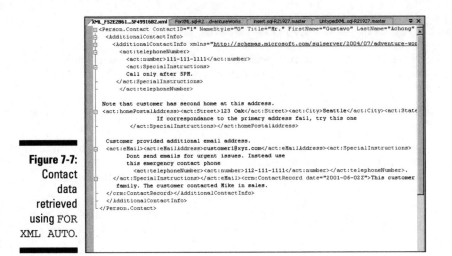

XML_F52E2B61...5F4991682.xml | ForXML.sql-R2...dventureWorks | insert.sql-R21927.master | UntypedXML.sql-R21927.master

```
<Person.Contact ContactID="1" NameStyle="0" Title="Mr." FirstName="Gustavo" LastName="Achong"
  <AdditionalContactInfo>
    <AdditionalContactInfo xmlns="http://schemas.microsoft.com/sqlserver/2004/07/adventure-wor
      <act:telephoneNumber>
        <act:number>111-111-1111</act:number>
        <act:SpecialInstructions>
        Call only after 5PM.
      </act:SpecialInstructions>
    </act:telephoneNumber>

  Note that customer has second home at this address.
  <act:homePostalAddress><act:Street>123 Oak</act:Street><act:City>Seattle</act:City><act:State
          If correspondance to the primary address fail, try this one
      </act:SpecialInstructions></act:homePostalAddress>

  Customer provided additional email address.
  <act:eMail><act:eMailAddress>customer1@xyz.com</act:eMailAddress><act:SpecialInstructions>
        Dont send emails for urgent issues. Instead use
        this emergency contact phone
        <act:telephoneNumber><act:number>112-111-1111</act:number></act:telephoneNumber>.
      </act:SpecialInstructions></act:eMail><crm:ContactRecord date="2001-06-02Z">This customer
      family. The customer contacted Mike in sales.
    </crm:ContactRecord></AdditionalContactInfo>
  </AdditionalContactInfo>
</Person.Contact>
```

**Figure 7-7:** Contact data retrieved using FOR XML AUTO.

## Using the OPENXML keyword

The OPENXML keyword takes an XML document and shreds it into rowsets that can be stored in relational columns in SQL Server.

The sp_xml_preparedocument stored procedure is used to parse the XML document. Then you specify which parts of the XML document are to constitute rows in SQL Server.

# Chapter 8

# Using the Common Language Runtime

●●●●●●●●●●●●●●●●●●●●●●●●●●●●●●●●●●●●●●●●●●●●●●

●●●●●●●●●●●●●●●●●●●●●●●●●●●●●●●●●●●●●●●●●●●●●●

*I*n SQL Server 2000 and earlier versions of SQL Server, you had one language to use in the database layer: T-SQL (Transact-SQL). T-SQL is well suited to tasks such as data storage and retrieval but it is not an all-purpose programming language. Many programming tasks were difficult or impossible to do with T-SQL.

If it was possible to do these tasks in T-SQL, often the code to carry out the tasks was verbose and complex. Writing the necessary code was difficult and maintaining the code was problematic. Another result of the limitations of T-SQL for tasks other than data manipulation was that developers often turned to *extended stored procedures* to carry out tasks that T-SQL was poorly suited to undertake. Problems with extended stored procedures include lack of security and reliability.

In SQL Server 2005, Microsoft has added support to allow you to use managed code in the database layer. *Managed code* is code that runs in the .NET Framework's Common Language Runtime (CLR). The support for the Common Language Runtime means that you, or developer colleagues, can use code created in Visual Basic .NET or Visual C# .NET inside SQL Server 2005.

Languages such as Visual Basic.NET and C#.NET are much better suited than T-SQL to many programming tasks, such as numeric manipulation, just to name one. So, for example, if you have complex number crunching that you want to do on some data, how could you best get the job done? In SQL Server 2000, you would probably have had to use an extended stored procedure. In SQL Server 2005, you have a new, more reliable, and more secure option to use the built-in Common Language Runtime capabilities.

SQL Server 2005 controls how the code runs in the CLR. If a CLR process is using too much memory or CPU cycles, SQL Server can shut the process down, which ensures that SQL Server continues to run efficiently.

# Introducing CLR Integration

SQL Server 2005 hosts the .NET Framework 2.0 Common Language Runtime (CLR). This is the same version of the .NET Framework that Visual Studio 2005 uses. You can write code in any .NET language including

- ✔ Visual Basic .NET
- ✔ Visual C# .NET
- ✔ Visual C++

Other .NET language can also produce the intermediate language (IL) that the CLR supports. In Visual Studio 2005, it is the previously listed languages that are supported in terms of creating .NET projects. Most developers of CLR code that's intended to run in SQL Server 2005 use one of these three languages and create the project in Visual Studio 2005.

You can possibly use a development environment other than Visual Studio 2005. However, Visual Studio 2005 provides such closely integrated support, including a SQL Server Project template, that many developers make it their first choice for creating managed code to run in SQL Server 2005.

You can use one of the .NET languages to create any of the following:

- ✔ Procedures
- ✔ Triggers
- ✔ Functions
- ✔ User-defined types
- ✔ User-defined aggregates

Visual Studio 2005 supports the following tasks for managed code intended for use in SQL Server 2005:

- ✔ Development
- ✔ Deployment
- ✔ Debugging

I briefly discuss each of these aspects of CLR use with SQL Server 2005 in the section that follows.

# Development

Visual Studio 2005 has a new project type — the SQL Server Project — for development of CLR projects in SQL Server 2005. You use that to create a CLR project.

The Visual Studio environment makes working with Visual C# code or Visual Basic .NET code easy. The SQL Server project has many new screens. Detailed steps of using the SQL Server project in the Visual Studio environment are beyond the scope of this chapter.

Visual Studio 2005 has support for many useful debugging features. You can debug seamlessly across the language boundaries between T-SQL and Visual Basic .NET or Visual C#. Equally, the type of connection to the SQL Server isn't important because both HTTP (*HyperText Transfer Protocol*, the protocol used on the World Wide Web) and TDS (*Tabular Data Stream*, the protocol used by SQL Server) are supported.

# Manual coding and deployment

If you choose to create your .NET code manually and deploy it in the same way, you need to follow these broad steps:

- When writing stored procedures, functions, and triggers, the .NET class is specified as `static` if written in C# or specified as `shared` if written in Visual Basic .NET.
- User-defined types and user-defined aggregates are written as full classes.
- The developer compiles the code that he has written. This creates an assembly.
- After creating the assembly, you use the `CREATE ASSEMBLY` statement to upload the assembly into SQL Server.
- To create a T-SQL object corresponding to a procedure contained in an assembly, you use the `CREATE PROCEDURE` statement. You use the `CREATE FUNCTION`, `CREATE TRIGGER`, `CREATE TYPE`, and `CREATE AGGREGATE` statements for the same purpose for functions, triggers, types, and aggregates respectively.
- After creating a T-SQL object, then you can use the object in your T-SQL code in the normal way.

To create a simple Visual C# example and deploy it manually to the local SQL Server instance, follow these steps:

1. **Open a text editor and type the following C# code:**

```
using System;
using System.Data;
using Microsoft.SqlServer.Server;
using System.Data.SqlTypes;

public class Chapter8Proc
{
  [Microsoft.SqlServer.Server.SqlProcedure]
  public static void Chapter8()
  {
    SqlContext.Pipe.Send("The Chapter 8 example
        works!\n");
  }
}
```

   Notice the use of the `System`, `System.data`, `Microsoft.SQLServer.Server`, and `System.Data.SqlTypes` namespaces. You use these namespaces often when writing .NET code for use in SQL Server 2005.

2. **Navigate to the location of the C# compiler. It's located in `C:\Windows\Microsoft.NET\Framework\v2.0.50727`. At the command line, type**

```
csc /target:library C:\location of CSharp
        File\Chapter8.cs
```

   A `dll` called `chapter8.dll` is created in the .NET Framework folder. More often, you would add the .NET Framework folder to your PATH environment variable.

3. **Open SQL Server Management Studio and click the Database Engine Query button to create a new database engine query. Create an assembly in the desired SQL Server 2005 instance, using this code:**

```
CREATE ASSEMBLY Chapter8
FROM
        'c:\windows\microsoft.net\framework\v2.0.50727
        \chapter8.dll'
WITH PERMISSION_SET = SAFE
```

   Notice the permission setting is `SAFE`, because the procedure does not need to access anything external to SQL Server.

4. **Create a procedure called `Chapter8` by using this code:**

```
CREATE PROCEDURE Chapter8
AS EXTERNAL NAME chapter8.Chapter8Proc.Chapter8
```

5. **Try to execute the `Chapter8` procedure by using the following code:**

```
EXEC Chapter8 --Will fail since CLR is not enabled
```

Unless you have explicitly turned on the CLR support, attempting to run the stored procedure fails.

6. **To enable the CLR, run the following code:**

```
sp_configure 'clr enabled', 1
GO
RECONFIGURE
GO
```

7. **Execute the `Chapter8` user-defined procedure that you created earlier.**

```
EXEC Chapter8 -- Now it will execute successfully
```

The result of execution is the display of a message in the Results pane, as shown in Figure 8-1.

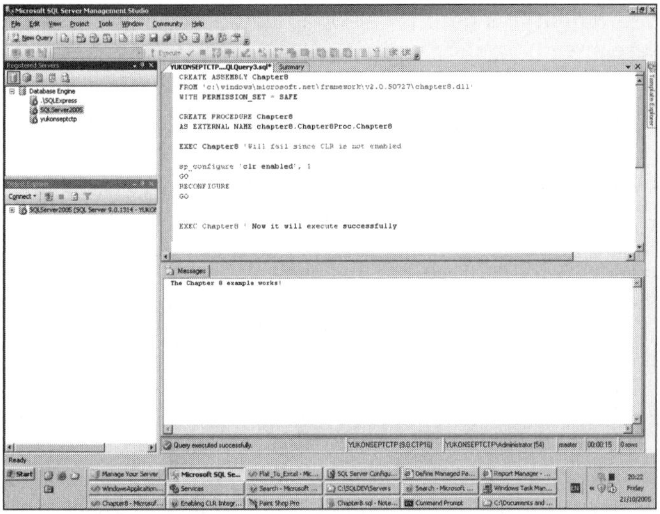

**Figure 8-1:** Successful execution of the `Chapter8` user-defined procedure.

# Comparison with Traditional Approaches

In this section, I look briefly at the potential benefits of CLR integration in SQL Server 2005 and then briefly compare using CLR with each of three traditional approaches:

- ✔ T-SQL
- ✔ Extended stored procedures
- ✔ Middle tier techniques

## *Potential benefits of CLR integration*

The integration of the CLR offers developers the following advantages:

- ✔ **A richer programming model:** You have access to programming constructs that are absent from T-SQL. In addition, you have access to the classes of the .NET Framework and can use those classes as a basis for your code.

- ✔ **Improved security:** Compared to the extended stored procedures you might have used with SQL Server 2000 to carry out tasks not possible or convenient with T-SQL, the CLR offers improved security.

- ✔ **User-defined types and aggregates:** You can use .NET languages to create your own user-defined types and aggregates.

- ✔ **Development in a familiar development environment:** Many developers are already familiar with using one of the versions of Visual Studio before Visual Studio 2005. For such developers, creating SQL Server projects in Visual Studio 2005 is an easy step, building on what they already know.

- ✔ **Potentially improved performance:** The .NET languages potentially offer improved performance and scalability.

T-SQL lacks many constructs used in more general purpose programming languages. For example, it does not have arrays, for each loops, collections, or classes. By contrast .NET languages, such as Visual Basic .NET and Visual C# .NET, has support for the preceding constructs and also has object-oriented capabilities such as inheritance, encapsulation, and polymorphism. When the purpose of the code is not simply to manipulate data, the .NET languages and the CLR can be a better choice.

The Base Class Library has many classes that support useful functionality including numeric manipulation, string manipulation, file access, and cryptography. If you need to carry out complex numeric manipulation of data, it is likely that Visual Basic .NET or Visual C# .NET is a better choice than T-SQL. Similarly, if you need to carry out complex text handling, the regular expression support in Visual Basic .NET and Visual C# .NET provides much more control than, for example, the LIKE keyword in T-SQL.

SQL Server 2005 doesn't support all the classes that are part of the .NET Framework 2.0. The code is intended to run inside SQL Server 2005, so some classes — for example, those for windowing — are inappropriate in that context and are not supported.

The Common Language Runtime provides a safer environment for code to run in. For example, it prevents code reading memory that hasn't been written and helps avoid situations where code accesses unmanaged memory. In addition, type safety in the CLR ensures that types are manipulated only in appropriate ways. Taken together, these features of the CLR remove many causes of errors.

For larger projects, the ability to organize code by using classes and namespaces allows the developer to structure the code in a way that is more easily understood. Such improved code structure allows you to easily create code and also more easily maintain the code.

## CLR and T-SQL comparison

T-SQL has two broad components: a Data Definition Language (DDL) and a Data Modification Language (DML). The DML has set-based constructs and procedural constructs. Set-based constructs include the SELECT and INSERT statements. Procedural constructs include stored procedures and triggers.

When the task you need to carry out is primarily or only a data manipulation task, then T-SQL is almost always the way to go. It is designed for data manipulation, whereas languages such as Visual Basic .NET and Visual C# are not. This means that the set-based processing of T-SQL give better performance.

The .NET languages have data structures, such as lists and arrays, which T-SQL lacks. In addition, the .NET languages are well suited to numerical computation. When complex calculations are required, the .NET languages can likely do what's needed even if it is beyond the capabilities of T-SQL.

The regular expression support in the .NET languages provides the ability to control the values in selected columns in ways that T-SQL cannot. User-defined datatypes, which use .NET languages, potentially provide tight control over desired values.

The .NET datatypes and the SQL Server datatypes are not the same. When running CLR code and T-SQL code together, take care to understand any differences between the two kinds of datatypes.

Because of similarities in using .NET languages to access data with the client layer and middle tier, developers can leverage their understanding of ADO.NET. However, code can be more verbose than when using T-SQL and using the right tool (often T-SQL) to access data is important, not least for reasons of performance.

In the situation in which data access is forward only, read only, the .NET languages, which use `SQLDataReader`, may be faster than using a T-SQL cursor. However, set-based operations may often be faster still.

# CLR and extended stored procedure comparison

In SQL Server 2000, if you needed to write code that T-SQL couldn't express, you had to write an extended stored procedure.

Using the CLR provides better control of security for administrators than was available with extended stored procedures. The CLR security permission sets of `SAFE`, `EXTERNAL_ACCESS`, and `UNSAFE` provide a consistent way for administrators to assess what a .NET language stored procedure is allowed to do.

Using .NET languages also provides a better degree of protection against stored procedures corrupting memory that belongs to SQL Server. Extended stored procedures could manipulate SQL Server's memory space without SQL Server having control over execution of the extended stored procedure. By contrast, managed code processes can be shut down by SQL Server if their execution uses too much memory or too many CPU cycles.

Data access to the local SQL Server instance is easier and more efficient than the loop-back mechanism used with extended stored procedures.

If you want to use the datatypes that are new in SQL Server 2005 — `xml`, `varchar(max)`, `nvarchar(max)`, and `varbinary(max)` in an extended stored procedure — you must use a .NET language. Extended stored procedures do not support these new datatypes.

When using managed code, SQL Server can monitor the execution of processes. Any process that runs for an unacceptably long time can be terminated to allow other SQL Server processes to run unhindered. SQL Server doesn't have comparable monitoring capabilities for extended stored procedures, so it can't automatically correct any runaway extended stored procedure.

# CLR and middle tier comparison

The introduction of CLR support inside the database management system in SQL Server 2005 gives developers an additional, but possibly controversial, choice about where to run code written in .NET languages. In principle, writing .NET code in SQL Server rather than on the middle tier reduces network traffic. The downside is that moving processing from the middle tier to the database tier uses valuable CPU cycles that may be better used by SQL Server for other purposes.

# CLR Code Access Security

Quite naturally, many database administrators are concerned about the security implications of allowing CLR-based code to run inside SQL Server 2005.

Managed code (code that runs in the CLR) uses Code Access Security to control what the code is allowed to do.

Managed code can run with the following settings:

- ✔ **Safe:** Only allows computation and local data access.
- ✔ **External access:** Same as for SAFE, plus access to files, environment variables, the registry, and the network.
- ✔ **Unsafe:** Unrestricted access to the environment in which SQL Server is running. In particular, code designated UNSAFE can call unmanaged code.

# Chapter 9

# Using Stored Procedures

● ● ● ● ● ● ● ● ● ● ● ● ● ● ● ● ● ● ● ● ● ● ● ● ● ● ● ● ● ● ● ● ● ● ● ● ● ● ● ● ● ● ● ● ● ● ● ● ● ●

● ● ● ● ● ● ● ● ● ● ● ● ● ● ● ● ● ● ● ● ● ● ● ● ● ● ● ● ● ● ● ● ● ● ● ● ● ● ● ● ● ● ● ● ● ● ● ● ● ●

*I*n this chapter, I introduce you to stored procedures, what they are, and how you can use them in SQL Server 2005.

Much of the system stored procedure functionality continues unchanged from previous versions of SQL Server but, when planning new code, you do need to read the SQL Server Books Online because some system stored procedures have been deprecated and marked for removal in a future version of SQL Server.

You can create user-defined stored procedures in SQL Server 2005 by using T-SQL or with the .NET languages and the Common Language Runtime (CLR).

## What a Stored Procedure Is

A *stored procedure* is a module of code that allows you to reuse a desired piece of functionality and call that functionality by name. Another way to look at a stored procedure is to view it as a routine that cannot be used in a scalar expression. This is a crucial way in which a stored procedure differs from a function (which you can use in a scalar expression).

A stored procedure is a database object in SQL Server 2005. You can assign permissions to individual stored procedures to control who can execute them.

Optionally, a stored procedure may take one or more parameters. I show you later in this chapter how to create and use stored procedures with and without parameters.

A user-defined stored procedure provides a way to store code, which you can call from applications that you or developer colleagues create. Such stored procedures offer security advantages. Text entered in, for example a Web page, isn't executed directly but is passed as a parameter to a stored procedure. This approach can prevent SQL injection attacks.

## Types of stored procedure

When using SQL Server 2005, you have several types of stored procedure available:

- ✔ **T-SQL user-defined stored procedures:** A T-SQL stored procedure consists of several T-SQL statements. It can, optionally, take one or more input parameters and output one or more output parameters.

- ✔ **CLR user-defined stored procedures:** A CLR stored procedure is a reference to a method written by using one of the .NET Framework languages. If you are unfamiliar with CLR in SQL Server 2005, turn to Chapter 8. Like a T-SQL stored procedure, it can optionally take one or more input parameters and/or output one or more output parameters.

- ✔ **Extended stored procedures:** An extended stored procedure is procedural code often written in C, which runs in the SQL Server memory space. These are now deprecated. However, existing extended stored procedures are fully supported in SQL Server 2005. You can still create extended stored procedures in SQL Server 2005 but Microsoft will drop them in a future release of SQL Server. I recommend using CLR stored procedures rather than creating new extended stored procedures. In addition, if you have any extended stored procedures in existing applications, you should replace them with CLR stored procedures when time and resources allow.

In addition to this list of user-defined stored procedures, SQL Server 2005 provides a large number of system stored procedures that I describe later in this chapter.

## What a stored procedure does

A stored procedure can, in principle, do anything that you can do using either T-SQL or a .NET language. For example, you can use a stored procedure to insert or update data in a table or you can use it to return data from one or more tables to a client application.

In an online scenario, a user may specify a locality where they want to find a company store. You can then pass the locality they choose to a stored procedure as an input parameter.

## *Reasons to use a stored procedure*

System stored procedures, which I describe in the next section, provide code to support many SQL Server administrative tasks. Because these system stored procedures are intended to support efficient execution of common tasks, it usually makes good sense to make use of them.

Another important reason for using stored procedures is to reuse code for tasks that you can use in several ways in a SQL Server database. If you later make changes in the code, you can potentially make those changes in a single place — inside the stored procedure. This helps to make maintenance of the functionality in response to changing business circumstances an easier task.

Another advantage of stored procedures is that you can make changes in the database layer in multi-tier applications without changing the client application. You can change the code inside a user-defined stored procedure but, so long as you don't alter the parameters it takes, you can leave the client application unchanged.

If you use a stored procedure that uses a parameter, it provides a level of protection against SQL injection attacks in a Web application. A SQL injection attack uses T-SQL code entered by a user to access unauthorized information. This can make SQL Server more vulnerable to future attack, as a hacker gathers information about the structures used in SQL Server. By using a stored procedure with a parameter, any information entered by a user doesn't execute. If it is not appropriately structured for use as the parameter, an ill-intentioned hacker is unlikely find out the structure of your SQL Server installation.

A SQL injection attack can occur when you create an application that executes dynamic T-SQL. Suppose you have a publisher that makes its catalog available online. A form might include a text box where a user can insert an author name. The application code might include code like this:

```
var sql = "SELECT * FROM Titles WHERE Author = '" +
SelectedAuthor + "'";
```

When the user enters a value of Andrew Watt, the T-SQL code returns titles for that author. However, if a malicious user enters the following in the text box, the Titles table is dropped.

```
Andrew Watt'; DROP TABLE Titles --
```

This happens because the T-SQL code to be executed becomes

```
SELECT * FROM Titles WHERE Author = 'Andrew Watt';
DROP TABLE Titles --
```

The first line executes as desired by the application developer. The DROP TABLE statement deletes the Titles table, which wasn't the expected effect of accepting user input.

On the other hand, if you created a user-defined stored procedure that accepts an Author parameter, the attempt to insert malicious code fails and an empty rowset is returned because there is no author whose name is Andrew Watt'; DROP TABLE Titles --.

## System stored procedures

SQL Server 2005 provides a huge range of stored procedures, ready made for your use. System stored procedures are stored in the Resource database. You can use these system stored procedures for a broad range of administrative purposes. System stored procedures can help you with several types of tasks, which Table 9-1 summarizes.

| Table 9-1 | Categories of System Stored Procedures |
| --- | --- |
| *Category* | *Purpose* |
| Active Directory | These stored procedures are used to register SQL Server instances and databases in Active Directory. |
| Catalog | These relate to ODBC functionality. |
| Cursor | These allow you to retrieve information relating to cursor variable functionality. |
| Database Engine | These are used in the maintenance of an instance of SQL Server. |
| Database Mail | These are used to support the new Database Mail functionality in SQL Server 2005. |
| Database Maintenance Plan | These support administrative tasks relate to database maintenance plans. These stored procedures have been replaced in SQL Server 2005 by maintenance plans that do not use this group of stored procedures. |

| Category | Purpose |
|----------|---------|
| Distributed Queries | These stored procedures are used to implement and manage distributed queries. |
| Full-text Search | These stored procedures allow you to create or remove full-text catalogs and to control indexing operations. |
| Log Shipping | These stored procedures allow you to configure, modify, and monitor log shipping configurations. |
| Notification Services | These stored procedures allow you to administer SQL Server 2005 Notification Services. For example, you can administer, debug, and troubleshoot Notification Services by using this group of stored procedures. |
| OLE Automation | These stored procedures allow you to use OLE automation objects from inside a T-SQL batch. |
| Replication | These stored procedures allow you to manage replication. You can use them for one-time tasks or in batch files and scripts. |
| Security | These stored procedures provide a wide range of techniques to manage SQL Server security. Some of these are deprecated and will be removed in a future version of SQL Server. |
| SQL Mail | These are used to support SQL Mail functionality. This group of stored procedures has been deprecated in SQL Server 2005 and will be removed in a future version of SQL Server. |
| SQL Server Agent | SQL Server Agent uses this large group of stored procedures to manage scheduled and event-driven subscriptions. |
| SQL Server Profile | SQL Server Profiler uses this group of stored procedures. |
| Web Task | These stored procedures are used to create Web pages. They are not enabled by default. This group of stored procedures has been deprecated. Use Reporting Services for new development work. |
| XML | These stored procedures support the management of in memory representations of XML documents based on the MSXML parser. |
| General Extended | These stored procedures provide an interface from an instance of SQL Server 2005 to external programs used for maintenance. These stored procedures are turned off by default. |

An alternative approach to replication stored procedures is to use the Replication Management Objects that are new to SQL Server 2005. Replication Management Objects are beyond the scope of this book.

To access some system stored procedures you need to use the sp_configure system stored procedure to enable advanced options. For example, to enable the Web Assistant that is required for the Web Task system stored procedures, use the following T-SQL code (which itself makes use of the sp_configure stored procedure):

```
sp_configure 'show advanced options', 1;
GO
RECONFIGURE;
GO
sp_configure 'Web Assistant Procedures', 1;
GO
RECONFIGURE
GO
```

When using XML system stored procedures, be aware that the MSXML parser uses one eighth of the memory in the SQL Server cache. To free up memory used by an XML document, use the sp_xml_removedocument stored procedure.

To use extended stored procedures you need to turn the relevant module on. To do that, use this code:

```
sp_configure 'show advanced options', 1
RECONFIGURE
GO
sp_configure 'xp_cmdshell', 1;
RECONFIGURE
GO
```

The preceding code enables you to use the xp_cmdshell system stored procedure. To run the xp_cmdshell extended stored procedure to show the files in the root directory on drive C use the following code:

```
EXEC master..xp_cmdshell 'dir c:\*.*'
```

Figure 9-1 shows the result from running the preceding code.

You can use many command-line commands as the argument to the xp_cmdshell extended stored procedure. This allows you to retrieve information from the operating system or manipulate aspects of the environment in which SQL Server operates.

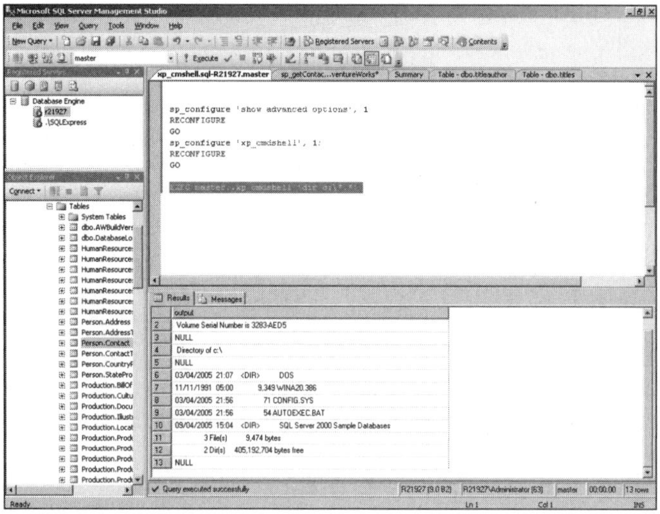

**Figure 9-1:**
Using the
`xp_cmd`
`shell`
stored
procedure
to list files.

Individual system stored procedures each have an associated permission level associated with them. A full description of the permission levels needed to use the large number of system stored procedures that SQL Server 2005 supports is beyond the scope of this chapter. The SQL Server 2005 Books Online describes the individual system stored procedures and the permission levels you need to use each one. Assuming you chose to install SQL Server 2005 Books Online, choose Start⇨All Programs⇨Microsoft SQL Server 2005⇨Documentation and Tutorials⇨SQL Server Books Online.

# Creating a Stored Procedure

To create a user-defined stored procedure, you use the CREATE PROCEDURE statement. You can create a stored procedure only in the current database.

In a T-SQL user-defined stored procedure, you cannot use some T-SQL statements inside the CREATE PROCEDURE statement. These are listed here:

- ✔ CREATE DEFAULT
- ✔ CREATE PROCEDURE
- ✔ CREATE RULE
- ✔ CREATE TRIGGER
- ✔ CREATE VIEW

To create a stored procedure, you need certain permissions. You need the CREATE PROCEDURE permission in the database. You also need the ALTER SCHEMA permission in that database, because stored procedures are schema-scoped objects.

To create a CLR stored procedure, you need to own the assembly referenced or have the REFERENCES permission on that assembly.

## Creating a procedure without parameters

In describing how to create a stored procedure, I assume that you have the permissions specified in the preceding section. If you are unfamiliar with how to grant permissions, see Chapter 11 on security in SQL Server 2005.

This example creates a stored procedure that retrieves name and e-mail information about contacts in the Person.Contact table of the AdventureWorks database. To do that, use this T-SQL code:

```
USE AdventureWorks
GO

CREATE PROCEDURE Person.sp_getContactNames
AS
  SELECT LastName, FirstName, EmailAddress
  FROM Person.Contact
GO
```

The first line of the CREATE PROCEDURE statement specifies the name of the stored procedure you create. Notice that the name of the stored procedure includes a schema name, Person. Because the stored procedure is in a schema other than the dbo schema, you run no risk of naming problems occurring if Microsoft adds a similarly named system stored procedure (which goes in the dbo schema) in a future version of SQL Server.

To run the stored procedure, run this code:

```
EXEC Person.sp_getContactNames
```

Figure 9-2 shows the result from running the stored procedure.

If you want to return the AdventureWorks database to its original state, you can drop the stored procedure by using the following code:

```
DROP PROCEDURE Person.sp_getContactNames
```

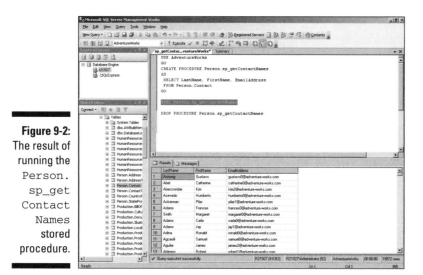

**Figure 9-2:**
The result of
running the
Person.
sp_get
Contact
Names
stored
procedure.

# Creating a stored procedure with a parameter

In this section, I show you how to create a stored procedure that takes a single parameter. The stored procedure makes the same selection as in the preceding stored procedure except that it has a single parameter. Use this code:

```
USE AdventureWorks
GO
CREATE PROCEDURE Person.sp_getContactNames2
 @lastName varchar(10)
 AS
 SELECT LastName, FirstName, EmailAddress
 FROM Person.Contact
 WHERE LastName = @lastName
```

Notice in the fourth line of the code, you specify a parameter @lastName whose type is varchar(10). That parameter is used in the WHERE clause of the SELECT statement.

To select contact details where the last name of the contact is Smith, use the following code:

```
EXEC Person.sp_getContactNames2 'Smith'
```

Figure 9-3 shows the result of running the preceding code.

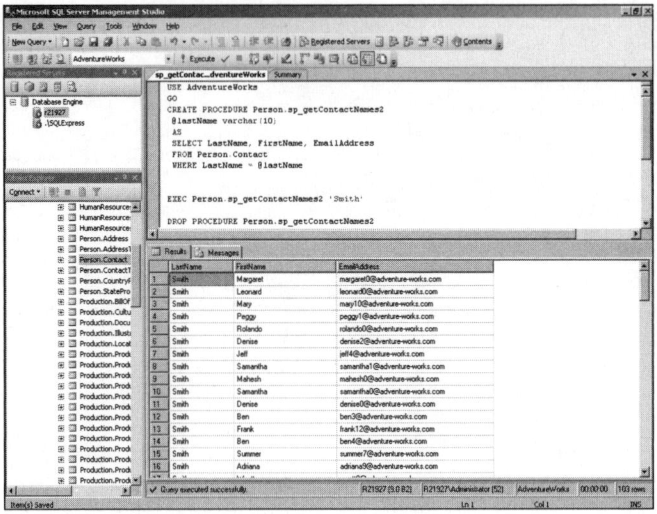

**Figure 9-3:**
Using a
parameter
when
executing a
stored
procedure.

To remove the `Person.sp_getContactNames2` stored procedure and return
the `AdventureWorks` database to its original state, use the following code:

```
DROP PROCEDURE Person.sp_getContactNames2
```

## Naming stored procedures

Many of the system stored procedures provided with SQL Server 2005 uses a
prefix of `sp_`. You can create your own stored procedures using that prefix,
but Microsoft strongly recommends that you don't. Microsoft may use the
name that you choose for a user-defined stored procedure in a future version
of SQL Server. This situation can cause unpredictable problems in your code.
If you create a user-defined stored procedure using the problematic prefix
(and it is either not schema-qualified or is in the `dbo` schema) and Microsoft
creates an identically named stored procedure, your code breaks.

You can avoid the risk of your code breaking two different ways. One way is
simply to avoid using the `sp_` prefix. The second option is to use schema-
qualified names for the user-defined stored procedures that you create. Using
the schema name makes it clear that your user-defined stored procedure is
not a system stored procedure. Therefore any future system stored procedure is in a different schema so the clash of names is avoided.

# Calling a Stored Procedure

Calling a stored procedure is straightforward. Use the EXEC statement together with the name of a system stored procedure or a user-defined stored procedure. Because a user-defined stored procedure is associated with an individual database, you must ensure that the correct database is the current database.

To execute a user-defined stored procedure called Person.sp_getContact Names that is associated with the AdventureWorks database, use the following code:

```
USE AdventureWorks
GO
EXEC Person.sp_getContactNames
```

The preceding code works with whatever the current database is when you execute it. The USE statement specifies that the current database is Adventure Works before executing the Person.sp_getContactNames stored procedure.

# CLR Stored Procedures

The presence of the Common Language Runtime (CLR) in SQL Server is new in SQL Server 2005. One of the uses for .NET language code is to create stored procedures written in a .NET language.

To create a CLR stored procedure, you need to follow these broad steps:

- ✔ Create a static method of a class using your .NET language of choice.
- ✔ Using the relevant language compiler, compile the class into an assembly.
- ✔ Register the assembly in SQL Server 2005 using the CREATE ASSEMBLY statement.
- ✔ When the assembly is registered, you can use the CREATE PROCEDURE statement to create a stored procedure that runs the method you created.

# Chapter 10

# Error Handling in T-SQL

● ● ● ● ● ● ● ● ● ● ● ● ● ● ● ● ● ● ● ● ● ● ● ● ● ● ● ● ● ● ● ● ● ● ● ● ● ● ● ● ● ● ● ● ●

## In This Chapter

▶ Catching errors with T-SQL

▶ Discovering the `TRY...CATCH` construct

▶ Using error functions and `@@Error`

● ● ● ● ● ● ● ● ● ● ● ● ● ● ● ● ● ● ● ● ● ● ● ● ● ● ● ● ● ● ● ● ● ● ● ● ● ● ● ● ● ● ● ● ●

*O*ne of the new features available to you in SQL Server 2005 is the ability to easily handle errors that occur in T-SQL code. In earlier versions of SQL Server, T-SQL visibly lacked well-structured error handling comparable to the approaches in languages such as Visual C++ or C#. The information available about individual errors was fairly limited. As the complexity and length of T-SQL code increased with time, the lack of easy-to-use error handling was a significant deficiency in T-SQL that needed to be corrected.

## Handling Errors with T-SQL

There are two broad approaches to working with errors in T-SQL. Using the `TRY...CATCH` construct that I describe in the next section is something new in SQL Server 2005. You can use the `TRY...CATCH` construct with error functions, but you can also use it with the `@@Error` function that was also supported in SQL Server 2000. I talk more about error functions in the "Using Error Functions" section, later in this chapter.

If you need to write code that runs on SQL Server 2005 and also on (for example) SQL Server 2000, you need to use the `@@Error` function that provides less information than the error functions introduced in SQL Server 2005. You also cannot use the `TRY...CATCH` construct in code intended to run on SQL Server 2000.

# The TRY...CATCH Construct

The `TRY...CATCH` construct is the pivot of error handling in T-SQL code in SQL Server 2005. The `TRY...CATCH` construct takes the following general form:

```
BEGIN TRY
  -- T-SQL code goes here.
  -- If an error is raised execution switches to the CATCH
        block
END TRY
BEGIN CATCH
  -- Other T-SQL code can go here which is executed
  -- when there is an error in the code between BEGIN TRY
  -- and END TRY
END CATCH
```

Inside the `TRY` block or inside the `CATCH` block you can have any T-SQL statement or block of T-SQL statements that you want. You can nest `TRY...CATCH` constructs and I show you how to do that later in the chapter in the "Using nested TRY...CATCH constructs" section.

If no error occurs during execution of the T-SQL code between `BEGIN TRY` and `END TRY`, then the code in the `CATCH` block doesn't execute. After all the code in the `TRY` block is done executing, control passes to the code that follows the `END CATCH` line.

## Rules for the TRY...CATCH construct

To use the `TRY...CATCH` construct correctly, you must follow these rules:

✔ There must be no code between the `END TRY` line and the `BEGIN CATCH` line. A syntax error occurs if you attempt to put any T-SQL code between those lines.

✔ A `TRY...CATCH` construct cannot span multiple batches.

✔ A `TRY...CATCH` construct cannot span multiple blocks of T-SQL code.

## Error message severity levels

In SQL Server, each error message has a severity level associated with it. The `TRY...CATCH` construct in SQL Server 2005 catches errors where the severity level is greater than 10. However, the `TRY...CATCH` construct doesn't catch errors with severity levels that exceed 10 if the error results in a loss of the database connection.

You can find a full list of error severity levels in SQL Server Books Online in the Database Engine Error Severity topic.

# Using Error Functions

Several error functions in SQL Server 2005 provide information that you can use inside the CATCH statement.

The error functions available in T-SQL in SQL Server 2005 are the following:

- ✔ **ERROR_LINE:** Gives the line at which the error appears to have occurred.

  The line given by the ERROR_LINE function may not be the line that actually contains the error. You may need to examine the control flow — for example, of nested script objects — to see exactly where the error occurs.

- ✔ **ERROR_MESSAGE:** Gives a brief message indicating the nature of the error.

  Many SQL Server error messages include parameters that provide information about the specific context in which an error arose. The ERROR_MESSAGE function substitutes values relevant to the context for those parameters and returns the substituted message. You can access error messages from the text column of the sys.messages catalog.

- ✔ **ERROR_NUMBER:** Gives the number of the error. If the error occurs in a stored procedure or trigger, it returns the line number in the routine.

  The ERROR_NUMBER function returns the number of an error when it is executed inside the CATCH block. If you attempt to use the ERROR_NUMBER function outside a CATCH block, it returns NULL.

- ✔ **ERROR_PROCEDURE:** Returns NULL if the error doesn't occur in a stored procedure. When the error occurs in a stored procedure or trigger, this function returns the name of the stored procedure or trigger.

- ✔ **ERROR_SEVERITY:** This returns the severity of a SQL Server error.

- ✔ **ERROR_STATE:** Returns an int value. Returns NULL if called outside a CATCH block. It provides information complementary to ERROR_NUMBER.

  The ERROR_STATE function provides additional information to help you understand the information returned by the ERROR_NUMBER function. Some error numbers can have different values returned by ERROR_STATE in different situations. When trying to understand and process errors, you may need to know both pieces of information — for example, to effectively use the Microsoft knowledge base.

The `sys.messages` catalog contains a complete list of error numbers and the corresponding messages. To view all errors and their corresponding messages, run this code:

```
SELECT * FROM sys.messages
ORDER BY message_id
```

Figure 10-1 shows the results grid scrolled to include error 8134.

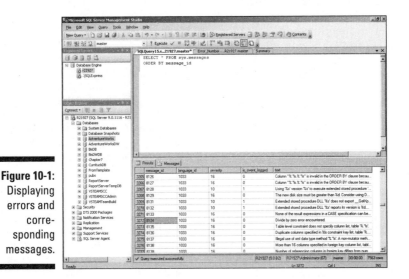

**Figure 10-1:** Displaying errors and corresponding messages.

Notice that the `severity` column indicates the severity of the error. The `is_event_logged` column shows whether or not the error is currently being logged. A value of 0 (zero) indicates that a particular error is not currently being logged.

To find the error number and severity for errors relating to a particular topic when you don't know the error number but do know part of the message, simply use code like the following:

```
SELECT * FROM sys.messages
WHERE text LIKE '%zero%'
```

This example finds all error messages that contain the word zero, including error 8134.

The LIKE keyword in the WHERE clause allows you to use the % wildcard character. The % wildcard character matches zero or more characters. By using it at the beginning and end of the word you're looking for, you find any occurrence of the word zero in the text column.

If you want to find information on errors that the TRY...CATCH construct can trap, use the following code.

```
SELECT * FROM sys.messages
WHERE severity > 10 AND severity < 20
ORDER BY severity
```

The TRY...CATCH construct allows you to trap errors where the severity level is greater than 10, except where the database connection is disrupted. Errors with a severity level of 10 or less provide warnings that are for information purposes only. Some errors of severity level 20 and above may also be processed using the CATCH block, if the database connection is not disrupted by the error.

## Using error codes

The following code demonstrates how you can use the error functions in SQL Server 2005 to display information about an error that occurs in the TRY block. It uses an attempt to divide by zero to raise an error:

```
USE master
GO

BEGIN TRY
SELECT 1/0 -- Produces a divide by zero error.
END TRY
BEGIN CATCH
  SELECT
  ERROR_LINE() AS ErrorLine,
  ERROR_MESSAGE() AS ErrorMessage,
  ERROR_NUMBER() AS ErrorNumber,
  ERROR_PROCEDURE() AS ErrorProcedure,
  ERROR_SEVERITY() AS ErrorSeverity,
  ERROR_STATE() AS ErrorState
END CATCH
```

Figure 10-2 shows the results of running the code.

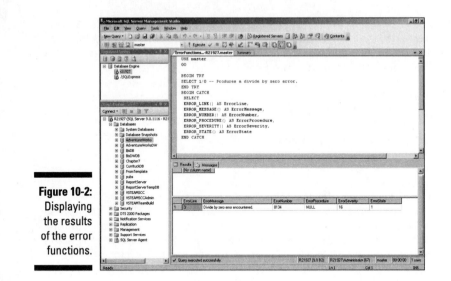

**Figure 10-2:**
Displaying
the results
of the error
functions.

The first result displays nothing because the attempt to divide by zero returns nothing. In the second grid, the result returned by each error function displays in its own named column.

If you want to store the values returned by the error functions, you must capture them in variables. You can then INSERT the values of the variables in an audit table.

## RAISERROR

The RAISERROR function can access a user-defined message that is stored in sys.messages or you can code an error dynamically by using RAISERROR.

When writing code with RAISERROR, the code takes the following form:

```
RAISERRROR(50100, 12, 1, 'Text of message goes here.')
```

Use the following code to add a new user-defined error to sys.messages, and then to raise an error with that number. In the next section, I look at using RAISERROR in nested TRY...CATCH constructs. To add a new message to sys.messages, use this code:

```
sp_addmessage @msgnum = 50100,
  @severity = 12,
  @msgtext = N'This is a test error.'
```

The `sp_addmessage` system stored procedure is used to add a new message to `sys.messages`. In this example, it takes three parameters that consist of the number, the severity, and the message text of the new message.

You can test that the new message has been added successfully by using this code:

```
SELECT * FROM sys.messages
WHERE message_id = 50100
```

You can then use `RAISERROR` inside a `TRY...CATCH` construct as follows:

```
BEGIN TRY
  RAISERROR(50100, 12, 1, '')
END TRY
BEGIN CATCH
  SELECT ERROR_MESSAGE() AS ErrorMessage
END CATCH
```

Figure 10-3 shows the result of running the preceding code.

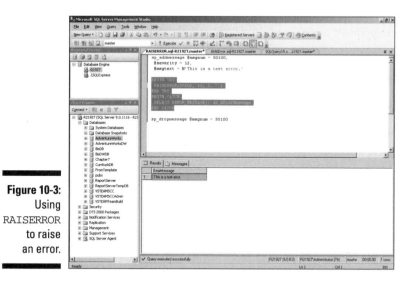

**Figure 10-3:**
Using
RAISERROR
to raise
an error.

You remove the message from `sys.messages` by using the following code:

```
sp_dropmessage @msgnum = 50100
```

# *Using nested TRY...CATCH constructs*

In some situations, you may want to nest TRY...CATCH constructs. The nested TRY...CATCH construct is nested inside the CATCH block of the outer TRY...CATCH construct.

The following example uses RAISERROR to demonstrate how to code nested TRY...CATCH constructs.

First add two new messages to the sys.messages catalog by using the following code. Notice that the message describes which construct it occurs in.

```
sp_addmessage
@msgnum = 50200,
@severity = 12,
@msgtext = N'This is in the outer TRY block.'

sp_addmessage
@msgnum = 50300,
@severity = 14,
@msgtext = N'This is in the **INNER** TRY block.'
```

Now that you have added two user-defined messages, you can use these to see how errors in a nested TRY...CATCH construct are handled. The following code shows a nested TRY...CATCH construct with RAISERROR used to raise an error in each of the constructs:

```
BEGIN TRY
  RAISERROR(50200,12,1,'')
END TRY
BEGIN CATCH
  SELECT ERROR_NUMBER() AS OuterErrorNumber,
   ERROR_MESSAGE() AS OuterErrorMessage
  BEGIN TRY
  RAISERROR(50300, 14, 1, '')
  END TRY
  BEGIN CATCH
    SELECT ERROR_NUMBER() AS InnerErrorNumber,
     ERROR_MESSAGE() AS InnerErrorMessage
  END CATCH -- Nested CATCH
END CATCH -- Outer CATCH
```

Figure 10-4 shows the result of running the code.

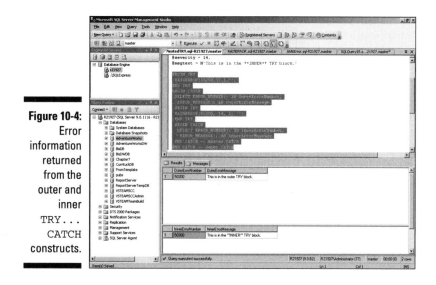

**Figure 10-4:**
Error
information
returned
from the
outer and
inner
TRY . . .
CATCH
constructs.

# @@Error

The @@Error function was the main way to get information about errors in SQL Server 2000 and earlier versions of SQL Server. If you need to write T-SQL code to run both on SQL Server 2005 and earlier versions, you need to understand how to use the @@Error function to capture information about errors.

The @@Error differs in several respects from the error functions described in earlier sections. The @@Error function returns the error number only in the next T-SQL statement after the occurrence of the error or when @@Error is used in the first statement in a CATCH block. If the preceding T-SQL statement executes correctly, @@ERROR returns zero.

The following code demonstrates that @@Error only contains a meaningful value in the first line of a CATCH block:

```
BEGIN TRY
  SELECT 1/0;
  PRINT @@ERROR;
END TRY
BEGIN CATCH
SELECT @@ERROR
SELECT @@ERROR
IF @@ERROR = 8134
  SELECT 'Divide by Zero Error found.'
ELSE
  SELECT 'No divide by Zero Error found.'
END CATCH
```

Notice that the first two lines of the CATCH block are the same. Figure 10-5 shows the appearance after running the code in SQL Server Management Studio.

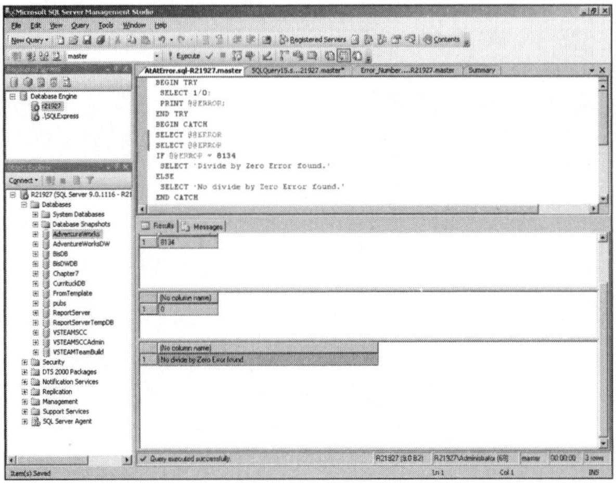

Figure 10-5:
Using the
@@Error
function.

The first result in the results grid is from the attempted division by zero, which fails; therefore, no value is displayed — in Figure 10-5, I had scrolled that blank result out of sight. The second result displays the value 8134, which indicates a divide by zero error and is produced by the first SELECT @@ERROR in the CATCH block. The third result displays the value 0, demonstrating that @@Error (in the second line of the CATCH block) is reset after each T-SQL statement executes. However when testing if @@Error = 8134 in the IF statement, you can see that @@Error no longer contains the value 8134 (in fact it is now 0) because the text "No divide by Zero Error found" is displayed.

If you comment out the two SELECT @@ERROR lines, then the first line of the CATCH block is IF @@ERROR=8134, which is now true (because this is the first line in the CATCH block) and the Divide by Zero Error found. error message displays in the results grid.

If, instead of using @@ERROR, you use the ERROR_NUMBER function, ERROR_NUMBER returns the same value whenever you use the function, as when you run the following code:

```
BEGIN TRY
  SELECT 1/0;
  PRINT @@ERROR;
END TRY
BEGIN CATCH
SELECT ERROR_NUMBER() AS ErrorNumber
```

```
IF ERROR_NUMBER() = 8134
  SELECT 'Divide by Zero Error found.'
ELSE
  SELECT 'No divide by Zero Error found.'
END CATCH
```

Figure 10-6 shows the result grid.

As you can see in Figure 10-6, the number returned in the second result is 8134. However, the test in the IF statement is TRUE (because ERROR_NUMBER still returns 8134) so the Divide by Zero Error found. error message displays.

If you need to use @@Error to give compatibility with earlier versions of SQL Server, then assign the value of @@Error to a variable. You can then use the value of that variable in a way similar to the way you can use ERROR_NUMBER.

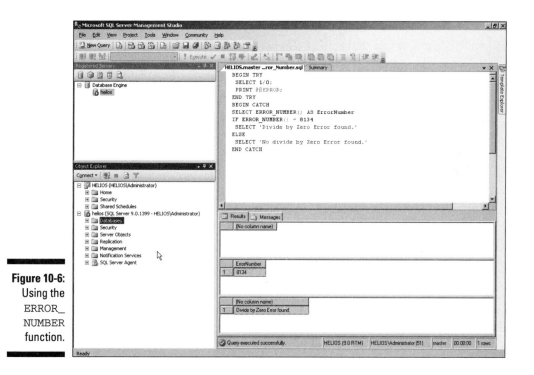

**Figure 10-6:**
Using the
ERROR_
NUMBER
function.

# Part IV
# Protecting Your Data

## The 5<sup>th</sup> Wave

By Rich Tennant

"Troubleshooting's a little tricky here. The route table to our destination hosts include a Morse code key, several walkie-talkies, and a guy with nine messenger pigeons."

## In this part . . .

I introduce you to techniques that will help you secure your data and prevent data loss.

I show you how to use transactions and how to create and use database triggers.

# Chapter 11

# Securing Your Data

● ● ● ● ● ● ● ● ● ● ● ● ● ● ● ● ● ● ● ● ● ● ● ● ● ● ● ● ● ● ● ● ● ● ● ● ● ● ● ● ● ● ● ● ● ● ● ●

● ● ● ● ● ● ● ● ● ● ● ● ● ● ● ● ● ● ● ● ● ● ● ● ● ● ● ● ● ● ● ● ● ● ● ● ● ● ● ● ● ● ● ● ● ● ● ●

*O*ne of the key considerations when you use any serious database management system is to control who has access to what data. For example, you don't want your competitors to see your financial data or to have access to information on a product that you haven't announced yet and you don't want your employees to see other employees' salary information or similar sensitive information. On the other hand, you must make it as easy and convenient as possible for your users to get access to the data that they legitimately should have access to in order to get their work done, place orders with your company, and so on.

The SQL Server 2005 security model attempts to enable you to both assure security and make SQL Server easy to use for authorized users and customers. In attempting to achieve that, SQL Server 2005 has several significant differences in its security model compared to the SQL Server 2000 security model.

The various parts of the SQL Server 2005 security model are interdependent. I suggest that you read quickly through this chapter initially so that you gain an overview of SQL Server 2005 security. Then read the chapter again carefully to understand the detail in context.

In the space available in this chapter, I can't cover every detail of every scenario in which you might use SQL Server 2005. When designing security in any particular situation, make sure that you consider all likely threats and then, with some careful thinking, try to identify less obvious threats too. Time spent in considering the risks to your data is time well spent. Microsoft tries to provide you with the tools to keep your data secure. Take time to understand those security tools and think through how they apply to your usage scenario.

# Introducing The New Security Model

Microsoft, after some embarrassing security problems with SQL Server 2000, has put great emphasis on improving security in SQL Server 2005. The broad aims are to make SQL Server 2005

- ✔ **Secure by design:** During the development of SQL Server 2005, Microsoft carried out a detailed threat analysis of SQL Server. All the possible threats that Microsoft could identify or imagine were considered. This analysis was, in part, stimulated by security problems that occurred with early versions of SQL Server 2000. Any potential security weaknesses in SQL Server 2005 that identified potential threats were addressed by improvements in the design of the security model and the design changes were rigorously tested.

- ✔ **Secure by default:** The default settings for a SQL Server 2005 installation are to have many features turned off. By turning off features, this reduces the *attack surface* of a default SQL Server 2005 installation, leaving fewer places for hackers to attack. Having features turned off by default avoids the situation where a new feature is active and potentially vulnerable to hackers but you, as the database administrator, don't know that the feature is there and therefore you don't realize that it may contain a potential security risk and take appropriate precautions. If you want one of those features to be turned on, you have to turn it on yourself. You are expected to take time to understand the feature and its security implications before turning it on.

  From a security point of view, turning features off by default is a good thing. From the point of view of the database administrator, you need to be aware that you need to explicitly turn on many features before you can use them. Increased security is achieved at a cost in convenience.

  The Surface Area Configuration tool provides a single place where you can configure the surface area of a SQL Server 2005 install. To open the Surface Area Configuration tool, choose Start⇨All Programs⇨Microsoft SQL Server 2005⇨Configuration Tools⇨SQL Server Surface Area Configuration.

- ✔ **Secure in deployment:** The *Principle of Least Privileges* is applied in SQL Server 2005 deployments. This means that you should use the account or login that has just enough security privileges to get the job done but avoid using accounts or logins that have unnecessary privileges. This means that if a hacker gets unauthorized access to the system (which you obviously take steps to avoid), he, generally, has access only to an account or login that has limited permissions. The result is that the hacker can do less damage or has to work much harder to cause serious damage than if he had gained access to an account with higher permissions. The fewer unnecessary permissions you grant a user, the less the damage that can result if a hacker impersonates a user.

The most dangerous accounts for a hacker to attack are the `sa` account and other administrator accounts.

## Security terminology

When you consider SQL Server 2005 security, it helps to think in terms of *securables* — things that can be secured, such as servers, databases, tables, and assemblies — and *principals* (for example, logins and users) to whom permissions on securables can be granted.

Both principals and securables belong to the hierarchies, which I describe next.

## Principals hierarchy

You can view security, as it applies to SQL Server 2005, as a three-level hierarchy relating to principals:

| Level | Principals |
| --- | --- |
| Windows | Groups |
| | Domain logins |
| | Local logins |
| SQL Server instance | Fixed server roles |
| | Logins |
| Database | Fixed database roles |
| | Users |
| | Application roles |
| | Groups |

I discuss several of these principals in more detail later in the chapter.

## Securables hierarchy

The Windows level has no SQL Server 2005 securables, but the schema level does have securables so again it has a three-level hierarchy:

### SQL Server Securables

SQL Server login          Endpoint      Database

### Database Securables

| | |
|---|---|
| Application role | Assembly |
| Asymmetric key | Certificate |
| Contract | Full-text catalog |
| Message type | Remote Service Binding |
| Role | Route |
| Schema | Service |
| Symmetric Key | User |

### Schema Securables

| | |
|---|---|
| Function | Table |
| Procedure | Type |
| Queue | View |
| Synonym | XML Schema Collection |

The T-SQL keywords GRANT, DENY and REVOKE handles the authorization for these securables. I demonstrate use of these later in the chapter.

## New security features

SQL Server 2005 introduces the following new or changed security features. I show several of these in use later in this chapter.

- **Logins:** Logins are (SQL Server) instance-level principals.

- **Users:** Users are database-level principals.

- **Separation of users and schemas:** Each schema has a user who is the owner of the schema. A schema is the owner of the objects in the schema. It is possible to change the owner of a schema without having to change any application code that uses objects in that schema. This avoids the problems that occur if a user who owns database objects, for example, leaves the company.

- **Catalog security:** Metadata is visible only for the tables that a user has permissions on. This helps to hide unauthorized information from users.

 ✔ **Module execution context:** This supplements Ownership Chaining that was present in SQL Server 2000.

 ✔ **Granular permissions control:** Granting of permissions is more granular than in SQL Server 2000. This means that you can now use lower privilege accounts to do some tasks for which you needed to use an administrator account in SQL Server 2000.

 ✔ **Password policy enforcement:** If you run SQL Server 2005 on Windows 2003 Server, you have the option to enforce in SQL Server any password policy that already exists for the Windows user accounts.

## Granular permissions control

In SQL Server 2000, permissions were granted in terms of the fixed server roles supported by SQL Server 2000. That does not provide a sufficiently granular approach to security. The least privileges principle specifies sufficient permissions to perform an action are granted without granting other potentially superfluous permissions.

In SQL Server 2005, the following levels of granular permissions control are supported:

 ✔ **Server:** At the server level, permissions can be granted to logins.

 ✔ **Database:** At the database level, permissions can be granted to users, database roles, or application roles.

 ✔ **Schema:** Each schema in a database has its own associated permissions.

 ✔ **Object:** Objects within schemas can have their own associated permissions.

## Permissions basics

SQL Server 2005 supports three keywords that affect permissions:

 ✔ **GRANT:** Gives a right.

 ✔ **DENY:** Explicitly denies a right.

 ✔ **REVOKE:** Revokes a previous GRANT or DENY.

A DENY at any level in a hierarchy of permissions always takes precedence. For example, if a user has been granted a read permission on a database but belongs to a group that has been denied the read on that database, the DENY takes precedence and the user can't read data in that database.

The GRANT and DENY keywords can apply together. For example, as a manager, Fred may be granted read access to a view because he is a member of the Managers group. However, he as an individual user may, for business reasons, be denied authorization to access the view. The denial of permission takes precedence.

## Permission levels

You can control a range of permission levels with the GRANT, DENY and REVOKE keywords. The SQL Server 2005 permission levels are listed here. In the following descriptions, a *grantee* is the person to whom a permission is granted.

- ✔ **CONTROL:** This effectively grants ownership-like rights on an object. A principal to whom CONTROL is granted has all defined permissions on the securable, including the ability to grant permissions on that securable to other principals.

- ✔ **ALTER:** Grants permission to alter an entity and to CREATE, ALTER, and DROP subentities. For example, granting ALTER permissions on a database also grants CREATE, ALTER, and DROP permissions for tables in that database. This permission does not allow the grantee to alter the ownership of the securable on which it is granted.

- ✔ **ALTER ANY *X*:** Grants permission to alter any object of the specified kind. This permission can be granted at the server level or at the database level. For example, ALTER ANY TABLE grants permission to alter any table in a database.

- ✔ **CREATE *<server securable>*:** Grants the permission to CREATE any server-level securable.

- ✔ **CREATE *<database securable>*:** Grants the permission to CREATE any database-level securable.

- ✔ **IMPERSONATE *<login>*:** Allows the grantee to impersonate the specified login.

- ✔ **IMPERSONATE *<user>*:** Allows the grantee to impersonate the specified user.

- ✔ **TAKE OWNERSHIP:** Gives the grantee the ability to take ownership of a securable.

## How permissions apply to specific securables

Table 11-1 summarizes which specific securables are affected by specific permissions.

| Table 11-1 | Permissions and Their Securables |
|---|---|
| *Permission* | *Securables* |
| ALTER | Assemblies |
| | Certificates |
| | Indexes |
| | Procedures (whether T-SQL or CLR) |
| | Scalar and aggregate functions (whether T-SQL or CLR) |
| | Schemas |
| | Service Broker queues |
| | Tables |
| | Table-valued functions (whether T-SQL or CLR) |
| | Views |
| CONTROL | Procedures (whether T-SQL or CLR) |
| | Scalar and aggregate functions (whether T-SQL or CLR) |
| | Service Broker queues |
| | Synonyms |
| | Tables |
| | Table-valued functions (whether T-SQL or CLR) |
| | Views |
| EXECUTE | Procedures (whether T-SQL or CLR) |
| | Scalar and aggregate functions (whether T-SQL or CLR) |
| | Synonyms |
| INSERT | Synonyms |
| | Tables and columns |
| | Views and columns |
| RECEIVE | Service Broker queues |
| REFERENCES | Scalar and aggregate functions (whether T-SQL or CLR) |
| | Service Broker queues |

*(continued)*

## Table 11-1 *(continued)*

| Permission | Securables |
| --- | --- |
| | Tables and columns |
| | Table-valued functions (whether T-SQL or CLR) and columns |
| | Views and columns |
| SELECT | Synonyms |
| | Tables and columns |
| | Table-valued functions (whether T-SQL or CLR) and columns |
| | Views and columns |
| TAKE OWNERSHIP | Procedures (whether T-SQL or CLR) |
| | Scalar and aggregate functions (whether T-SQL or CLR) |
| | Synonyms |
| | Tables |
| | Table-valued functions (whether T-SQL or CLR) |
| | Views |
| UPDATE | Synonyms |
| | Tables and columns |
| | Views and columns |
| VIEW DEFINITION | Procedures (whether T-SQL or CLR) |
| | Services broker queues |
| | Scalar and aggregate functions (whether T-SQL or CLR) |
| | Synonyms |
| | Tables |
| | Table-valued functions (whether T-SQL or CLR) |
| | Views |

A complete listing of all SQL Server 2005 permissions is available in SQL Server 2005 Books Online. To access SQL Server 2005 Books Online, choose Start⇨ All Programs⇨Microsoft SQL Server 2005⇨Documentation and Tutorials⇨ SQL Server Books Online. You can also list all permissions from inside SQL Server Management Studio query pane by running the following code:

```
SELECT * FROM sys.fn_builtin_permissions(default)
```

It returns over 180 rows in the results grid. You can supply a parameter to view the permissions that apply to a particular class of object. The following code shows how you retrieve all permissions that apply to a database object:

```
SELECT * FROM sys.fn_builtin_permissions('database')
```

To view permissions on a server, use the following T-SQL code:

```
SELECT * FROM sys.server_permissions
WHERE class = 100
```

To view permissions for endpoints on a server, use the following code:

```
SELECT * FROM sys.server_permissions
WHERE class = 105
```

# Working with the New Security Model

In this section, I show you examples of how you can use the SQL Server 2005 security model and permissions to carry out common security tasks.

The code examples shown in this section assume that you're running the T-SQL inside the Query Editor in SQL Server Management Studio. To run the code, type the code in the Query Editor, select it, and press F5.

The system catalog and metadata are more secure than in SQL Server 2000. Previously you could see database objects that you didn't have permissions on. A hacker could use that information to plan further attacks. In SQL Server 2005, you can see only those database objects for which you have permissions. A hacker who gains unauthorized access to your login sees only what you can see and can't see other database objects. For example, if you use

```
SELECT * FROM sysobjects
```

to see system objects, you see only objects for which you have permissions.

## Logins and users

Logins are SQL Server instance-level objects. Users are database-level objects. To create a user JSmith with a specified password, use the following statement:

```
CREATE LOGIN JSmith WITH PASSWORD = 'ABC123'
```

You have created a login with access to a SQL Server instance. You now need to specify a corresponding user for one or more databases. To create a user JSmith for the Sales database, use the following statement:

```
USE Sales
CREATE USER JSmith
```

## Separation of users and schemas

In SQL Server 2000 the concepts of a user and a schema were, for practical purposes, one and the same. This caused problems when, for example, a user User1 left a company. The schema disappeared when you removed the user. So you had to make edits, possibly many of them, in an application that referenced User1.Object to keep the application working or delete objects in the schema, delete the schema, or create a new schema and add schema objects.

In SQL Server 2005, a user User1 can own a schema, say, Accounts. If User1 leaves the company, you can change the owner of the Accounts schema. You don't need to make changes to an application that uses the Accounts schema because the Accounts schema still exists and the schema name hasn't been changed.

More strictly, the separation is between *principals* and schemas. To see all principals in a SQL Server instance, use the following T-SQL:

```
SELECT * FROM sys.server_principals
```

The preceding code displays all the built-in principals plus any principals you have added. To view the built-in principals and any added principals at the level of an individual database, use the following code:

```
USE databaseName
SELECT * FROM sys.database_principals
```

To see all schemas in a SQL Server instance, use the following T-SQL statement:

```
SELECT * FROM sys.schemas
```

To create a schema, `Accounts`, and specify the schema owner as `JohnJones`, use the following T-SQL (this assumes that the principal `JohnJones` already exists):

```
CREATE SCHEMA Accounts AUTHORIZATION JohnJones
```

## The default schema

A principal has a default schema. I show here how to create a login, a corresponding user, and specify which schema is the default for that user.

To specify a user, you must first create a login. To specify the login `FredHamid`, use the following T-SQL:

```
CREATE LOGIN FredHamid WITH PASSWORD = 'TemporaryPassword'
```

The login `FredHamid` is now created on the current SQL Server instance. After you create the login, you can create a user for a specified database. To specify a default schema `Accounts` for a user `FredHamid`, use the following statement:

```
USE FinanceDB
CREATE USER FredHamid
FOR LOGIN FredHamid
WITH DEFAULT_SCHEMA = Accounts
```

If you omit the `WITH DEFAULT_SCHEMA` clause, the default schema for the user is the `dbo` schema.

If the `Accounts` schema does not already exist, you can create it and assign permissions to the user `FredHamid` using

```
CREATE SCHEMA Accounts AUTHORIZATION FredHamid
```

To see the default schema for a principal — for example a user — use the following T-SQL statement:

```
SELECT name, default_schema_name
FROM sys.database_principals
WHERE name= 'FredHamid'
```

If Fred Hamid tries to access a table named `Sales`, the `Accounts` schema is searched first, because that is his default schema. If a table `Accounts.Sales` is found, it is used. If such a table is not found, SQL Server looks for a table named `Sales` in the `dbo` schema.

To retrieve the name of the owner of each schema, use the following:

```
SELECT S.name AS schema_name, S.schema_id,
O.name as owner_name, O.principal_ID as owner_id
FROM sys.database_principals AS O, sys.schemas AS S
WHERE O.principal_id = S.principal_id
```

This returns system schemas and user-created schemas, as shown in Figure 11-1. You can see that I created the `Accounts` schema as `dbo`, and therefore `dbo` is the owner of the `Accounts` schema.

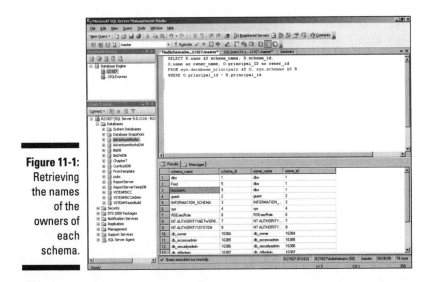

**Figure 11-1:**
Retrieving
the names
of the
owners of
each
schema.

## *Granting permissions to a user*

At this point, Fred Hamid is identified as the user `FredHamid`. To see the permissions he has on the `FinanceDB` database, follow these steps:

1. **In the Object Explorer, expand the Databases node to display the FinanceDB database node.**

   If you already have the Object Explorer open, you may need to right-click Databases and choose Refresh from the context menu.

2. **Navigate through the tree until you get to the Users node by expanding the FinanceDB, Security, and Users nodes in turn.**

The user FredHamid is listed among the users. (See Figure 11-2.)

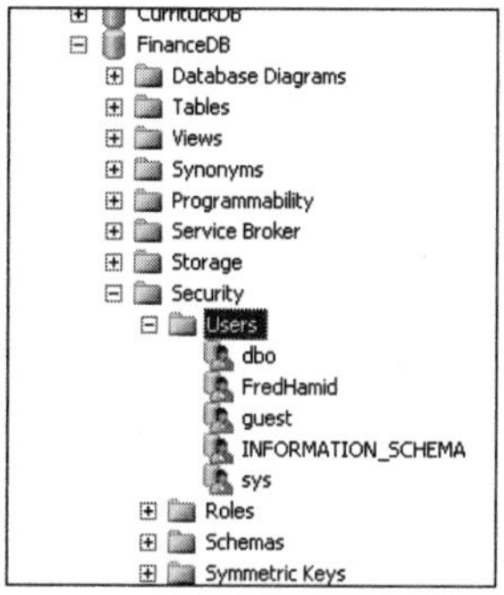

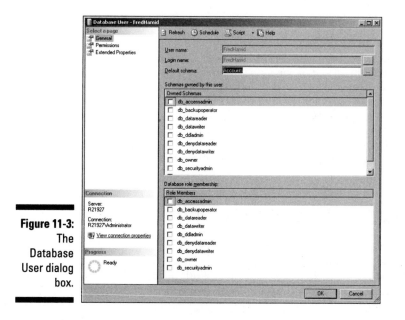

**Figure 11-2:**
Listing users
for a
database.

3. **Right-click FredHamid and choose Properties from the context menu.**

The Database User – FredHamid dialog box opens, as shown in
Figure 11-3.

**Figure 11-3:**
The
Database
User dialog
box.

As you can see in Figure 11-3, the user FredHamid exists but initially has no
permissions (all the options are unchecked). You click the appropriate check
boxes to add any desired permissions for the user FredHamid. This provides
a convenient alternative to using T-SQL code to achieve the same end.

# Module Execution Context

The concept of *Module Execution Context* means the login or user who executes a module. In this context, a module can be a stored procedure, a function, or a trigger.

- **Execute as caller:** The user executes the module. The user needs to have permissions on the module and appropriate permissions for anything that's referenced by the module — for example, any databases.

- **Execute as a specified username:** The username must exist in the relevant database and be a *singleton principal* (not a group). The statements in the module execute in the context of the named user.

- **Execute as owner:** Executes as the owner of a module. If the owner of a module changes in the future, the user runs as that new owner.

- **Execute as self:** Executes as the original owner of a module. If the owner of the module changes, the user still runs as the original owner.

# Catalog security

You can use the built-in catalog security in SQL Server 2005 to secure metadata.

At the server level, the sa login can see everything on the server. At the database level, the dbo can see everything in the database. Other logins and users see only metadata on objects where they have relevant permissions. In previous versions of SQL Server, a user could see metadata for objects to which he had no permissions. A malicious user could use that information to plan or attempt unauthorized access to such database objects. By hiding metadata, in SQL Server 2005, such a malicious user can't see what objects exist. This makes any attack on data more difficult.

# Password policy enforcement

Microsoft recommends that Windows Integrated Security is the preferred authentication mechanism for SQL Server 2005. However, Microsoft also recognizes that some SQL Server 2005 installations also allow SQL Server logins. Therefore, you need to ensure that SQL Server logins are as secure as practicable.

If you're running SQL Server 2005 on Windows Server 2003, you can enforce an existing password policy on SQL logins.

The following aspects are supported:

- ✔ **Password Strength:** You can specify to use strong passwords.
- ✔ **Password Expiration:** You can specify that SQL passwords expire regularly.
- ✔ **Account Lockouts:** If the SQL Server is under a brute force attack, it is helpful if the account(s) being attacked are locked out before a hacker gains access to the server through those accounts.

This improves on the SQL Server 2000 situation where you could only specify the password strength for the SQL Server.

To create a strong password for login `FredHamid`, use the following T-SQL:

```
CREATE LOGIN FredHamid WITH PASSWORD = 'Passw0rd!'
```

Notice that the fourth to the last character in the password is a zero. The password has both upper and lowercase characters, a numeric character, and a punctuation character, so it meets the requirements for password complexity.

In SQL Server 2005, you have an option to turn off the password policy for selected logins. You can also specify that some passwords never expire. For example, if applications use a particular login, it makes sense not to enforce a need to change passwords in applications. An application obviously has no way to change its password.

If you want to continue to enforce password complexity policy on the `FredHamid` login but not enforce password expiration, you can use the following T-SQL:

```
ALTER LOGIN FredHamid WITH CHECK_EXPIRATION = OFF
```

If you want to create a login with a simple password, you can turn off password policy for that login by using syntax like the following:

```
CREATE LOGIN TooSimple
WITH PASSWORD = 'Fred', CHECK_POLICY = OFF
```

Turning off the password policy is not recommended, however; it allows users to create passwords that are more vulnerable to cracking than strong passwords.

To check the status of password policy enforcement on all logins, you can use the following T-SQL:

```
SELECT name, is_policy_checked, is_expiration_checked
FROM sys.sql_logins
```

A value of 1 in the relevant columns indicates that the policy indicated in the column name is enforced.

# Using Common Language Runtime Security

The Common Language Runtime (CLR) allows .NET code to be run inside the SQL Server 2005 database engine. Three levels of security are specified:

- ✔ **Safe:** Code that runs under the Safe setting is unable to access anything external to SQL Server. Specifically, the code cannot access environment variables, the registry, files, and the network. Code running with a Safe permission set poses minimal or no security risk.

  If you don't specify a permission set, then Safe is used as a default.

- ✔ **External Access:** Code running with an External Access permission set can access environment variables, the registry, files, and the network. Unmanaged code cannot be run.

- ✔ **UnSafe:** UnSafe doesn't mean that the code is necessarily dangerous. It means that the code is permitted unlimited access outside the SQL Server database engine. That means that the code is potentially unsafe. A database administrator has to be very sure about what is in the code and be sure that he understands what the code does.

You specify the permission set by using the CREATE ASSEMBLY statement. For example, to add an assembly called myAssembly that uses the Safe permission set, use the following code:

```
CREATE ASSEMBLY myAssembly
WITH PERMISSION_SET = SAFE
```

# Chapter 12

# Availability and Preventing Data Loss

*I*n a connected world, your colleagues and customers need almost continuous access to data. This means that you need to avoid users temporarily losing access to data. Or, if you can't completely avoid such temporary problems, make sure that you can recover from them quickly. More important, you must take careful steps to ensure that the chance of users permanently losing access to data is as close to zero as possible.

SQL Server 2005 supports many features that improve the chances of keeping your SQL Server databases available to users. For example, database mirroring is a new feature that allows almost instant switching to a backup SQL Server if a primary server goes down.

As well as achieving high availability of data, it is crucially important that you avoid the permanent loss of any business data that is needed for the running of your business. Losing important business data can be fatal for your continued employment and can, in some cases, also be fatal for the business. Taking appropriate steps to back up data and ensure that you can restore it is of enormous importance.

# *Availability Overview*

Preventing poor availability is not simply a matter of using SQL Server 2005 features. Availability of data can be threatened in several layers:

- **Hardware:** Modern computer hardware is highly reliable, but reliability is not quite 100 percent. Therefore, you need to plan for the possible failure of hardware. Among the approaches you should consider are

    - Redundant servers (with failover clustering or database mirroring)

    - RAID rather than single hard drives

    - Uninterruptible power supplies to allow SQL Server to shut down properly in the case of a local power failure

    - Hot swapping of RAM (requires special hardware)

- **System Software:** Specifically, SQL Server 2005.

- **Application Software:** Improperly written application software can also produce errors or loss of data. For example, application software needs to protect against SQL injection attacks and potential loss or corruption of data.

- **User/Operator Error:** User or operator error forms an increasing proportion of total downtime as the reliability of hardware and system and application software improves. To achieve improved availability and avoid data loss, properly train your users and colleagues on how to use SQL Server.

Among the most important issues is ensuring that one individual is responsible for carrying out data backups and that appropriate procedures are in place to carry out and test backups if that individual is absent for any reason. A manager should be responsible for ensuring that backing up and testing of backups has been done every time!

# *Reducing Downtime with Database Mirroring*

Database mirroring is an option to improve the availability of a SQL Server database or databases. Database mirroring is new in SQL Server 2005. You choose to mirror the databases on a SQL Server instance on a database-by-database basis.

Database mirroring was intended to be available in the November 2005 release of SQL Server 2005. Microsoft has delayed support of the database mirroring feature in a production environment, although you can enable it in the November 2005 release for evaluation purposes by using trace flag 1400. Microsoft recommends that you do not use database mirroring in the original release in a production environment.

## Database mirroring overview

You have three server machines in a common setup for database mirroring. One machine (the *principal*) has the copy of a database that applications read and write to. Another machine (the *mirror*) has a copy of the principal database. The mirror database is kept almost instantaneously in synch with the principal database via a network connection. All transactions that are applied to the principal database are also applied to the mirror database.

You might wonder how, with two copies of the data, applications know which copy of the database to read and write to. The third machine is a witness and has the "casting vote" as to which of the other two machines is running the principal database.

Database mirroring gives very fast switching if the principal database becomes unavailable. Typically, it takes less than three seconds to be up and running again, using the mirror database. Many users don't notice an interruption of response; at the most, perhaps just a slightly slower response than normal.

Microsoft claims zero data loss for database mirroring. Transactions are sent to the mirror database's log at the same time as they are written to the principal database's log. The chances of any transaction being lost on the mirror are extremely low.

*Note:* You cannot mirror the `master`, `msdb`, `tempdb`, or `model` databases.

You can switch control to the mirror database either manually or automatically. Given that one of the advantages of database mirroring is the really rapid switching that can occur automatically, I envisage automatic switching being the typical scenario.

Another useful feature of database mirroring is that any changes that are made on the new principal database (the former mirror database) are automatically synchronized with the former principal database when the former principal server is available again.

You can use database mirroring together with replication. For example, if you're replicating the data from a headquarters SQL Server instance to branch offices, all or any of the headquarters or branch office instances to which replication takes place can be a database mirroring configuration. While replication and database mirroring are separate processes, you can, in appropriate circumstances, usefully combine them.

## Transparent client redirect

Database mirroring depends on a companion new technology on the client side that is called *transparent client redirect*. Essentially the client knows about both the principal database and the mirror database. While the principal database is working correctly, the client only connects to it. When the principal database fails and the former mirror database becomes the new principal database, the client automatically connects to the new principal database.

## Database views

You can use another new feature, called *database views*, with database mirroring. Database views allow you to make read-only use of the mirror database. The mirror database is only minimally out of synchronization with the principal database, because the transaction log of the principal database is immediately sent to and applied to the mirror database. For any data retrieval that doesn't require absolutely up-to-date, real-time information, the mirror database is satisfactory. Any database access that involves writing to the database must use the principal database.

One important potential use of database views is as the data source for Reporting Services. Because reporting requires only read access to the database, you can retrieve any data you need while taking some load off the principal database.

## Differences from failover clustering

I list here some key differences between database mirroring and failover clustering (discussed later in the chapter):

- ✔ **Database mirroring allows failover at the database level.** Failover clustering allows failover at the server level or SQL Server instance level.

- ✔ **Database mirroring works with standard computers, standard storage, and standard networks.** Failover clustering requires specific, certified hardware.

- ✔ **Database mirroring has no shared storage components.** Failover clustering uses shared hard drives.

- ✔ **Database mirroring allows Reporting Services to run against the mirror database.** Reporting Services cannot be run against a currently inactive node in a failover cluster.

- ✔ **Database mirroring has two (or more) copies of a database.** Failover clustering works with a single copy of databases, which are stored on shared hard drives.

- ✔ **Database mirroring is *much* faster than failover clustering.** Typical figures might be 3 seconds versus 60 seconds, although exact figures depend on various factors specific to your setup.

## Similarities to failover clustering

The following points apply to both database mirroring and failover clustering:

- ✔ Both support automatic detection and failover.
- ✔ Each has a manual failover option.
- ✔ Each supports transparent client connection to the backup database or server.
- ✔ Each achieves "zero" work loss.
- ✔ Database views minimize the effects of DBA or application errors.

## Recovery models

Database mirroring is available only on databases that have the full recovery model associated with them. In this list, I briefly summarize the available recovery models so that you can make a decision regarding whether you need to consider database mirroring:

- ✔ **Simple:** You are likely to use simple recovery only on test or development machines. Data is recoverable only as far as the most recent full backup or differential backup.

  You should not use simple recovery on a production system where the loss of recent changes is unacceptable.

- ✔ **Full:** The full recovery model provides protection against data loss in many scenarios and provides complete protection against media failure. The full recovery model supports all restore scenarios.

- ✔ **Bulk-logged:** Bulk-logged recovery may be an appropriate choice for production systems. It has less flexibility to recover to a point in time than full recovery. When bulk-loading data, you can switch from full recovery model to bulk-logged recovery model to achieve better performance during the bulk-load operation.

# Speeding Recovery with Checkpointing

To achieve best performance, SQL Server performs many operations in memory. At a *checkpoint,* the cache buffer that holds information about committed transactions not yet written to disk is flushed so that all dirty (changed) data pages are then written to disk.

As time increases since the most recent checkpoint (or, more precisely, as the number of changes since the most recent checkpoint increases) the time to write all changes to disk takes longer. Each time SQL Server starts, a checkpoint is created automatically so all changes not already written to disk are written to disk at startup. In the absence of a recent checkpoint, more operations need to be written to disk at startup for each database. If many operations need to be written for each database, the SQL Server instance can be unavailable for longer than it needs to be.

To avoid lengthy startup delays when you restart SQL Server for any reason, you need to make sure that checkpoints are created at appropriate intervals or in appropriate circumstances. The following activities cause a checkpoint to be created:

- ✔ You execute a T-SQL CHECKPOINT statement.
- ✔ You perform a minimally logged operation on the database. One example is a bulk copy operation when you're using the bulk-logged recovery model.
- ✔ You use the ALTER DATABASE statement to add or remove database files.
- ✔ You change to the simple recovery model.
- ✔ You stop a SQL Server instance by using the T-SQL SHUTDOWN statement or by stopping the MSSQLSERVER service.
- ✔ A SQL Server instance automatically generates a checkpoint to keep recovery time within the specified limit.
- ✔ You back up the database.

## Automatic checkpoints

To ensure that checkpoints are made at appropriate intervals, you can use the automatic checkpointing facility of SQL Server 2005.

The need for a checkpoint depends on how many changes have been made in a particular database. If many changes are made, the interval between checkpoints decreases. For rarely used databases, you don't need to have checkpoints made often.

SQL Server doesn't require that you make complex calculations to determine how often checkpoints are created automatically. You specify how long a database should take to have outstanding operations written to disk on startup, which is called the *recovery interval*. By setting the recovery interval, SQL Server then works out when an automatic checkpoint is created for you.

## Setting the recovery interval

To set the recovery interval, follow these steps:

1. **Open SQL Server Management Studio. If the Object Explorer is not already open, choose View⇨Object Explorer.**

2. **Right-click a SQL Server instance in the Object Explorer and choose Properties from the context menu.**

   The Server Properties dialog box opens.

3. **In the left pane of Server Properties, select the Database Settings option.**

   In the main pane, the Recover Interval text box displays, about halfway down the pane.

4. **Enter a desired value for the recovery interval (in minutes).**

*Note:* SQL Server 2005 has improved recovery times compared to SQL Server 2000. After the redo portion of recovery is complete, a database is brought online. This can significantly increase availability.

# Using Failover Clustering

Failover clustering was introduced in SQL Server 7, was refined in SQL Server 2000, and has been further improved in SQL Server 2005.

Failover clustering depends on Microsoft Clustering Services. A failover cluster typically consists of two or more servers that use two or more shared disks. A failover cluster is also known as a *virtual server* or a *resource group*.

Having two servers is the simplest situation. One server has a SQL Server service running. If that server fails (due to hardware or operating system failure, for example), the other server in the cluster starts the SQL Server service. Apart from the time required to start up the SQL Server service, the cluster continues to operate despite the failure of the server to which connections were originally made.

The new features or improvements in failover clustering in SQL Server 2005 are

- ✔ Increase in number of nodes supported (now limited only by operating system limits).
- ✔ Unattended setup is supported.
- ✔ All SQL Server 2005 services participate. Now supports database engine, SQL Server Agent, Analysis Services, Full-text Search.

A virtual server appears on the network as if it were a single machine.

The time taken to failover from one server to another in a virtual server is significantly longer than the equivalent time for database mirroring. For failover clustering, time taken to have a standby server up and running can vary from tens of seconds up to two or three minutes. Database mirroring uses a standby server within two or three seconds.

# *Database Snapshots*

Any real-world SQL Server installation periodically needs maintenance. When you carry out maintenance tasks, it is important that SQL Server or individual databases are unavailable for as short a time as possible.

When you work with databases, you always have the possibility of human error. With any luck, it's a low risk most of the time. No matter the risk involved, though, you need to be able to undo any changes you make.

*Note:* Database snapshots are available only on Microsoft SQL Server 2005 Enterprise Edition.

Database snapshots allow you to take a snapshot of a database before you carry out a major operation. If something goes wrong, you can simply revert to the snapshot (assuming that the database is not live). The important thing is to realize that you must make the snapshot before carrying out the major or risky operation.

You can use database snapshots on a single server install of SQL Server, with database mirroring, or with failover clustering.

# Naming database snapshots

When creating database snapshots, make sure you choose a naming scheme that contains the following pieces of information:

- ✔ The database of which it is a snapshot.
- ✔ That it is a snapshot.
- ✔ A sequence number or date and time that indicates the time when you made the snapshot or its place in a sequence of snapshots (so that you can easily identify the most recent snapshot).

How you name snapshots may depend on the way you use them. If you have a daily cycle of four snapshots made regularly for a database in use around the clock, then a name similar to

```
databaseName_snapshot_0800
```

lets you know that this is the daily snapshot made at 08:00. Alternatively, if you want to create snapshots on an as needed basis, a name similar to

```
databaseName_snapshot_20060418
```

can tell you that this is the snapshot made on April 18, 2006. If you're carrying out several operations that need snapshots on the same day, simply add a time also.

# Creating a database snapshot

To create a database snapshot, you use the CREATE DATABASE statement with code like this, which you run in SQL Server Management Studio:

```
CREATE DATABASE myDatabaseName_snapshot_20060418 ON
( NAME = myDatabaseName_Data, FILENAME =
'C:\Program Files\Microsoft SQL
        Server\MSSQL.1\MSSQL\Data\myDatabaseName_snapsh
        ot_20060418.ss' )
AS SNAPSHOT OF myDatabaseName;
GO
```

When you create a database snapshot, consider whether the target disk has enough disk space. The size of the snapshot may be as large as the database on which the snapshot is being made.

## Deleting unwanted database snapshots

If you keep creating database snapshots without deleting them, they take up unnecessary disk space. When reverting to a snapshot (which I describe in the next section), you need to delete any unwanted snapshots before doing so.

To view the existing database snapshots in SQL Server Management Studio, follow these steps:

1. **Open SQL Server Management Studio. If the Object Explorer is not visible, choose View⇨Object Explorer.**

2. **Connect to the relevant SQL Server instance.**

3. **Expand the Databases node and the Database Snapshots node.**

4. **Delete the database snapshot that you want to delete by using the following T-SQL:**

   ```
   DROP DATABASE databaseSnapshotName
   ```

## Reverting to a database snapshot

If a significant error occurs during an administrative operation, you likely need to revert to the database snapshot you made immediately before starting the operation that failed.

To revert to a database snapshot, follow these steps:

1. **In SQL Server Management Studio, open the Object Explorer by choosing View⇨Object Explorer, if it is not already open. Connect to the relevant SQL Server 2005 instance.**

2. **Navigate to the desired database under the Databases node.**

3. **Delete any database snapshots other than the one you want to revert to.**

   I cover how to delete a database snapshot in the preceding section.

4. **Remove any full-text catalogs on the database.**

5. **If the database uses the full recovery model, back up the log.**

6. **To revert to the snapshot, use the following T-SQL code:**

   ```
   RESTORE databaseName
   FROM DATABASE_SNAPSHOT = databaseSnapshotName
   ```

   During the revert operation, both the database and the database snapshot are unavailable.

*Note:* The reverted database retains the permissions and configuration options used when the database snapshot was created.

7. **Start the database.**

8. **Back up the reverted database.**

# Backing Up and Restoring Data

Losing access to data for a short time can be a significant inconvenience for your business. Losing the data permanently can be a major disaster and for some businesses losing important data can be fatal to the business. For many businesses, cash flow can be a situation that has to be fine-tuned. If you lose key data, it can take weeks to reconstitute the data. Technically, you may be able to reproduce the data at the time of the problem. In the meantime, cash flow has potentially become a serious problem and many of your customers may have left, perhaps forever. The business message is clear. Take adequate steps to protect important data!

## Assessing the risks to protect against

One of the key things to do in order to avoid being thrown into a crisis is to consider the scenarios where data loss can occur and to plan an approach that minimizes or, better, totally avoids the risks you can anticipate.

Among the scenarios that you need to consider are the following:

- ✔ Hardware failure
- ✔ Theft of hardware
- ✔ Unauthorized access to data and damage to the data

## Backing up data

Typically, you use scripts to create backups. In this section, I briefly describe how to back up a database.

*Note:* Before a backup, SQL Server 2005 automatically creates a checkpoint so that the data you back up contains all changes to database pages.

To back up a database, use the BACKUP DATABASE statement. You specify the database to be backed up and the destination it is to be backed up to. For example, to back up to a hard drive, use the following T-SQL code (which assumes you've formatted the destination drive):

```
USE myDatabaseName
GO
BACKUP DATABASE myDatabaseName
TO DISK = 'C:\filePath\myDatabaseName.bak'
  NAME = 'The name of the back up.'
```

## Checking backups

I give this topic a separate section because it is crucially important and all too easy to overlook. You must check that you can restore from the backup tapes or other backup media. Just imagine — you've been backing up faithfully for months, secure in the knowledge that you're safe if disaster happens, only to discover that you can't use the backups.

The longer you leave between checking that you can restore a backup, the greater the possibility that *none* of the backups are usable! Therefore, you should frequently check that you can restore your backup tapes or other backup media. Bypassing this crucially important task is false economy.

The exact frequency that you choose to check backups depends on your situation. The more important the data, the more often you need to confirm that you can restore from tapes or other media.

## Restoring data

Backups are only useful if you know how to restore the data. You can carry out a simple full restore by using T-SQL code like the following:

```
RESTORE databaseName
FROM DISK = 'C:\filePath\backupFilename'
```

The RESTORE command has many options that are described in SQL Server 2005 Books Online.

# Chapter 13

# Maintaining Integrity with Transactions

. . . . . . . . . . . . . . . . . . . . . . . . . . . . . . . . . . . . . . . . . . . . .

. . . . . . . . . . . . . . . . . . . . . . . . . . . . . . . . . . . . . . . . . . . . .

*M*any business activities depend on an action being accompanied by a corresponding action. For example, if you are a customer and pay for goods but don't receive them, something is wrong. Similarly, if you take goods and don't pay for them, again, something is wrong. The expected typical scenario is a *transaction* where you pay for goods and you receive the goods. More than one action is required to make up a transaction.

Another common example of more than one operation making up a transaction is when you transfer money from one bank account to another. Suppose you're transferring a regular payment to a company. Your bank takes the money out of your account and puts it into the account of the company or person that you're paying. You would be annoyed if the money was taken out of your account and didn't reach the account where it was supposed to go. If the money was never transferred to the company's account you, as a customer of a bank, would not be happy whether the money was put in the wrong account or just disappeared. The different parts of that transaction must be kept together. There are two possible scenarios:

✔ No money is taken from your account and nothing is transferred to the other account (possibly because of insufficient funds in your account or a network problem is preventing the transfer).

✔ The right amount of money is taken from your account and is placed in the other account.

In a SQL Server transaction, either all the component parts of a transaction are carried out or none of them are. This concept is called *atomicity*.

# Understanding Transactions

In SQL Server 2005, there are several levels of transaction. In the preceding paragraphs, I mention *business level* transactions. These are the subject of this chapter. Behind the scenes in SQL Server 2005, other transactions take place routinely. For example, if you add data to a table that has an index, both the table and the index need to be updated or neither is updated. If that coordination of operations doesn't happen, then the index and table are inconsistent with each other, which is unacceptable.

## ACID

ACID describes four essential characteristics of a transaction:

- ✔ **Atomicity:** *Atomicity* means that the transaction cannot be divided and still make sense. With the transfer between bank accounts, either both parts of the transaction take place successfully or neither happens.

- ✔ **Consistency:** *Consistency* means that the database is in a consistent state before the transaction takes place and remains in a consistent state after the transaction. For example, if you add a row to a table, then the index must also be updated.

- ✔ **Isolation:** This is the idea that a transaction should be able to proceed as if it were completely isolated from any other transaction. For multi-user databases, it is increasingly important that the product supports this.

- ✔ **Durability:** This is the concept that a transaction survives even if there is a hardware failure. It should be possible to re-create the data up to the last completed transaction that completed a split second before the hardware failure.

## The transaction log

Each SQL Server 2005 database has an associated transaction log. The transaction log contains information about recent changes that have been made in the database that have not yet been committed to disk. When SQL Server is restarted, any transactions not yet committed to disk are committed to disk during startup. This facility supports durability of the ACID acronym that I discuss in the preceding section.

# Coding Transactions

When a transaction involves, for example, removing money from one account and transferring it to another account, then both accounts are updated. First, look at how SQL Server carries out a simple update.

## A simple update

Imagine that you have a database called `Departments` that has columns, which include `DepartmentName` and `DepartmentManager`. When the manager of the IT department is replaced, you need to update the information in the `DepartmentManager` column. To do this, you use code like the following:

```
UPDATE Departments
  SET DepartmentManager = 'John Smith'
WHERE Department = 'IT'
```

The `WHERE` clause works much as it does in a `SELECT` statement. It selects the rows where the `Department` column contains the `IT` value and the `SET` clause causes the value in the `DepartmentManager` column to update to the `John Smith` value.

## A simple transaction

To demonstrate a simple transaction, I create a database called `Chapter13`. In that database, I create a couple of tables called `PersonalAccount` and `CompanyAccount`:

```
CREATE DATABASE Chapter13

USE Chapter13
CREATE TABLE PersonalAccount (AccountID INT PRIMARY KEY,
        Name VARCHAR(30), BALANCE MONEY)
```

I create two accounts, one for John Smith and one for Jane Doe, with each individual having a balance of $100.00:

```
INSERT INTO PersonalAccount
VALUES (1, 'John Smith', 100.00)
INSERT INTO PersonalAccount
VALUES (2, 'Jane Doe', 100.00)
```

Similarly, I create a `CompanyAccount` table:

```
CREATE TABLE CompanyAccount (AccountID INT PRIMARY KEY,
             Name VARCHAR(30), BALANCE MONEY)
```

Then I create two rows in it, with each company having a balance of $10,000:

```
INSERT INTO CompanyAccount
VALUES (1, 'Acme Company', 10000.00)
INSERT INTO CompanyAccount
VALUES (2, 'XMML.com', 10000.00)
```

To confirm that the two tables have been created with appropriate values in each column, use the following code:

```
SELECT * FROM PersonalAccount
SELECT * FROM CompanyAccount
```

Figure 13-1 shows the initial values in each column of the two tables.

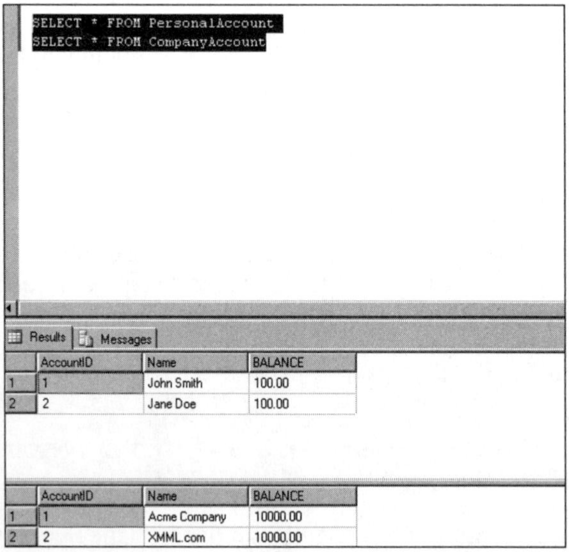

**Figure 13-1:**
Initial values
in the
Personal
Account
and
Company
Account
tables.

The following code transfers $50.00 from John Smith's personal account to XMML.com's company account by using a transaction:

```
BEGIN TRANSACTION
UPDATE PersonalAccount
 SET BALANCE = 50.00
WHERE Name = 'John Smith'
UPDATE CompanyAccount
```

```
    SET BALANCE = 10050.00
WHERE Name = 'XMML.com'
COMMIT TRANSACTION
GO
```

Confirm that the balance in John Smith's personal account and XMML.com's company account have changed appropriately by using the following code:

```
SELECT * FROM PersonalAccount
SELECT * FROM CompanyAccount
```

Figure 13-2 shows the changed balances in the two desired accounts.

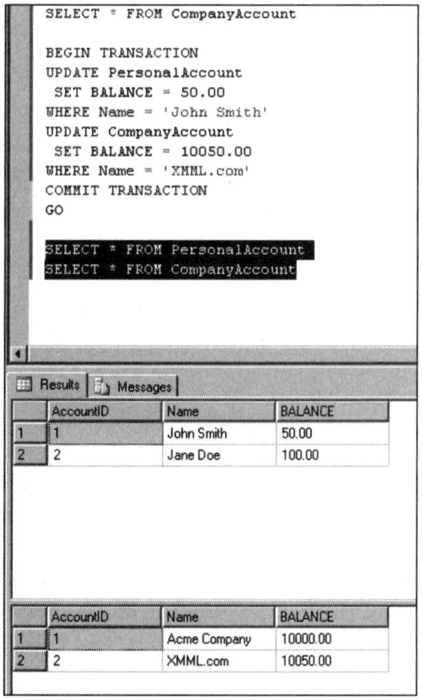

**Figure 13-2:** Changed balances in the Personal Account and Company Account tables.

Often, a transaction has some error checking included in the code. To include error checking when making a transfer from Jane Doe to Acme Company, you can use @@ERROR:

```
BEGIN TRANSACTION
UPDATE PersonalAccount
  SET BALANCE = 0.00
WHERE Name = 'Jane Doe'
IF @@ERROR <> 0
  PRINT N'Could not set balance in PersonalAccount.'
UPDATE CompanyAccount
  SET BALANCE = 10100.00
```

```
WHERE Name = 'Acme Company'
IF @@ERROR <> 0
PRINT N'Could not set balance in CompanyAccount.'
COMMIT TRANSACTION
GO
```

To confirm that you have changed the row for Jane Doe in the `Personal Account` table and the row for Acme Company in the `CompanyAccount` table, use the following code:

```
SELECT * FROM PersonalAccount
SELECT * FROM CompanyAccount
```

The `BEGIN TRANSACTION` statement marks the beginning of the T-SQL code to be treated as a transaction. If the T-SQL code in the transaction executes successfully, the `COMMIT TRANSACTION` statement is reached and the transaction is committed.

If an error occurs during processing, the `ROLLBACK TRANSACTION` statement executes. After the `COMMIT TRANSACTION` statement executes, you cannot use a `ROLLBACK TRANSACTION` statement to roll back the transaction.

## *Implicit transactions*

The preceding examples showed *explicit transactions*. T-SQL also supports *implicit transactions*.

To start implicit transactions, you use the `SET IMPLICIT_TRANSACTIONS ON` statement. Each statement after that statement until a transaction is committed is considered to be part of that transaction. After you do that, you must explicitly commit the statements that make up each transaction by using the `COMMIT TRANSACTION` statement. The statements after the `COMMIT TRANSACTION` statement are considered to be the first statement of the next transaction. Again, that transaction must be explicitly committed.

To turn implicit transactions off, you use the `SET IMPLICIT_TRANSACTIONS OFF` statement.

The default behavior, if you do not `SET IMPLICIT TRANSACTIONS ON`, is that each individual T-SQL statement is treated as a transaction rather than as a group of T-SQL statements.

You can't combine Data Definition Language (DDL) statements in a single transaction.

# Chapter 14

# Maintaining Data Integrity with Constraints and Triggers

● ● ● ● ● ● ● ● ● ● ● ● ● ● ● ● ● ● ● ● ● ● ● ● ● ● ● ● ● ● ● ● ● ● ● ● ● ● ● ● ●

*In This Chapter*

▶ Ensuring data integrity with constraints

▶ Adding check constraints to your data

▶ Keeping track of changes with DDL triggers

▶ Adding and deleting data with DML triggers

● ● ● ● ● ● ● ● ● ● ● ● ● ● ● ● ● ● ● ● ● ● ● ● ● ● ● ● ● ● ● ● ● ● ● ● ● ● ● ● ●

*M*aintaining the integrity of the data in a SQL Server 2005 instance is cru- cially important to the reliable operation of your business that uses SQL Server data. SQL Server uses several mechanisms, including constraints and triggers, to help ensure data integrity. In this chapter, I tell you about constraints and triggers that are tools to help maintain data integrity in SQL Server 2005.

A *constraint* is a rule that is enforced by SQL Server 2005. Microsoft suggests that, in SQL Server 2005, constraints are the preferred way to enforce busi- ness rules.

A *trigger* is a special kind of stored procedure that executes in response to an event inside SQL Server. A common use of triggers is to create an audit trail. For example, suppose you want to keep an audit trail of who makes changes to prices in your online store. Each time someone modifies a row in the rele- vant table, a trigger executes, which could store information such as the time of the change, who made the change, what the original price was, and what the new price is. Such information allows your business to monitor trends in prices and also to find out who made any possibly wrong changes in price.

# Understanding Constraints, Defaults, Rules, and Triggers

In this section, I describe constraints, defaults, rules, and triggers, which provide a range of ways to enforce business rules inside SQL Server databases.

In this chapter, I create a simple database by using the following code. Examples later in this chapter use the Chapter14 database.

```
CREATE DATABASE Chapter14
```

## Constraints

*Constraints* (rules enforced by SQL Server 2005) provide a key way to ensure several aspects of data integrity. Microsoft recommends that you use constraints rather than triggers in SQL Server 2005 to ensure data integrity.

The constraints supported in SQL Server 2005 are

- ✔ **Primary key:** Provides a way to uniquely identify each row in a table. A primary key constraint is a specialized form of a unique constraint.

- ✔ **Unique constraint:** Specifies that each value in a column is unique.

  One difference between a unique constraint and a primary key constraint is that a column with a unique constraint can contain NULL values, which are not permitted in a column that has a primary key constraint. If a column is a primary key or part of a primary key, you cannot also set up a unique constraint for that column.

- ✔ **Check constraint:** Specifies rules that values in a column must obey. A check constraint uses an expression to define the permitted values in a column. Later in this chapter, I show you how to define check constraints on a column.

## Defaults

A *default* is a database object that you define and bind to a column. If during an insert operation, you don't supply a value for a column to which the default is bound, then the default is inserted into that column.

The following example creates a default of Unknown for values inserted into a table that records student grades.

First, specify that you use the `Chapter14` database:

```
USE Chapter14
```

Then create the default called `StudentGradeUnknown`, specifying that it is the string `Unknown`:

```
CREATE DEFAULT StudentGradeUnknown AS 'Unknown'
```

Then create a simple table to store student grades:

```
CREATE TABLE StudentGrades
  (StudentID int PRIMARY KEY,
   Examination varchar(10),
   Grade varchar(7))
```

At this stage, the `StudentGradeUnknown` default exists in the `Chapter14` database. You need to bind it to the `Grade` column in the `StudentGrades` table. Use this code, which makes use of the `sp_bindefault` system stored procedure:

```
sp_bindefault 'StudentGradeUnknown', 'StudentGrades.Grade'
GO
```

To confirm that the default operates, use the following `INSERT` statement. Notice that no value is supplied for the `Grade` column:

```
INSERT INTO StudentGrades(StudentID, Examination)
  VALUES(1, 'XML101')
```

Also, insert a row where you supply a value in the `Grade` column:

```
INSERT INTO StudentGrades
  VALUES(2, 'SVG101', 'A')
```

You can confirm the values in the `StudentGrades` table by using the following code:

```
SELECT * FROM StudentGrades
```

In the first row shown in Figure 14-1, the value `Unknown` in the `Grade` column was supplied by the default bound to that column. In the second row, you supplied a value for the `Grade` column so the default was not used.

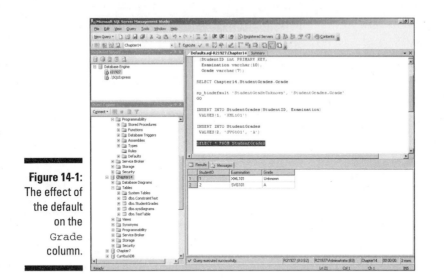

**Figure 14-1:**
The effect of
the default
on the
`Grade`
column.

## Rules

*Rules* are included in SQL Server 2005 for backwards compatibility with SQL Server 2000. Check constraints in SQL Server 2005 provide similar functionality. Microsoft recommends that you use check constraints rather than rules in new code.

The following example that demonstrates how to create and use a rule uses a test table called `TestTable` in the `Chapter14` database, which I created with this code:

```
USE Chapter14
CREATE TABLE TestTable
(ID int PRIMARY KEY,
Data char(1))
```

To create a rule in the `Chapter14` database, use the following code:

```
CREATE RULE aThroughcOnly
AS
@ruleval >= 'a' AND @ruleval <= 'c'
```

The preceding rule specifies that the value must be lowercase, between lowercase a and lowercase c. You also need to bind the rule you have created to a column. The following code binds it to the `Data` column in the `TestTable` table:

```
sp_bindrule aThroughcOnly, 'TestTable.[Data]'
```

To insert a row with an allowed value, use the following code:

```
INSERT INTO dbo.TestTable
VALUES (1, 'b')
```

You should be prevented from entering a value that doesn't correspond to the rule you created. The following attempts to insert a disallowed character in the Data column.

```
INSERT INTO dbo.TestTable
VALUES (2, 'd')
```

After you create a rule, you're likely to leave it in place unless you want to convert it to a constraint as described in the preceding section. To unbind a rule from a specified column, use the following code:

```
sp_unbindrule 'dbo.TestTable.Data'
```

# Triggers

*Triggers* are used to help maintain data integrity and enforce business rules. (Remember that a trigger is a special kind of stored procedure that executes in response to an event inside SQL Server.) They complement the protection of data integrity that constraints, defaults, and rules can provide.

A trigger is a specialized stored procedure. Unlike regular stored procedures, you cannot use an input parameter with a trigger, nor can a trigger return a value. A trigger is associated with a particular table. When a specified event occurs, the trigger executes.

Triggers are broadly divided into two groups:

- ✔ **DDL triggers:** Data Definition Language triggers
- ✔ **DML triggers:** Data Modification Language triggers

Triggers are classified as follows:

- ✔ **INSTEAD OF triggers:** These execute instead of the statement to which they are related.
- ✔ **AFTER triggers:** These execute after the statement to which they are related.

I describe and demonstrate several of these types of triggers later in this chapter.

Auditing who does what in your database is one of the most important uses of triggers. Depending on which actions of users you want, or are required by legislation to monitor, you may choose to audit Data Definition Language statements, Data Modification Language statements, or both.

# Using Check Constraints

You have two options to create and *drop* (delete) check constraints. You can either use the visual tools in SQL Server Management Studio or you can use T-SQL (either in the query pane of SQL Server Management Studio or from the command line with the SQLCMD utility). I show you both techniques.

Check constraints can use simple and complex expressions. You specify that the value in some column meets some specified criterion or criteria. For example, an expression to specify that the value in an InStock column must be greater than zero would look like this:

```
InStock > 0
```

You can use the keywords AND, OR, and NOT to combine conditions. For example, to specify that the quantity purchased of a special offer must be at least 1 and less than 5, you could use the following expression:

```
QtyBought > 0 AND QtyBought < 5
```

In this section, I use a sample table named ConstraintTest. To create the table, use the following T-SQL code:

```
USE Chapter14
CREATE TABLE ConstraintTest
(ID int PRIMARY KEY,
PartNum char(6))
```

You can use the limited regular expression support for the T-SQL LIKE keyword to create a check constraint based on a pattern. For example, suppose a valid part number in your company consists of three uppercase characters followed by three numeric digits. To specify that a value in the PartNum column must consist of exactly six characters with the first three being uppercase alphabetic characters and the last three being numeric digits, use the following regular expression:

```
[A-Z][A-Z][A-Z][0-9][0-9][0-9]
```

The [A-Z] pattern is a regular expression *pattern* that matches any uppercase character. Because there are three in a row of those, a sequence of exactly three uppercase alphabetic characters is matched. Similarly, the [0-9] pattern matches any numeric digit. The full expression for the check constraint uses this regular expression with the LIKE keyword and column name:

```
PartNum LIKE '[A-Z][A-Z][A-Z][0-9][0-9][0-9]'
```

## Creating a check constraint visually

To create a check constraint with the visual tools, follow these steps:

1. **Open SQL Server Management Studio. Use the Registered Servers pane to connect to the desired SQL Server instance, which contains the Chapter14 database, in the Object Explorer.**

2. **Expand the Databases node, the Chapter14 node, and then the Tables node.**

   You should see the node for the dbo.ConstraintTest database.

3. **Right-click the dbo.ConstraintTest node and choose Modify from the context menu.**

   The Table Designer opens in the right pane of SQL Server Management Studio (see Figure 14-2).

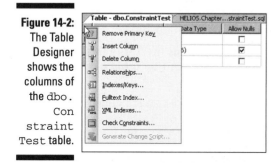

**Figure 14-2:**
The Table Designer shows the columns of the dbo. Con straint Test table.

4. **Right-click in the left area of the Table Designer (note where the cursor is visible in Figure 14-2 to see where). Select the Check Constraints option on the context menu.**

   The Check Constraints dialog box opens (see Figure 14-3).

5. **Click the Add button in the Check Constraints dialog box.**

   Some text boxes appear in the right part of the Check Constraints dialog box.

6. **In the Expression text box, type the following expression:**

   ```
   PartNum LIKE '[A-Z][A-Z][A-Z][0-9][0-9][0-9]'
   ```

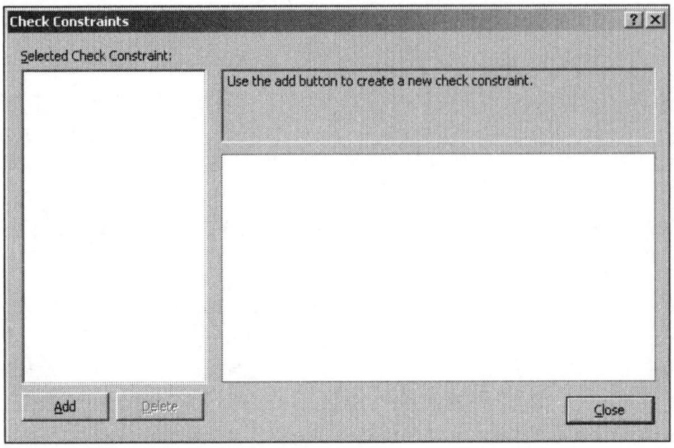

**Figure 14-3:**
The Check
Constraints
dialog box.

Attempting to insert any other pattern than the three uppercase alphabetic characters (followed by three numeric digits) in the PartNum column is a violation of the check constraint.

7. **In the Name text box, type** PartNum_Constraint.

Notice that you have options in the lower part of the Check Constraints dialog box to check existing data and to enforce the check constraint for inserts and updates (see Figure 14-4). The default behavior is for existing data to be checked and for the check constraint to be enforced on inserts and updates.

8. **Click Close to close the Check Constraint dialog box.**

9. **Right-click the tab for the pane that contains the Table Designer (refer to Figure 14-2). Click Save** ConstraintTest **(the table name may be different if you created a different table).**

10. **To test that you have successfully created the check constraint, create a new query.**

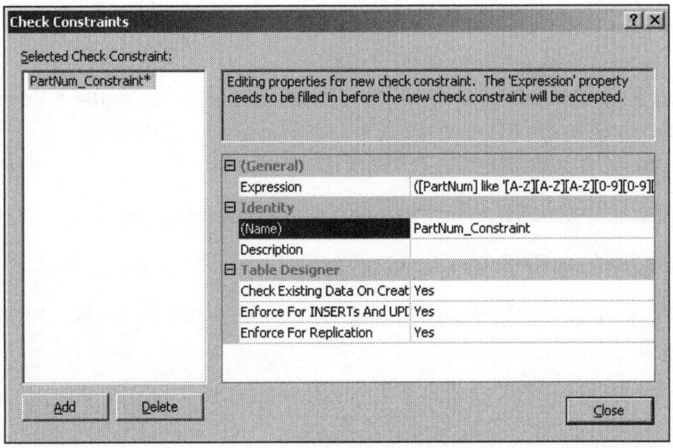

**Figure 14-4:**
The
completed
Check
Constraint
dialog box
for the
PartNum_
Con
straint
check
constraint.

To do that, click the Database Engine Query button. In the Connection dialog box, connect to the appropriate SQL Server instance.

11. **Test that the table is correctly created by using this code:**

```
SELECT *
FROM dbo.ConstraintTest
```

The ID and PartNum columns display in the results grid but with no rows displayed.

12. **Add two rows with a correctly constructed part number by using the following code:**

```
INSERT INTO dbo.ConstraintTest
VALUES (1, 'ABC123')

INSERT INTO dbo.ConstraintTest
VALUES (2, 'XYZ234')
```

13. **Confirm that the two rows have been inserted successfully by running this code:**

```
SELECT *
FROM dbo.ConstraintTest
```

14. **Attempt to update the second row with an incorrect value in the PartNum column by using the following code:**

```
UPDATE dbo.ConstraintTest
  SET PartNum = 'ABC23A'
WHERE ID = 2
```

The following error message displays:

```
Msg 547, Level 16, State 0, Line 1
The UPDATE statement conflicted with the CHECK
        constraint
"PartNum_Constraint". The conflict occurred in
        database
"Chapter14", table "ConstraintTest", column 'PartNum'.
The statement has been terminated.
```

15. **Attempt to insert a row that doesn't have a correctly constructed part number:**

```
INSERT INTO dbo.ConstraintTest
VALUES (3, '123ABC')
```

The following error message displays:

```
Msg 547, Level 16, State 0, Line 1
The INSERT statement conflicted with the CHECK
        constraint
"PartNum_Constraint". The conflict occurred in
        database
Chapter14", table "ConstraintTest", column 'PartNum'.
The statement has been terminated.
```

As you can see in the two preceding error messages, the check constraint constrains both the `INSERT` and `UPDATE` statements. The check constraint is evaluated before the `INSERT` or `UPDATE` operation takes place, so in both cases no change is made to the table.

## Dropping a check constraint visually

When business rules change, you may need to drop an existing check constraint. To drop the check constraint created in the preceding section, follow these steps. If you left SQL Server Management Studio open, you can skip to Step 4.

1. **Open SQL Server Management Studio and connect to the desired SQL Server instance by using the Registered Servers pane.**

2. **In the Object Explorer, expand the Databases node, the Chapter14 node.Tables node, the dbo.ConstraintTest node, the Constraints node, and then the PartNum_Constraint nose.**

3. **Right-click the PartNum_Constraint node and select the Delete option.**

   The constraint is deleted.

## Creating a check constraint with T-SQL

To create a check constraint in a table called `ConstraintTest2` with T-SQL, follow these steps:

1. **Open SQL Server Management Studio.**

2. **Click the Database Engine Query option.**

3. **Enter and execute the following T-SQL code to create the `ConstraintTest2` table:**

```
USE Chapter14

CREATE TABLE ConstraintTest2
  (ID int PRIMARY KEY,
   PartNum char(6),
   CHECK (PartNum LIKE '[A-Z][A-Z][A-
       Z][0-9][0-9][0-9]'))
```

Notice that the `CHECK` clause uses the expression that you used earlier when you created a check constraint with the visual tools.

4. **Try to insert a value with an incorrectly constructed part number:**

```
INSERT INTO ConstraintTest2
  VALUES (1, 'ABCDEF')
```

An error message displays, similar to those shown in the preceding section.

5. **Insert a correctly formed part number into the PartNum column.**

```
INSERT INTO ConstraintTest2
  VALUES (1, 'ABC123')
```

6. **Confirm the successful insert by using the following code:**

```
SELECT * FROM ConstraintTest2
```

# DDL Triggers

DDL triggers respond to an event associated with a Data Definition Language (DDL) statement. These DDL statements are

- ✔ CREATE
- ✔ ALTER
- ✔ DROP

You use DDL triggers for the following purposes:

- ✔ To prevent changes being made to a schema
- ✔ To log who makes changes to a schema
- ✔ To respond in some desired way to changes made in a schema

## Preventing undesired changes

The following example shows you how to prevent undesired changes being made to the tables of the Chapter14 database.

1. **Use SQL Server Management Studio to connect to the desired SQL Server 2005 instance.**

2. **Click the New Database Query button.**

3. **Ensure you're using the Chapter14 database:**

```
USE Chapter14
```

4. **Create a trigger to prevent changes being made to the Chapter14 database:**

```
CREATE TRIGGER PreventChanges
ON DATABASE
FOR DROP_TABLE, ALTER_TABLE, CREATE_TABLE
AS
```

```
PRINT 'Making alterations to the Chapter14 database
      is not permitted.'
PRINT 'To make changes you must disable this DDL
      trigger.'
ROLLBACK
```

The first line provides a name for the trigger. The second line specifies that the trigger apply the database changes. A trigger is bound to a database object; in this case, the current database, Chapter14. The third line specifies that the trigger executes for DROP TABLE, ALTER TABLE, and CREATE TABLE statements. The FOR keyword indicates that the trigger runs *before* the DDL statement executes.

**5. Attempt to create a new table called DDLTriggerTest:**

```
CREATE TABLE DDLTriggerTest
  (ID int PRIMARY KEY,
   SomeColumn varchar(30))
```

An error message displays, as shown in Figure 14-5.

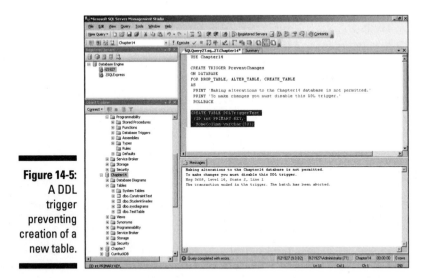

**Figure 14-5:**
A DDL trigger preventing creation of a new table.

**6. Attempt to drop the dbo.ConstraintTest table that you created earlier in this chapter:**

```
DROP TABLE dbo.ConstraintTest
```

The attempted change is prevented with a message similar to the message shown in Figure 14-5.

**7. Drop the trigger:**

```
DROP TRIGGER PreventChanges
ON DATABASE
```

**8. Retry creating the DDLTriggerTest table, which failed in Step 5:**

```
CREATE TABLE DDLTriggerTest
 (ID int PRIMARY KEY,
  SomeColumn varchar(30))
```

Because you dropped the trigger in Step 7, you can now successfully create the DDLTriggerTest table.

## Auditing changes

Another use of a DDL trigger is to log how and when changes are made in database or table structure.

In the following example, I show you how to create a DDL trigger for the ALTER TABLE statement. Follow these steps:

**1. Ensure you are using the Chapter14 database:**

```
USE Chapter14
```

**2. Create a table called AuditedTable. Later you monitor this table for changes in its structure made by using the ALTER TABLE statement.**

```
CREATE TABLE AuditedTable
 (MessageID int PRIMARY KEY,
  Message varchar(100))
```

**3. Insert a sample row into the AuditedTable table.**

```
INSERT INTO AuditedTable
 VALUES (1, 'Hello World!')
```

**4. Confirm that the row has been inserted (see Figure 14-6).**

```
SELECT *
FROM AuditedTable
```

**5. Create a table DDLAudit to contain the information used for auditing.**

Using a TIMESTAMP column allows easy monitoring of the sequence of alterations made:

```
CREATE TABLE DDLAudit
 (
  Changed TIMESTAMP,
  DateChanged DateTime,
  TableName char(30),
  UserName varchar(50)
  )
```

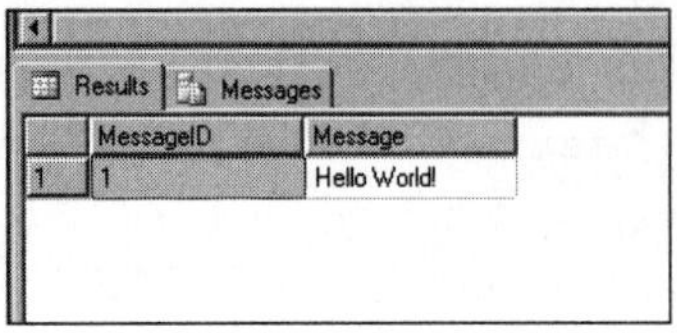

**Figure 14-6:**
A sample
row inserted
into the
`Audited`
`Table`
table.

6. **Confirm that the `DDLAudit` table has been created and is empty.**

```
SELECT *
FROM DDLAudit
```

7. **Insert a sample row manually into the `DDLAudit` table.**

```
INSERT INTO DDLAudit (DateChanged, UserName)
  VALUES (GetDate(), 'John Smith')
```

8. **Confirm that the sample row has been inserted (see Figure 14-7).**

```
SELECT *
FROM DDLAudit
```

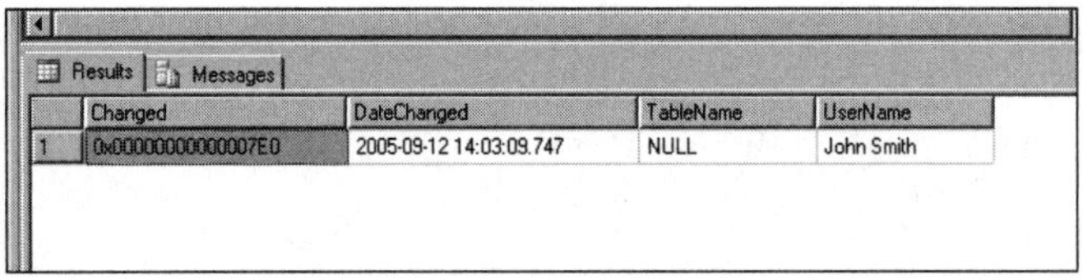

**Figure 14-7:**
A sample
row in the
`DDLAudit`
table.

9. **Create a trigger named `AuditDDL`, which responds to an `ALTER`**
   **`TABLE` statement.**

   Notice that in the FOR clause, you write ALTER_TABLE with an underscore. Notice too that the GetDate() function is used to retrieve the
   date and time when the row is inserted into the DDLAudit table. The
   suser_sname() function is used to retrieve the system name of the
   user making the change in the table schema.

```
CREATE TRIGGER AuditDDL
ON DATABASE
FOR ALTER_TABLE
AS
INSERT INTO dbo.DDLAudit(DateChanged,
  TableName, UserName)
  SELECT GetDate(), 'AuditedTable', suser_sname()
-- End of Trigger
```

The trigger now responds to any attempt to use the ALTER TABLE statement to alter the structure of the AuditedTable table.

**10. Use the following code to attempt to add an additional column to the AuditedTable table.**

```
ALTER TABLE AuditedTable
  ADD Comment varchar(30)
```

**11. Inspect the content of the DDLAudit table.**

```
SELECT *
FROM DDLAudit
```

Figure 14-8 shows two rows in the DDLAudit table. The first row you added manually in Step 7. The DDL trigger added the second row when you executed the ALTER TABLE statement in Step 10.

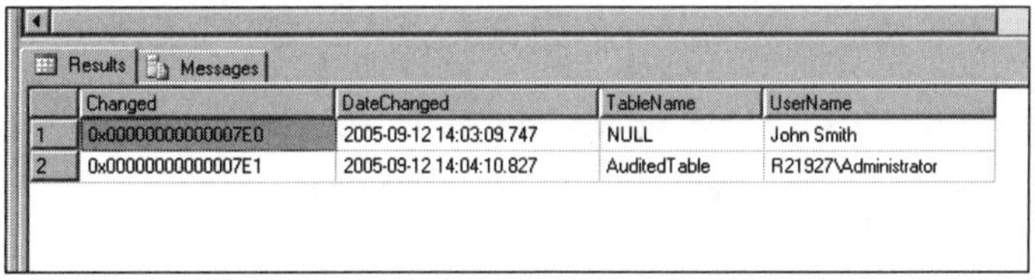

**Figure 14-8:**
An
additional
row added
to the
DDLAudit
table
following
the ALTER
TABLE
statement.

# DML Triggers

A DML trigger is executed in response to an event associated with a Data Modification Language (DML) statement. A DML trigger is associated with one of the following statements:

✔ INSERT

✔ UPDATE

✔ DELETE

You can use DML triggers either to replace a DML statement or to execute after a DML statement. A trigger that replaces a DML statement is called an INSTEAD OF trigger. A trigger that executes after a DML statement is called an AFTER trigger.

## The inserted and deleted tables

SQL Server automatically manages the `deleted` and `inserted` tables. If you delete rows from a table, the `deleted` table contains a row that matches the rows deleted from the other table. Similarly, if you update a row, the `deleted` table contains a row with the old values. When you execute an `UPDATE`, values are inserted into both the `inserted` and `deleted` tables.

If you insert data into a table, a copy of that row or those rows is contained in the `inserted` table.

You can use the `inserted` and `deleted` tables to determine what kind of change has been made to the data, as I show you in the next section.

## Triggers for auditing DML

A common use for DML triggers is to record, for audit purposes, changes made to data. The following steps show you how to create a DML trigger to store information about who changed data:

1. **Open a new database engine query in SQL Server Management Studio.**

2. **Ensure you are working in the `Chapter14` database.**

   ```
   USE Chapter14
   ```

3. **Create a table to store messages called `DMLAuditedTable`:**

   ```
   CREATE TABLE DMLAuditedTable
     (MessageID int PRIMARY KEY,
      Message varchar(100))
   ```

   This is the table you want to audit.

4. **Enter a sample value in the `DMLAuditedTable` table:**

   ```
   INSERT INTO DMLAuditedTable
     VALUES (1, 'Hello World!')
   ```

5. **Confirm the successful `INSERT` operation:**

   ```
   SELECT *
   FROM DMLAuditedTable
   ```

6. **Create a table, `DMLAudit`, to store the audit information:**

   ```
   CREATE TABLE DMLAudit
     (
      Changed TIMESTAMP,
      DateChanged DateTime,
      TableName char(30),
      UserName varchar(50),
      Operation char(6)
      )
   ```

The changed column is of type TIMESTAMP to store information about the sequence in changes made to the DMLAuditedTable table. In the Operation column, you store information about whether the DML change was an INSERT or an UPDATE operation.

7. **Enter a sample row manually into the DMLAudit table:**

```
INSERT INTO DMLAudit (DateChanged, UserName)
  VALUES (GetDate(), 'John Smith')
```

8. **Confirm the successful INSERT operation into the DMLAudit table:**

```
SELECT *
FROM DMLAudit
```

9. **Create a DML trigger called AuditDML:**

```
CREATE TRIGGER AuditDML
ON dbo.DMLAuditedTable
AFTER INSERT, UPDATE
-- NOT FOR REPLICATION
AS
DECLARE @Operation char(6)

IF EXISTS(SELECT * FROM deleted)
  SET @Operation = 'Update'
ELSE
  SET @Operation = 'Insert'

INSERT INTO dbo.DMLAudit(DateChanged,
  TableName, UserName, Operation)
  SELECT GetDate(), 'DMLAuditedTable', suser_sname(),
       @Operation
-- End of Trigger
```

Notice the IF clause that uses information from the deleted table to determine whether the operation is an UPDATE or an INSERT. That information is stored in the @Operation variable. The GetDate() function retrieves the data and time of the operation and the suser_sname() function retrieves the username. The Operation column stores the value in the @Operation variable.

10. **Test whether the DML trigger responds to an INSERT operation on the DMLAuditedTable table by using the following code:**

```
INSERT INTO DMLAuditedTable
  VALUES (2, 'To be or not to be, that is the
       question.')
```

11. **Execute a SELECT statement on the DMLAudit table to confirm that the INSERT operation has been executed:**

```
SELECT *
FROM dbo.DMLAudit
```

Notice in Figure 14-9 that the AuditDML trigger added a second row to the DMLAudit table.

12. **Execute an UPDATE statement against the DMLAuditedTable table:**

```
UPDATE DMLAuditedTable
  SET Message = 'Goodbye World!'
WHERE MessageID = 1
```

13. **Test whether the AuditDML trigger has added a row to the DMLAudit table by using the following code:**

```
SELECT *
FROM DMLAudit
```

Figure 14-10 shows that the UPDATE operation also caused a row to be added to the DMLAudit table. Notice that the value in the Operation column is Update.

The information you store in an audit table can be much more extensive than shown in this example. The scope is limited only by your knowledge of T-SQL and your business setting.

# Part V
# Administering a SQL Server System

The 5th Wave                    By Rich Tennant

"Maybe your keyword search, 'legal secretary, love, fame, fortune', needs to be refined."

## In this part . . .

**1** show you techniques to configure SQL Server and how to create SQL Server Agent jobs.

I introduce you to SQL Server Notification Services, show you how to create maintenance plans, and introduce you to topics relevant to working with multiple servers.

# Chapter 15

# Configuring a SQL Server System

● ● ● ● ● ● ● ● ● ● ● ● ● ● ● ● ● ● ● ● ● ● ● ● ● ● ● ● ● ● ● ● ● ● ● ● ● ● ● ● ● ● ● ● ● ● ● ● ●

## In This Chapter

▶ Configuring using SQL Server Configuration Manager

▶ Configuring using SQLCMD

▶ Configuring using SQL Server Management Studio

● ● ● ● ● ● ● ● ● ● ● ● ● ● ● ● ● ● ● ● ● ● ● ● ● ● ● ● ● ● ● ● ● ● ● ● ● ● ● ● ● ● ● ● ● ● ● ● ●

*M*icrosoft has put a lot of thought into making SQL Server work well out of the box. However, over time, almost inevitably you will want to configure some of the settings to make SQL Server better suited to work optimally in your own environment. In this chapter, I show you how to use the configuration tools available with SQL Server 2005 to carry out several configuration tasks.

Microsoft has given you several tools that you can use to configure a SQL Server 2005 instance. In this chapter, I describe three configuration tools:

✔ SQL Server Configuration Manager

✔ The SQLCMD command-line utility

✔ SQL Server Management Studio

## Using SQL Server Configuration Manager

SQL Server Configuration Manager is a GUI tool that is new in SQL Server 2005. It is intended to replace Client Network Utility, Server Network Utility, and Service Manager. You still use those tools to manage instances of SQL Server 2000 in your network. You use SQL Server Configuration only for configuring SQL Server 2005 instances.

SQL Server Configuration Manager allows you to carry out the following tasks:

- ✔ Manage the services associated with the various components of SQL Server 2005
- ✔ Configure the network protocols used by SQL Server 2005
- ✔ Manage the configuration of network connectivity for client computers

You can use SQL Server Configuration Manager to manage the following services:

- ✔ **Database engine:** MSSQLServer for a default instance and MSSQLServer$*instanceName* for a named instance. Each instance of SQL Server 2005 is managed separately but in the same interface. This lets you run the SQL Server relational database engine.
- ✔ **Analysis Services:** This lets you run the Analysis Services service. I describe Analysis Services in Chapter 21.
- ✔ **Integration Services:** This lets you run the Integration Services service. (In some places, this is still referred to as "DTS.") I describe Integration Services in Chapter 20.
- ✔ **Reporting Services:** This lets you run the Reporting Services service. I describe Reporting Services in Chapter 22.
- ✔ **SQL Agent:** This lets you execute scheduled tasks in SQL Server 2005.
- ✔ **SQL Browser:** This enables SQL Server to match ports with SQL Server instances.
- ✔ **SQL Server Full Text Search:** This enables full-text search.

SQL Server Configuration Manager lets you enable or disable the following network protocols:

- ✔ Shared Memory
- ✔ Named Pipes
- ✔ TCP/IP
- ✔ VIA

You can use SQL Server Configuration Manager in two ways:

- ✔ As a stand-alone application
- ✔ As part of a Microsoft Management Console (MMC)

Using SQL Server Configuration Manager as a stand-alone application is particularly convenient on a development machine when you may only want to configure local settings. However, you cannot use stand-alone SQL Server Configuration Manager to manage a remote machine.

# *Adding SQL Server Configuration Manager to an MMC console*

SQL Server Configuration Manager uses Microsoft Management Console (MMC) snap-in technology. On a typical SQL Server 2005 install, the SQL Server management console is installed as a stand-alone application that you can access from the Start menu: Start⇨All Programs⇨Microsoft SQL Server 2005⇨Configuration Tools⇨SQL Server Configuration Manager.

Alternatively, you can add SQL Server Configuration Manager inside another Microsoft management console. You can add it to a new MMC console or to an existing one. To add it to a new MMC console, follow these steps:

1. **Choose Start⇨Run.**

2. **In the Run dialog box, type** MMC **and click OK.**

   A blank Microsoft Management Console opens, as displayed in Figure 15-1.

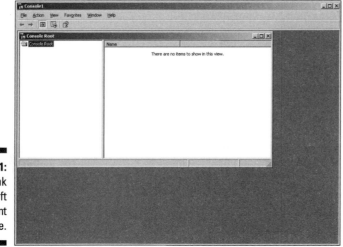

**Figure 15-1:** A blank Microsoft Management Console.

If you want to add SQL Server Configuration Manager to an existing Microsoft Management Console, start your selected MMC application at this step, and then continue to Step 3.

3. **Choose File⇨Add/Remove Snap-in in the Microsoft Management Console.**

   The Add/Remove Snap-in dialog box opens, as shown in Figure 15-2.

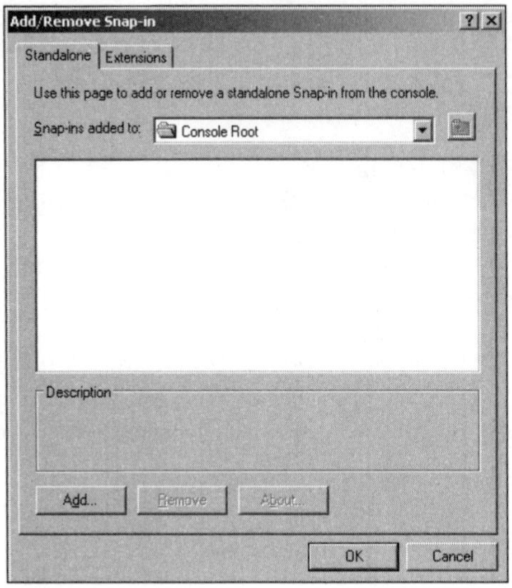

**Figure 15-2:**
The Add/
Remove
Snap-in
dialog box.

4. **Click the Add button.**

5. **In the Add Standalone Snap-in dialog box that appears, scroll down until you see the SQL Server Configuration Manager option. Highlight it as shown in Figure 15-3 and then click the Add button.**

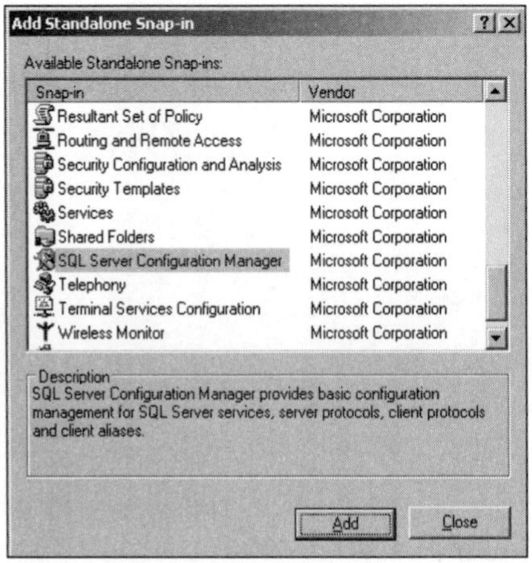

**Figure 15-3:**
Select the
SQL Server
Configuration
Manager in
the Add
Standalone
Snap-in
dialog box.

The SQL Server Configuration Manager is added to the Add/Remove Snap-in dialog box.

6. **Click the Close button in the Add Standalone Snap-in dialog box.**

7. **Click OK in the Add/Remove Snap-in dialog box.**

   SQL Server Configuration Manager displays in the Microsoft
   Management Console window, as shown in Figure 15-4.

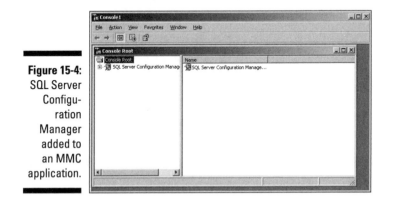

**Figure 15-4:**
SQL Server
Configu-
ration
Manager
added to
an MMC
application.

You can now use SQL Server Configuration Manager inside the Microsoft
Management Console. Figure 15-5 shows the nodes of SQL Server Configuration Manager expanded in the left pane of the management console, with the
node for management of network protocols for a default instance of SQL
Server 2005 selected.

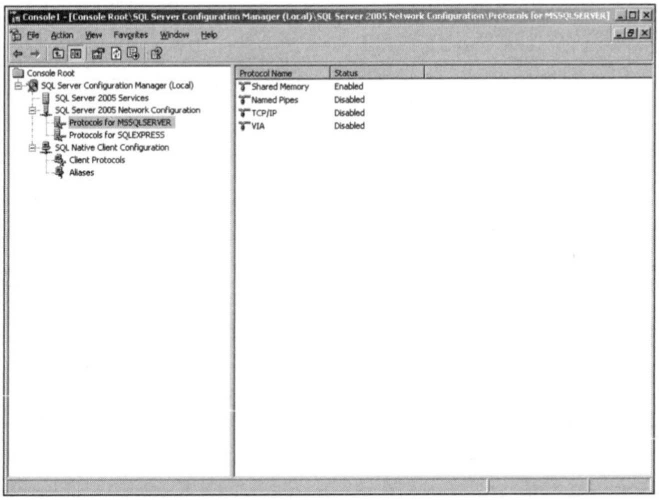

**Figure 15-5:**
The nodes
contained in
SQL Server
Configuration
Manager.

## Managing SQL Server services

SQL Server Configuration Manager provides an alternative way to manage services associated with SQL Server.

The conventional way to access and manage services is to choose Start➪ Control Panel ➪Administrative Tools➪Services (Windows XP with Classic view). If you're using Windows 2003 Server, you can access the Services window by choosing Start➪Administrative Tools➪Services. The big downside to the conventional Services window is that you can have a large number of services running and it is difficult to clearly view all services together that relate to SQL Server. SQL Server Configuration Manager makes it much easier to see what is happening with SQL Server-related services. Another advantage of using SQL Server Configuration Manager is that it forces a checkpoint on all databases. That speeds recovery and SQL Server startup.

To view the installed SQL Server-related services on the local machine, follow these steps:

1. **Start SQL Server Configuration Manager by choosing Start➪ All Programs➪Microsoft SQL Server 2005➪Configuration Tools➪ SQL Server Configuration Manager.**

   SQL Server Configuration Manager opens (see Figure 15-6).

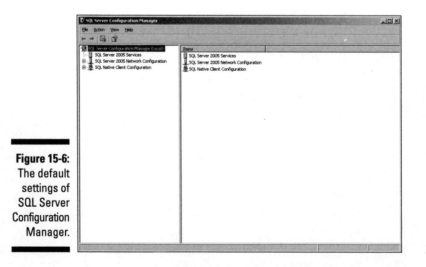

**Figure 15-6:**
The default
settings of
SQL Server
Configuration
Manager.

2. **Choose one of two ways to open the Services pane: Either single-click SQL Server 2005 Services in the left pane or double-click SQL Server 2005 Services in the right pane.**

   The services display in the right pane; see Figure 15-7.

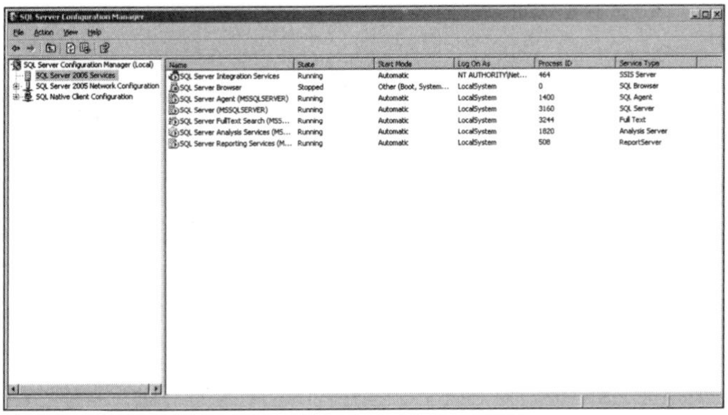

**Figure 15-7:**
The SQL
Server 2005
services
display in
the right
pane.

If a service that relates to SQL Server 2005 doesn't display, then it's likely not installed or some problem occurred during installation.

Notice that several pieces of information display about each service. Most important is whether or not the service is running. A small right-pointing green arrow indicates that a service is running. A small red square indicates that the service is not running.

To start, stop, or inspect the properties of a service, you must first select the service.

3. **To stop a running service, right-click the service and select Stop from the context menu.**

   The dialog box shown in Figure 15-8 displays.

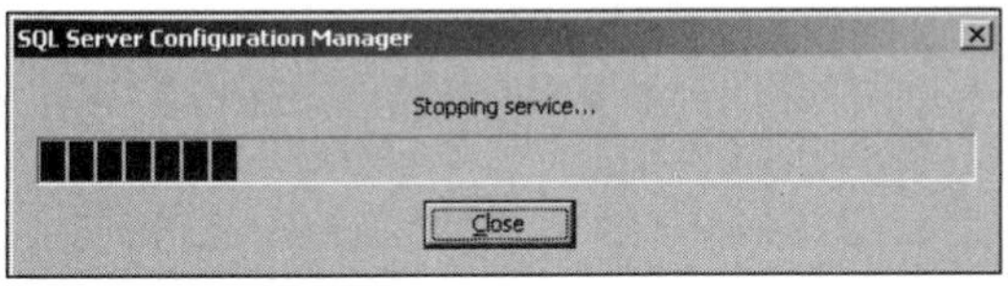

**Figure 15-8:**
The dialog
box displays
when
stopping a
service.

4. **To start a stopped service, right-click the service and select Start from the context menu.**

5. **To display the properties of a service, right-click the service and select Properties from the context menu.**

   Figure 15-9 shows the Log On tab of the SQL Server (MSSQLServer) Properties dialog box. The name of the service displays in brackets in the title bar of the dialog box.

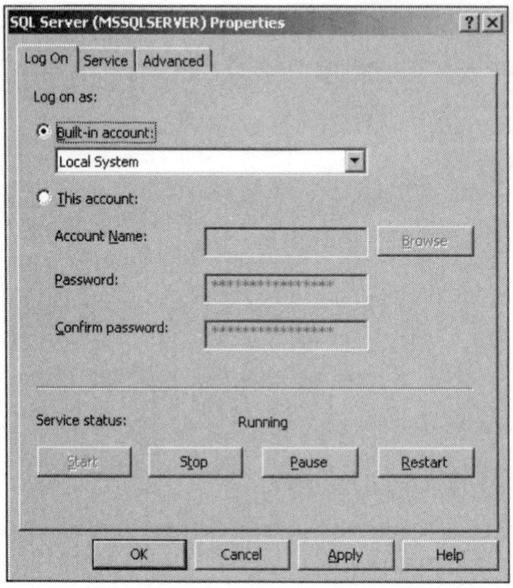

**Figure 15-9:**
The SQL
Server
(MSSQL
Server)
Properties
dialog box.

If the dialog box relates to Integration Services, Analysis Services, or
Reporting Services, the service name displays in the title bar of the
Properties dialog box. In the Reporting Services properties dialog box, you
can access the Reporting Services Configuration tool by clicking the
Configure button (see Figure 15-10).

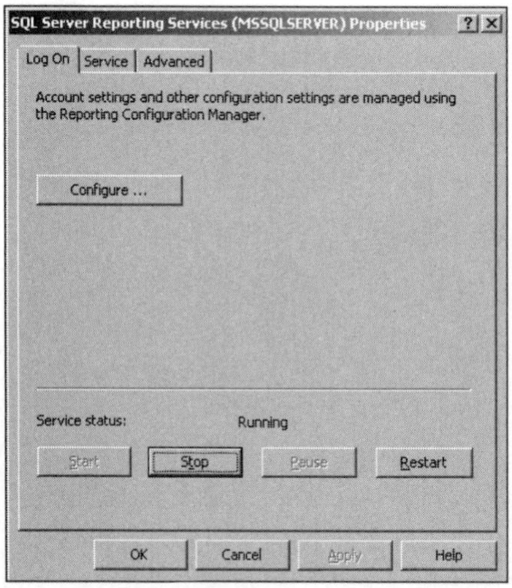

**Figure 15-10:**
The
Reporting
Services
Properties
dialog box.

Chapter 21 goes into more detail about Analysis Services; Chapter 20 includes Integration Services; and you find more about Reporting Services in Chapter 22.

You can use the preceding steps to start and stop services on a remote computer after you connect to the remote computer. Connecting to a remote computer is described in the next section.

## Connecting to a remote computer

The stand-alone SQL Server Configuration Manager has no functionality to allow an administrator to connect to a remote computer. To connect to a remote computer, you must use Windows Computer Management MMC console. The following steps show you how to make the connection to the remote computer:

1. **Click the Start button. Right-click My Computer and select Manage from the context menu.**

   Windows Computer Management console opens.

2. **Expand the Services and Applications node in Windows Computer Management console and you see the SQL Services Configuration Manager as a node under the Services and Applications node (see Figure 15-11).**

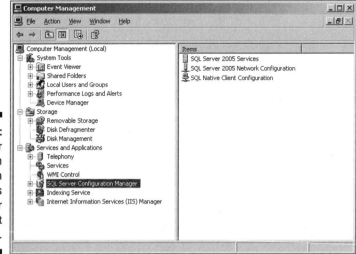

**Figure 15-11:**
SQL Server Configuration Manager in Windows Computer Management console.

3. **Right-click the Computer Management (Local) node and select Connect to Another Computer from the context menu (see Figure 15-12).**

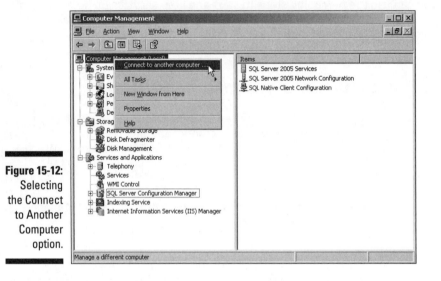

4. **In the Select Computer dialog box that appears, enter the name of a remote computer to which you have access and click OK.**

Figure 15-13 shows a connection targeted at a computer named SQLSERVER2005.

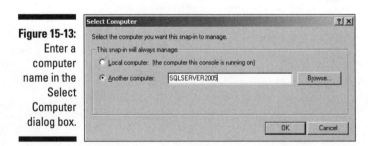

After you click OK, the Select Computer dialog box closes. You're returned to Windows Computer Management console. Notice in Figure 15-14 that the name of the remote computer you've connected to displays in the top node (highlighted in the figure).

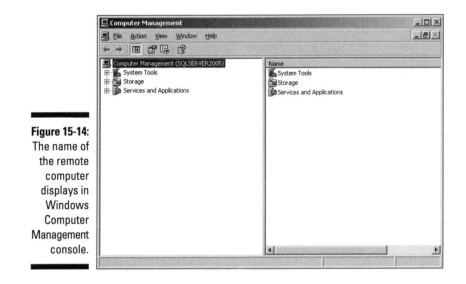

You can now (on the remote computer) stop, start, or inspect services as described in the preceding section. Or configure network protocols as described in the next section.

SQL Server Configuration Manager supports the Shared Memory Named Pipes, TCP/IP, and VIA protocols only.

## Configuring network protocols

To configure network protocols, follow these steps. The steps are the same whether you are connected to a local machine or connected remotely. Be sure that you know which machine you are connected to when making changes.

1. **Open SQL Server Configuration Manager by choosing Start⟹ All Program⟹Microsoft SQL Server 2005⟹Configuration Tools⟹ SQL Server Configuration Manager.**

2. **If appropriate, switch to the machine where you want to configure SQL Server 2005.**

3. **Click the SQL Server 2005 Network Configuration node in the left pane of Configuration Manager.**

   The node expands to display each SQL Server 2005 instance that is available for configuration on the chosen machine. Figure 15-15 shows the situation on a machine that has a default instance of SQL Server 2005 and a named instance (SQLExpress).

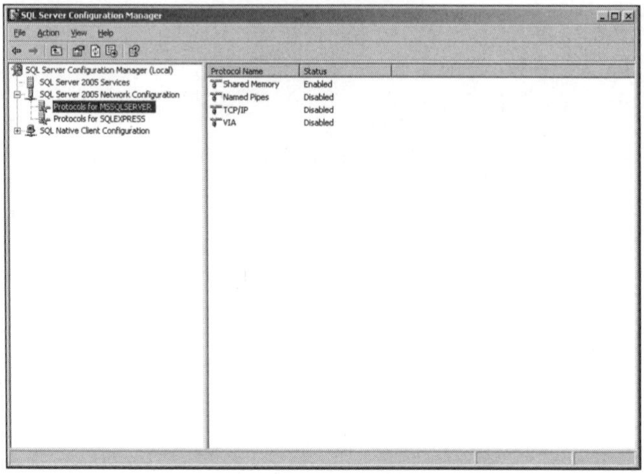

**Figure 15-15:**
The SQL Server 2005 Network Configuration node.

Notice in the right pane in Figure 15-15 that the network protocols for a SQL Server 2005 instance display together with their current status.

4. **To change the status of a protocol, right-click the protocol and select Enable or Disable from the context menu.**

   If the protocol is currently disabled, only the Enable option displays on the context menu. Similarly, if the protocol is currently enabled, only the Disable option displays.

5. **To inspect, and optionally change, the properties of a protocol, right-click the desired protocol and select Properties from the context menu.**

   The content of the Properties dialog box for each protocol is different. Figure 15-16 shows the Properties dialog box for the TCP/IP protocol.

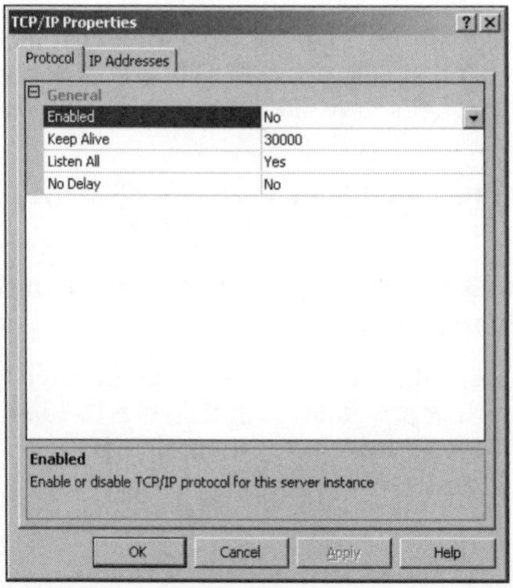

**Figure 15-16:**
The TCP/IP Properties dialog box.

## Configuring client computers

Many client computers will already be configured to use a network protocol like TCP/IP. If you need to configure a client computer to run a network protocol, follow these steps after installing SQL Server Configuration Manager on the client machine or using SQL Server Configuration Manager inside Windows Computer Management to connect to a client machine across the network:

1. **Navigate to the SQL Native Client Configuration node and expand it.**

2. **Click the Client Protocols option in the left pane.**

   The available network protocols display in the right pane. If the network protocol you desire to enable is already enabled you don't need to do anything more.

3. **To enable a protocol, select the protocol and then right-click and select Enable from the context menu.**

# Configuring Using SQLCMD

The SQLCMD utility allows you to send T-SQL code to an instance of SQL Server 2005 from the command prompt and, assuming you have the necessary permissions, configure the SQL Server instance or database objects to behave in desired ways.

## Getting started with SQLCMD

SQLCMD is installed if you select client tools when you install SQL Server 2005.

If SQLCMD is installed and you're connecting to a local instance of SQL Server — for example, on a development machine — follow these steps to connect to the default instance of SQL Server 2005:

1. **Open a Windows command prompt by choosing Start⇨Run, typing CMD in the Run dialog box, and then clicking OK.**

   A command line console opens.

2. **At the command line, type** SQLCMD.

   The prompt changes to:

   ```
   1>
   ```

   and you can then type T-SQL commands. Figure 15-17 shows the prompt.

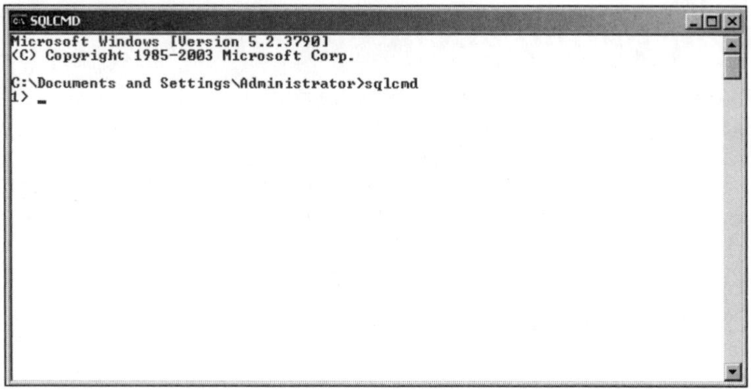

**Figure 15-17:**
The
SQLCMD
prompt.

You can now execute any T-SQL command. In this example, you create a database and add a new login and user. Because this is a command-line interface, you must type each line, and then press Return to get to the next line. The number that makes up part of the command prompt increases at each line.

3. **To create a database called** `Chapter15`, **type this code (I have included the prompts; DO NOT type those when you enter the T-SQL):**

```
1>CREATE DATABASE Chapter15
2>GO
```

and then press Return. The `GO` statement is not a T-SQL statement. SQLCMD interprets `GO` to mean that a batch of T-SQL statements are to be sent for execution. The prompt changes back to `1>` indicating that the command has run without errors. If there are any error messages, those are displayed.

4. **To add a** `CMDTest` **table, use the following code:**

```
1>CREATE TABLE CMDTest
2> (ID int PRIMARY KEY,
3> Message varchar(150))
4>GO
```

and then press Return to execute it. Again the prompt returns to `1>`.

5. **To add a login, type the following code and then press Return:**

```
1>CREATE LOGIN CMDTest WITH PASSWORD = 'abc123'
2>GO
```

6. **Before you add a user, which has permissions in the scope of a database, switch the context to the** `Chapter15` **database:**

```
1>USE Chapter15
2>GO
```

7. **Add the user to the `Chapter15` database:**

```
1>CREATE USER CmdTest
2>GO
```

8. **Open SQL Server Management Studio and connect to the SQL Server instance.**

9. **In the Object Explorer, expand the Security node for the SQL Server instance.**

10. **Expand the Logins node.**

    The new login, CMDTest, is listed in the logins, as shown in Figure 15-18.

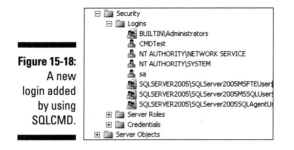

**Figure 15-18:**
A new
login added
by using
SQLCMD.

11. **To confirm that the user `CMDTest` has been added to the `Chapter15` database, expand the node with this path: Databases⇨Chapter15⇨ Security⇨Users.**

    The CMDTest user is listed, as shown in Figure 15-19.

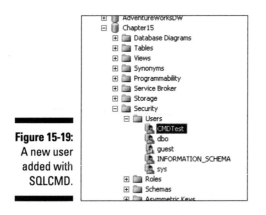

**Figure 15-19:**
A new user
added with
SQLCMD.

You can carry out any configuration task that you have permissions for and the knowledge of T-SQL to carry out.

## Executing a T-SQL script with SQLCMD

You can execute any saved T-SQL script with the SQLCMD utility. The example accesses a `GetDate.sql` script, which has a single line of T-SQL code that retrieves the current date and time:

```
SELECT GetDate()
```

To run the `GetDate.sql` script, type the following at the command prompt on a single line, and then press Return. (The instructions assume that `GetDate.sql` is in the Chapter15 folder.)

```
sqlcmd -i "C:\Documents and Settings\All Users\Documents\
            Chapter15\GetDate.sql"
```

The current date and time displays, as shown in Figure 15-20.

**Figure 15-20:**
Using
SQLCMD to
run a T-SQL
script to
find the date
and time.

## Logging in as a specified user

To log in as a particular user to an instance of SQL Server 2005 by using SQLCMD, follow these steps:

1. **Open a command window prompt by choosing Start⇨Run, typing CMD in the Run dialog box, and then clicking OK.**

2. **At the command prompt type**

   ```
   sqlcmd -U username
   ```

   For example, if you want to log in as the `sa` user, type the following:

   ```
   sqlcmd -U sa
   ```

   The *username* in the preceding code is a login for SQL Server 2005. Unlike T-SQL code, the login is case sensitive. The `-U` argument is also case sensitive.

A prompt displays.

3. **You type in the password and you have access to the SQL Server instance as before.**

   When you type the password, the keystrokes are not echoed to the console. So you need to be precise about pressing the keys in order to avoid a mistake.

You can log in to SQLCMD by using the -U and -P arguments as in the following command:

```
sqlcmd -u sa -p myPassword
```

This does not conceal the characters in the password on-screen. If there is any possibility of somebody watching over your shoulder while you type or having access to an open command console that you used to log in, you should avoid this approach, because the password is readable in plain text. I suggest that if you don't use Windows Authentication to log in that you only use -U and avoid the -P argument. By doing that, you supply the password separately and it is not echoed to the screen.

## Connecting to a remote SQL server instance

You can also use SQLCMD to connect to an instance of SQL Server 2005 across a Windows network. To do that, use the -S argument. You use the CmdTest login that I show you how to create in the "Getting started with SQLCMD" section, earlier in the chapter. You must have Named Pipes enabled on both machines for the remote login to work. I show you earlier in this chapter (in the "Configuring network protocols" section) how to enable network protocols by using SQL Server Configuration Manager. Named Pipes is one of the network protocols that you can use SQL Server Configuration Manager to enable.

To connect to the default instance of SQL Server 2005 on a server that is named SQLServer2005, follow these steps:

1. **At the command line, type the following:**

```
sqlcmd -S SQLServer2005 -U CmdTest
```

   The prompt displays, requesting a password.

2. **Enter the password and press Return.**

   The 1> prompt displays, shown in Figure 15-21, indicating a successful connection to the remote instance of SQL Server 2005.

```
SQLCMD                                                    _□×
C:\Documents and Settings\Administrator>sqlcmd -S SQLServer2005 -U CmdTest
Password:
1> _
```

**Figure 15-21:**
Connecting
remotely
by using
SQLCMD.

# Configuring Using SQL Server Management Studio

SQL Server Management Studio, which I introduce you to in Chapter 3, has many options that allow you to configure aspects of a SQL Server 2005 installation. The examples I show assume that you're connecting locally to a default instance of SQL Server 2005.

## SQL Server instance level configuration

You can carry out many tasks at the SQL Server instance level by using SQL Server Management Studio. To access the dialog boxes to allow you to carry out those tasks, follow these steps:

1. **Open SQL Server Management Studio and open the Object Explorer with the desired instance of SQL Server 2005 selected.**

2. **Right-click the name of the instance and choose Properties from the context menu.**

   The Server Properties dialog box opens, as shown in Figure 15-22.

Notice in Figure 15-22 the names in the left pane. Clicking these names allows you to access and configure a large number of server properties. At the risk of stating the obvious, be sure that you only configure properties if you understand the effects of the changes you make.

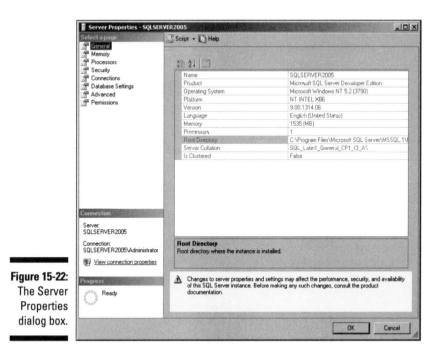

**Figure 15-22:**
The Server
Properties
dialog box.

The following panes contain configuration options:

- ✔ Memory
- ✔ Processors
- ✔ Security
- ✔ Connections
- ✔ Database settings
- ✔ Advanced
- ✔ Permissions

Inspect the different panes to see which properties are read only and which you can change.

## Configuring at the database level

SQL Server Management Studio gives you access to many properties that you can configure at the database level. To configure properties for the Chapter15 database, follow these steps:

1. **Open the Databases node.**

2. **Right-click the Chapter15 node and select Properties from the context menu.**

   The Database Properties dialog box, shown in Figure 15-23, opens.

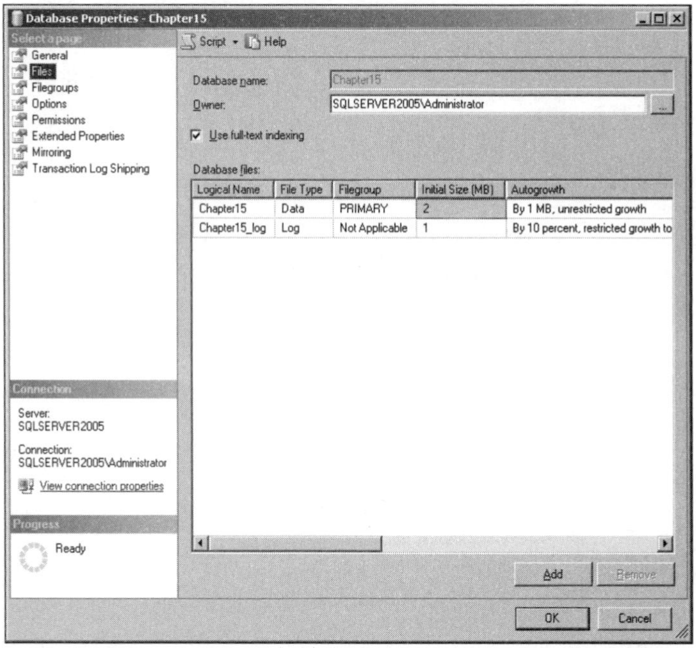

**Figure 15-23:**
The
Database
Properties
dialog box.

The Database Properties dialog box gives you access to properties under the following headings:

- ✔ Files
- ✔ Filegroups
- ✔ Options
- ✔ Permissions
- ✔ Extended Properties
- ✔ Mirroring
- ✔ Transaction Log Shipping

# Chapter 16

# Scheduling SQL Server Agent Jobs

- - - - - - - - - - - - - - - - - - - - - - - - - - - - - - - - - - - - - - - -

## In This Chapter

▶ Discovering SQL Server Agent

▶ Setting permissions for SQL Agent

▶ Setting up SQL Server Agent

▶ Enabling jobs and alerts

▶ Controlling SQL Server Agent with T-SQL

▶ Setting up automated maintenance tasks

- - - - - - - - - - - - - - - - - - - - - - - - - - - - - - - - - - - - - - - -

*A*s a database administrator, you must carry out many tasks several times in order to keep a SQL Server 2005 database installation in good shape. Often such repeated tasks must be done at particular times. For example, some must be done every day, some every week. Because of the repetitive, but essential, nature of these tasks, SQL Server supports a way to carry out such necessary tasks automatically. Carrying out the tasks individually by hand is expensive in time (and therefore money) and can produce boredom and error (after all, most administrators are human). Therefore an automated approach is preferable. SQL Server Agent is in charge of automated tasks.

In SQL Server Agent, you create a *job* to carry out a task in an automated way. You use an *alert* to inform a database administrator or other human being of a particular situation that needs human assessment or intervention. You may want, for example, to back up SQL Server data on a fixed schedule. SQL Server Agent is ideal to carry out this task.

In this chapter, I often refer to SQL Server Agent simply as SQL Agent. I use the terms interchangeably. Microsoft uses both terms.

In the final part of the chapter, I introduce the Maintenance Plan Wizard that allows you to automate maintenance tasks. The Maintenance Plan Wizard creates SQL Server Agent jobs under the covers.

# Introducing SQL Server Agent

SQL Server Agent is a service that allows you to automate administrative tasks. It stores the information needed to carry out its function in SQL Server.

You can use SQL Server Agent for two types of tasks: monitoring and maintenance. You can use SQL Server Agent to do two types of thing:

- ✔ Carry out a task, whether monitoring or maintenance, on one or several instances of SQL Server.
- ✔ Inform, or alert, a database administrator or other professional if certain situations arise.

The two preceding bullet points relate, respectively, to a *job* and an *alert* in SQL Server Agent.

The following are examples of tasks that you might want to use SQL Server Agent to carry out:

- ✔ Backing up data
- ✔ Moving or copying data to a data warehouse
- ✔ Scheduled database maintenance

# Managing Agent from SQL Server Management Studio

You can manage SQL Server Agent from SQL Server Management Studio. A basic task is to find out whether or not SQL Server Agent is running. To access information on SQL Server Agent, follow these steps:

1. **Start SQL Server Management Studio.**

   Use the Registered Servers pane to connect to the desired SQL Server instance by using the Object Explorer.

2. **If the Registered Servers pane is not visible, choose View⇨Registered Servers. In the Registered Servers pane, select the desired instance, and then right-click and choose Connect⇨Object Explorer from the context menu.**

3. **In the Object Explorer, click the desired SQL Server instance. Expand the instance node, if it is not already expanded.**

   The SQL Agent icon is visible below all other nodes for that SQL Server instance. In Figure 16-1, you see the appearance when SQL Agent is not running. Notice the message that Agent XPs are disabled. Later in this chapter, in the "Enabling SQL Agent extended stored procedures" section, I explain how to enable Agent extended stored procedures. Notice, too, that no + sign allows you to expand the SQL Agent node.

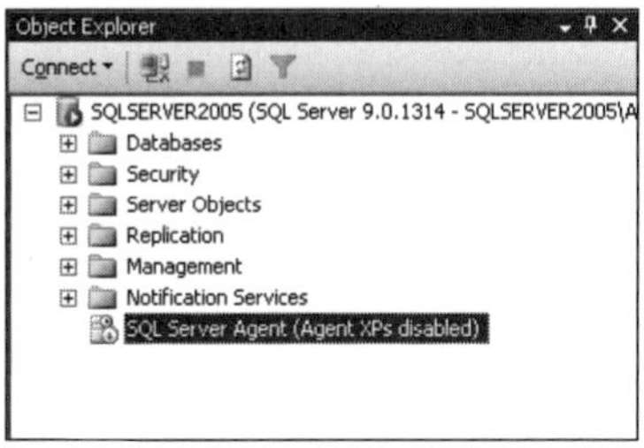

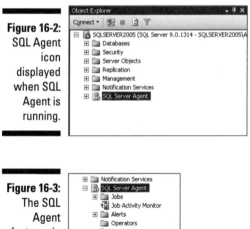

**Figure 16-1:**
SQL Agent icon displayed when SQL Agent is not running.

Figure 16-2 shows the appearance when SQL Agent is running. Notice in Figure 16-2 that, when SQL Agent is running, the node can be expanded. Figure 16-3 shows the features that display when the SQL Agent node is expanded.

**Figure 16-2:**
SQL Agent icon displayed when SQL Agent is running.

**Figure 16-3:**
The SQL Agent features in Object Explorer.

The most important nodes in Figure 16-3 are Jobs, Alerts, and Operators, which you use to create and configure jobs, alerts, and operators, respectively. I show you how to carry out those tasks later in this chapter.

A SQL Server Agent proxy allows SQL Agent to carry out a job step by using the security credentials of an appropriate user.

## Starting and stopping SQL Server Agent

Using SQL Server Management Studio, you can easily start or stop the SQL Server Agent service.

The following descriptions assume you have SQL Server Management Studio open as described in the preceding section.

To start SQL Agent if it's stopped, right-click the SQL Agent node in the Object Explorer and select the Start option from the context menu.

To stop SQL Agent when it's running, right-click the SQL Agent node in the Object Explorer and select the Stop option from the context menu.

As well as needing to be able to start and stop SQL Agent, you also need to be able to configure SQL Agent to start when the server on which SQL Server 2005 is installed is restarted.

## Setting SQL Agent to start automatically

All SQL Server automation depends on the SQL Server Agent service. If you configure SQL Agent to carry out a task at specified times and forget to ensure that the SQL Agent service is running, then the task isn't carried out. Depending on how often you monitor the results of SQL Agent jobs, you may be unaware of this for some time.

If you stop the SQL Server service the SQL Server Agent service is also stopped.

To ensure that SQL Agent is always running, be sure to set it, and the SQL Server service, to start automatically when the SQL Server machine starts. Then if the machine reboots after a software update or reboots after a temporary power outage, you can be sure that the SQL Agent service is running.

SQL Agent is a Windows service. You have two options to make SQL Agent start automatically when the server machine starts: SQL Server Configuration Manager or the Services utility.

To use SQL Server Configuration Manager to set SQL Agent to start automatically, follow these steps:

1. **Open SQL Server Configuration Manager (or a Microsoft Management Console to which SQL Server Configuration Manager has been added, as I describe in Chapter 15).**

2. **Select SQL Server 2005 Services in the left pane.**

   The SQL Server services display in the right pane.

3. **Select the SQL Server Agent service, right-click, and choose Properties from the context menu.**

   The SQL Server Agent Properties dialog box opens.

4. **On the Service tab (shown in Figure 16-4), check the Start Mode drop-down menu to see when (or if) the SQL Agent service starts when the server restarts. If you want the SQL Agent service to start automatically, select the Automatic option.**

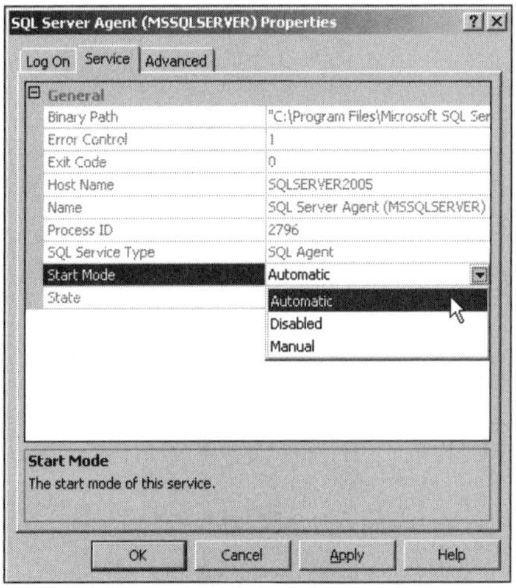

**Figure 16-4:**
Selecting the Automatic option for SQL Agent.

5. **Assuming that you don't want to make any other changes to SQL Agent properties, click Apply and then click OK.**

You can also set the SQL Agent service to start automatically by using the SQL Server Surface Area Configuration Manager. Follow these steps:

1. **Choose Start➪All Programs➪Microsoft SQL Server 2005➪ Configuration Tools➪SQL Server Surface Area Configuration.**

   Figure 16-5 shows the SQL Server 2005 Surface Area Configuration tool.

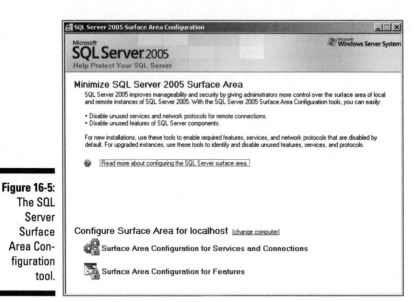

**Figure 16-5:**
The SQL Server Surface Area Configuration tool.

2. **Select the Surface Area Configuration for Services and Connections.**

   The Surface Area Configuration for Services and Connections dialog box opens (see Figure 16-6).

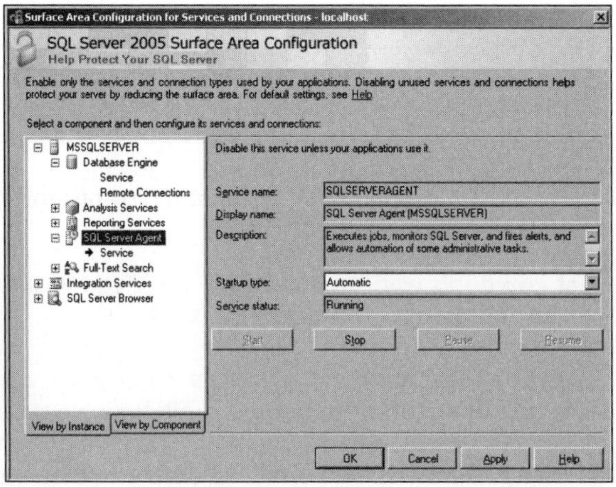

**Figure 16-6:**
The Surface Area Configuration for Services and Connections dialog box.

3. **Select the SQL Agent option in the left pane.**

   The right pane displays information about the SQL Agent service.

4. **Select Automatic from the Startup Type drop-down menu.**

5. **Click Apply and then click OK.**

## Using Agent in Business Intelligence

In addition to handling routine administration tasks, you can use SQL Server Agent to schedule the execution of Integration Services packages or the execution or distribution of Reporting Services reports.

You might want to run a SQL Server Integration Services package to transform and transport a day's data each evening to a data warehouse. SQL Server Agent is used to schedule running of the Integration Services package. Similarly, if you schedule report delivery in Reporting Services, SQL Server Agent is responsible for correct scheduling.

I describe SQL Server Integration Services in Chapter 20 and SQL Server Reporting Services in Chapter 22.

# Security

In SQL Server 2005, you must use Windows Authentication when using SQL Agent. SQL Server Authentication is available only when using SQL Agent with instances of earlier versions of SQL Server.

Each job step can have its own security context. This provides granular security so that each step is carried out with minimum permissions, so cutting down the risk of inappropriate use of a SQL Agent task.

You should create specific proxy user accounts (they display in the Proxies node in Object Explorer) to run job steps. Each proxy user account should be granted only the permissions necessary to carry out a particular job step.

For SQL Agent to automate tasks successfully, it must have appropriate permissions for each aspect of what it needs to do.

## Permissions for SQL Agent

You can use the SQL Agent service to carry out jobs locally or across a network. When SQL Agent is carrying out jobs only on a local server, you can run SQL Agent as a local machine account. When you want SQL Agent to carry out jobs across a network, you use a domain user account.

After you install SQL Server Agent and start the service, you can view or change the account under which SQL Agent runs by following these steps:

1. **Start SQL Server Configuration Manager by choosing Start⇨ All Programs⇨Microsoft SQL Server 2005⇨Configuration Tools⇨ SQL Server Configuration Manager.**

**2. Select SQL Server 2005 Services in the left pane.**

The available SQL Server services display in the right pane.

**3. Right-click the desired SQL Agent service and select the Properties option from the context menu.**

The SQL Server Agent Properties dialog box opens (see Figure 16-7). The Log On tab displays by default.

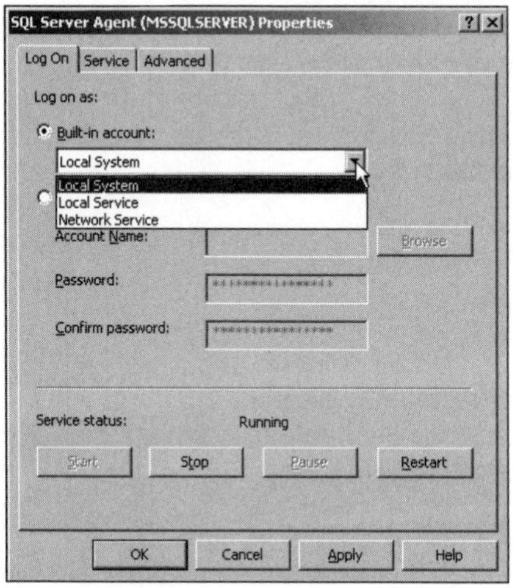

**Figure 16-7:**
The SQL
Server
Agent
Properties
dialog box
showing the
Log On tab.

**4. You can view the options by clicking the Built-in Account drop-down menu, as shown in Figure 16-7.**

**5. To change to a specified account other than one of the built-in accounts, select the This Account radio button, and then supply an account name and password.**

## Permissions for users

Following installation of SQL Server 2005, only system administrators can view, modify, create, or execute SQL Server Agent jobs. For any other type of user to even view the Agent node in SQL Server Management Studio, the administrator must grant the relevant permissions.

To grant `sysadmin` permissions to the login `CMDTest` that you create in Chapter 15, follow these steps. Choose another appropriate login, if needed, as appropriate to your circumstances.

1. **Open SQL Server Management Studio. Select the instance in Registered Servers. Right-click and choose Connect⊅Object Explorer.**

2. **Expand the Security node.**

3. **Right-click the CMDTest login (or other desired login). Select Properties from the context menu.**

   The Login Properties dialog box displays (see Figure 16-8).

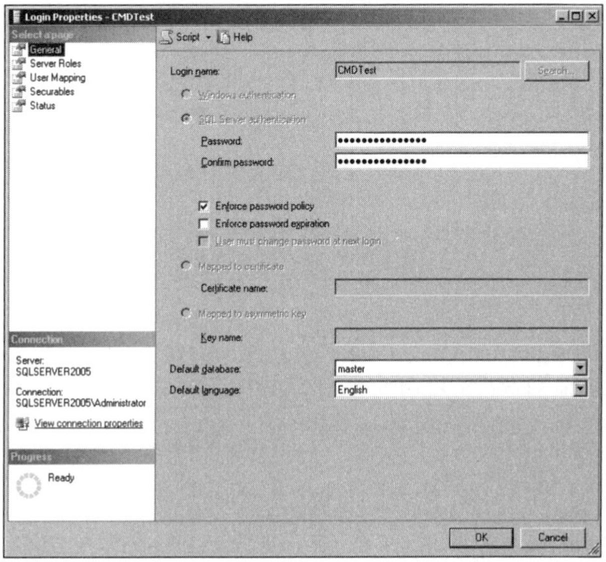

**Figure 16-8:**
The Login
Properties
dialog box.

4. **Select the User Mapping option in the left pane of the Login Properties dialog box.**

   The right pane changes to show options for User Mapping.

5. **In the Users Mapped to This Login area of the right pane, select the check box for the msdb database.**

   The options in the lower part of the right pane become available for selection.

6. **Scroll down the Database Role Membership For list.**

   The options relevant to SQL Agent display (see Figure 16-9).

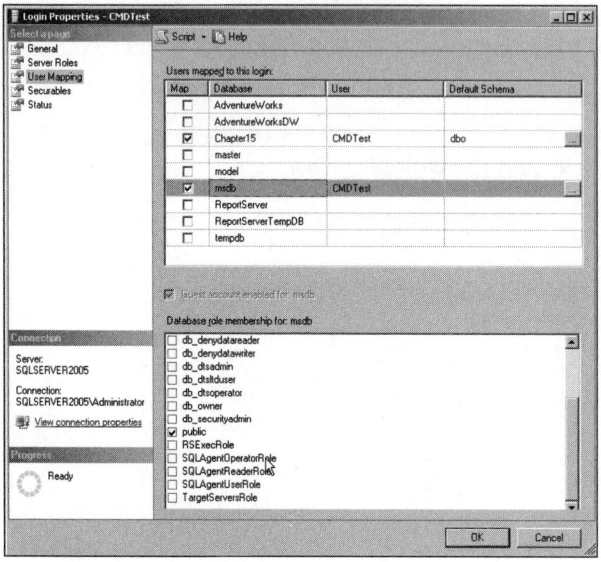

**Figure 16-9:**
Selecting
SQL Agent
roles in
the msdb
database.

   7. **Check the options SQLAgentOperatorRole, SQLAgentReaderRole
      and/or SQLAgentUserRole, as appropriate.**

   8. **Click OK to confirm the changes that you've made.**

To enable other users to use SQL Server Agent, you must assign a user to one
of two roles: SQLAgentUserRole or MaintenanceUserRole. Users to
whom you grant permissions for these roles can create SQL Server agent
jobs. They can manage jobs that they have created.

# Configuring SQL Server Agent

You need to correctly set several configuration options for SQL Agent to perform some or all the actions you're likely to need.

## Windows permissions

To run successfully, SQL Agent needs the following Windows permissions:

   ✔ Adjust memory quotas for a process

   ✔ Act as a part of the operating system

   ✔ Bypass traverse checking

   ✔ Log in as a batch job

> ✔ Log in as a service
>
> ✔ Replace a process level token

If you're having problems running SQL Agent, you may want to check that each of these permissions has been granted to the `SQLAgentUserRole` account. To check granting of those Windows permissions locally, follow these steps:

1. **Choose Start➪Administrative Tools➪Local Security Policy (Windows 2003) or Start➪Control Panel➪Administrative Tools➪Local Security Policy (Windows XP).**

   Figure 16-10 shows the appearance of the Local Security Settings dialog box on Windows 2003.

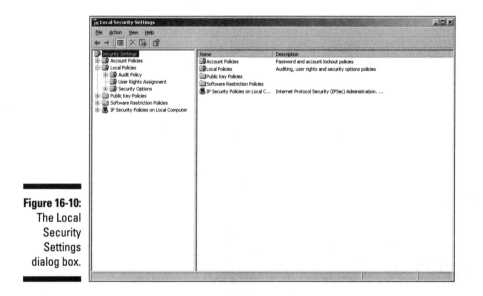

**Figure 16-10:**
The Local
Security
Settings
dialog box.

2. **Expand the Local Policies node, and then select User Rights Assignment.**

   The individual policies display in the right pane.

3. **To check whether SQL Agent has permissions — for example, to log in as a service — select the Log On as a Service option in the right pane. Right-click and select Properties from the context menu.**

   The Log On as a Service Properties dialog box displays.

4. **Examine the list in the dialog box and check whether the `SQLAgentUser` role is listed.**

   It is highlighted in Figure 16-11.

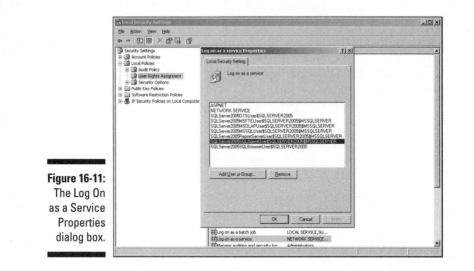

**Figure 16-11:**
The Log On
as a Service
Properties
dialog box.

5. **Repeat Steps 3 and 4 to check the status of the other permissions listed in the preceding bulleted list.**

## Enabling SQL Agent extended stored procedures

To enable SQL Server Agent extended stored procedures, you use the `sp_configure` system stored procedure. To turn on Agent extended procedures, follow these steps.

1. **Open SQL Server Management Studio.**

2. **Click the Database Engine Query button.**

3. **Because you must enable the advanced options to make the necessary change, run this T-SQL code:**

```
sp_configure 'show_advanced_options', 1
GO
```

4. **Run the following code to apply the change:**

```
Reconfigure
GO
```

5. **Run the following code to enable Agent extended stored procedures:**

```
sp_configure 'Agent XPs', 1
GO
Reconfigure
GO
```

6. **Check that the `config_value` column now contains a value of 1 by using the following code.**

```
sp_configure
GO
```

Figure 16-12 shows the desired appearance.

| | name | minimum | maximum | config_value | run_value |
|---|---|---|---|---|---|
| 1 | Ad Hoc Distributed Queries | 0 | 1 | 0 | 0 |
| 2 | affinity I/O mask | -2147483648 | 2147483647 | 0 | 0 |
| 3 | affinity mask | -2147483648 | 2147483647 | 0 | 0 |
| 4 | Agent XPs | 0 | 1 | 1 | 1 |
| 5 | allow updates | 0 | 1 | 0 | 0 |
| 6 | awe enabled | 0 | 1 | 0 | 0 |
| 7 | blocked process threshold | 0 | 86400 | 0 | 0 |
| 8 | c2 audit mode | 0 | 1 | 0 | 0 |
| 9 | clr enabled | 0 | 1 | 0 | 0 |
| 10 | cost threshold for parallelism | 0 | 32767 | 5 | 5 |
| 11 | cross db ownership chaining | 0 | 1 | 0 | 0 |
| 12 | cursor threshold | -1 | 2147483647 | -1 | -1 |

# Creating Jobs and Alerts

When using SQL Server Agent in a production setting, you'll likely want to create both jobs and alerts.

## Creating a SQL Agent job

The following example uses a database, Chapter16, which you create by using the following T-SQL code:

```
CREATE DATABASE Chapter16
```

Add a DateTimeInserts table by using the following code:

```
CREATE TABLE DateTimeInserts
  (ID INT PRIMARY KEY,
  DateFromAgent DateTime)
```

Insert a sample value into the table and view it by using the following code:

```
INSERT INTO DateTimeInserts
  VALUES(1, GetDate())

SELECT *
FROM DateTimeInserts
```

The example job inserts a row into the `DateTimeInserts` table with the value of the current date and time stored in the `DateFromAgent` column.

To create a SQL Server Agent job in SQL Server Management Studio, follow these steps:

1. **Open SQL Server Management Studio. Select a desired SQL Server instance in Registered Servers. Right-click the desired instance and choose Connect⇨Object Explorer from the context menu.**

   The desired instance displays in the Object Explorer.

2. **Expand the SQL Agent node.**

   You can expand it only if the SQL Agent service is running. If the service is not running, follow the steps in the "Starting and stopping SQL Server Agent" section, earlier in this chapter.

3. **Right-click the Jobs node and select New Job from the context menu.**

   The New Job dialog box opens, as shown in Figure 16-13.

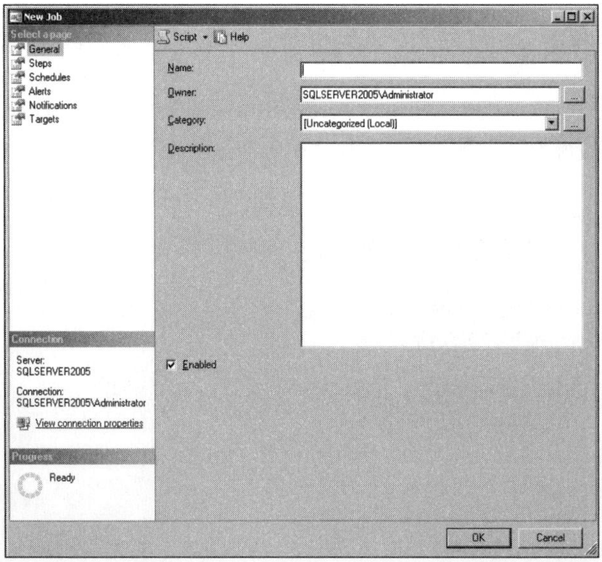

**Figure 16-13:**
The New Job dialog box.

4. **Give the new job a name and description, as shown in Figure 16-14.**

   You can leave the category as unclassified.

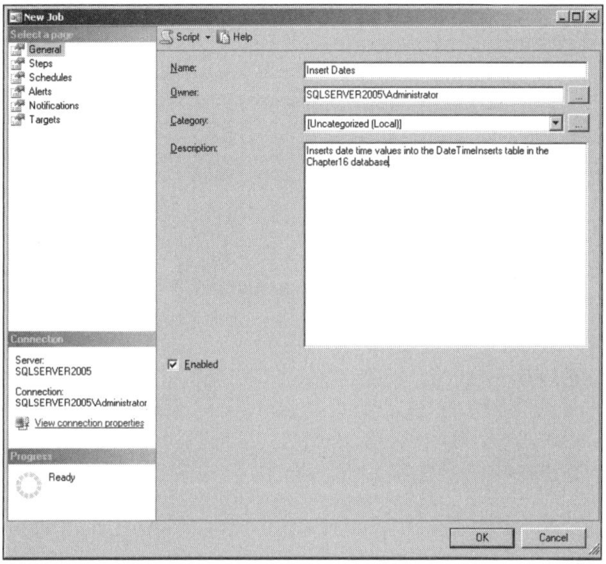

**Figure 16-14:**
Supplying a
name and
description
for the
new SQL
Agent job.

5. **Select Steps in the left pane of the New Job dialog box. In the right pane, click the Add button to add a new step (the only step in this example) to the job.**

The New Job Step dialog box displays as shown in Figure 16-15.

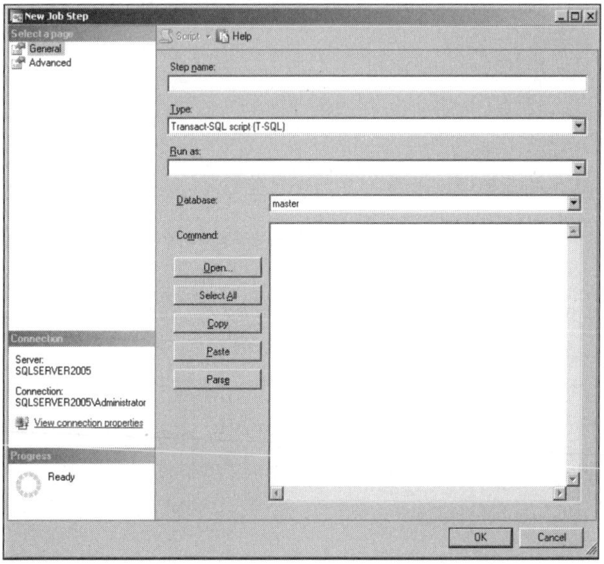

**Figure 16-15:**
The New
Job Step
dialog box.

6. **Give the step a name such as "Inserting a date value". In the code area, insert the following code:**

```
USE Chapter16

INSERT INTO DateTimeInserts (DateFromAgent)
  VALUES(GetDate())
```

7. **Click the OK button.**

You return to the New Job dialog box. In Figure 16-16, you can see that the new step has been added to the job.

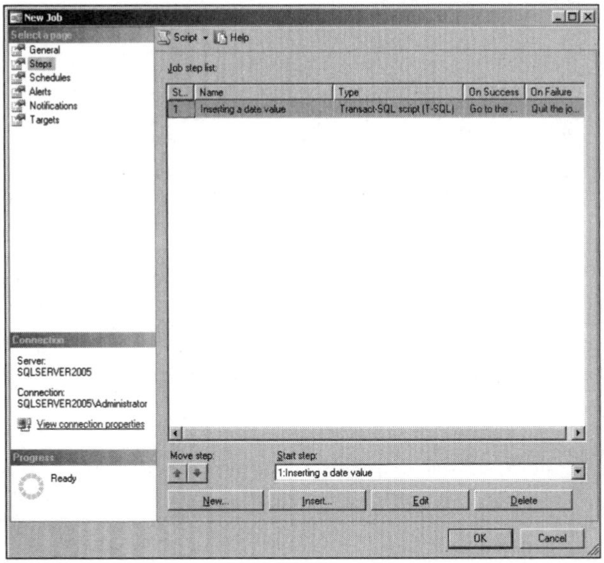

**Figure 16-16:**
A step added to the SQL Agent job.

8. **Click Schedules in the left pane of the New Job dialog box.**

9. **Give the schedule a name. Specify a schedule of every 1 minute and give the schedule a name, as shown in Figure 16-17. Click OK.**

You can have more than one schedule, so be sure that you use a unique name for each schedule.

In this example, you won't define alerts or notification for the job.

10. **Return to SQL Server Management Studio and run this code:**

```
USE Chapter16
SELECT *
FROM DateTimeInserts
```

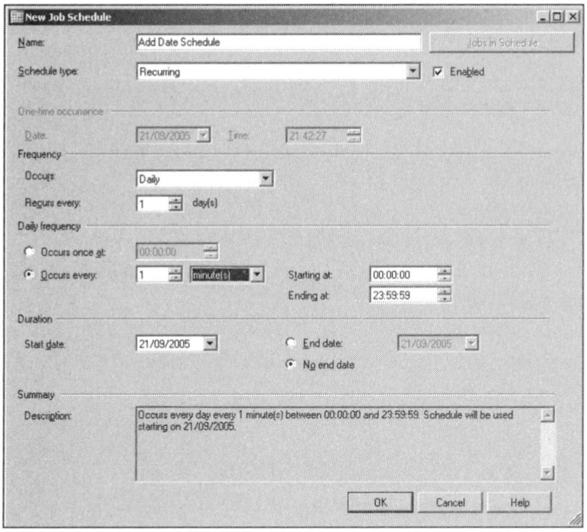


**Figure 16-17:** Defining a schedule for the SQL Agent job.

11. **Wait a few minutes and then execute the preceding `SELECT` statement again.**

    The appearance is similar to Figure 16-18, with several rows added to the `DateTimeInserts` table by the SQL Agent job.

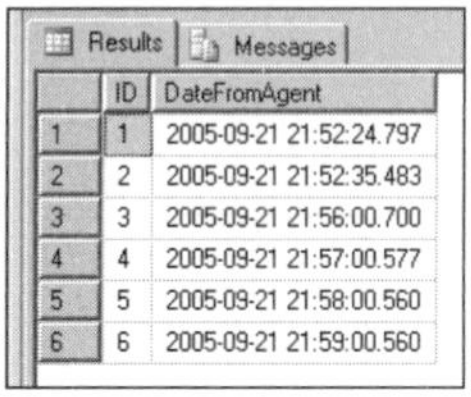

|  | ID | DateFromAgent |
|---|---|---|
| 1 | 1 | 2005-09-21 21:52:24.797 |
| 2 | 2 | 2005-09-21 21:52:35.483 |
| 3 | 3 | 2005-09-21 21:56:00.700 |
| 4 | 4 | 2005-09-21 21:57:00.577 |
| 5 | 5 | 2005-09-21 21:58:00.560 |
| 6 | 6 | 2005-09-21 21:59:00.560 |

**Figure 16-18:** Several rows added by the SQL Agent job to the `DateTimeInserts` table.

12. **To monitor the activity of SQL Agent jobs, expand the SQL Agent node, if necessary. Double-click the Job Activity Monitor icon.**

    The Job Activity Monitor opens. Figure 16-19 shows the appearance after the SQL Agent job has failed to run successfully.

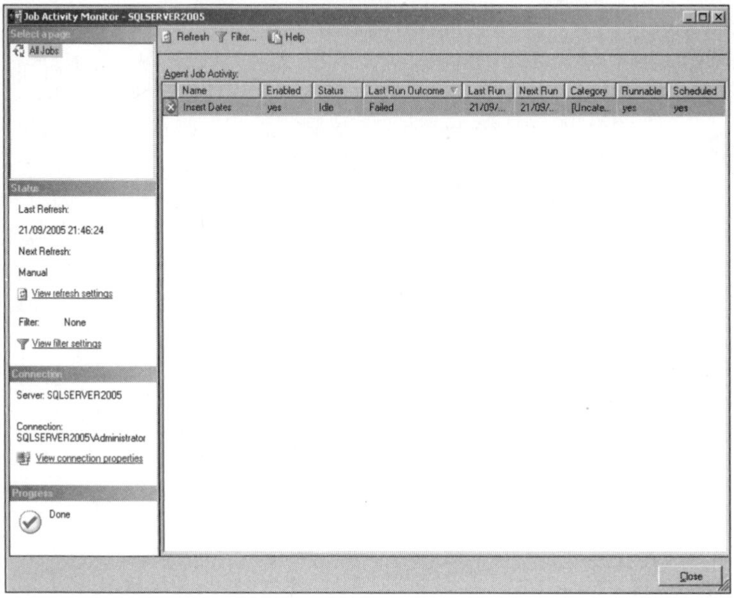

**Figure 16-19:**
The Job
Activity
Monitor.

13. **You can also check error logs. Expand the Error Logs node and double-click the Current log.**

The Log File Viewer opens. The appearance is similar to Figure 16-20.

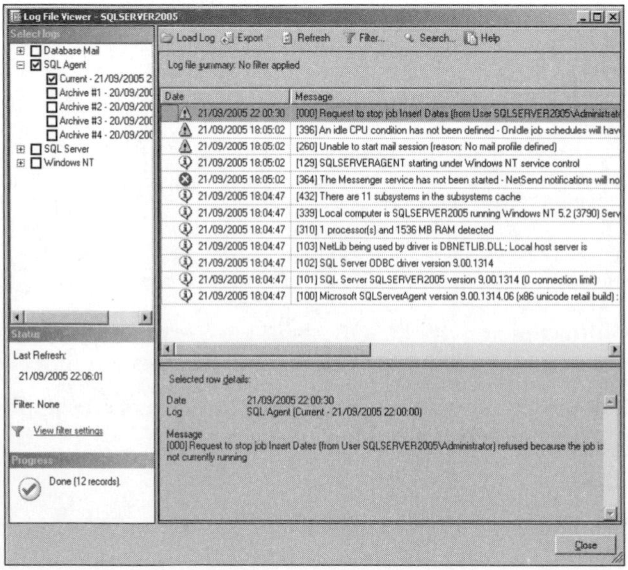

**Figure 16-20:**
Viewing SQL
Agent error
logs in Log
File Viewer.

# Creating a SQL Agent alert

At Step 9 of the preceding example, you could have added an alert or a notification to the SQL Agent job you created.

To add an alert to an existing job, follow these steps:

1. **Right-click the name of the SQL Agent job to which you want to add an alert and select Properties from the context menu.**

2. **Select Alerts in the left pane of the Job Properties dialog box.**

3. **Click the Add button.**

   The New Alert dialog box opens, as shown in Figure 16-21. The General tab allows you to give the alert a name, specify which database it applies to, and specify when the alert will be generated depending on criteria such as error severity or a specific error message.

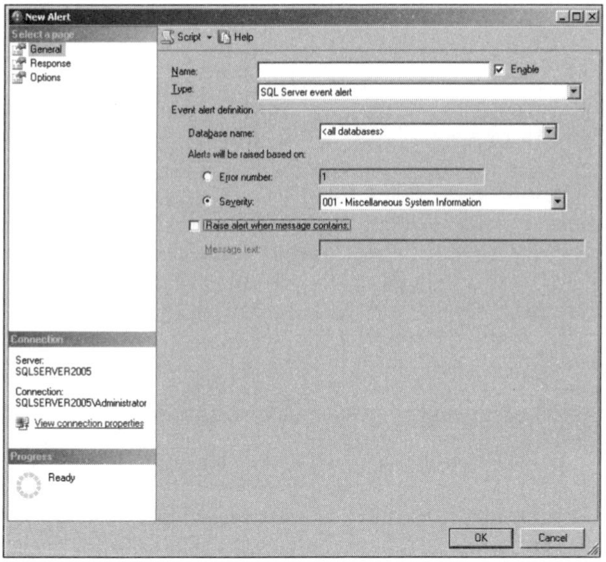

**Figure 16-21:** The General tab of the New Alert dialog box.

4. **Click the Response option in the left pane.**

   You then have the option to specify one or more operators (human beings) to be notified when an alert occurs.

5. **Click the Options option in the left pane.**

   You then have options of whether to include the error text in the alert.

# Using T-SQL with SQL Server Agent

You can control SQL Server Agent by using T-SQL code. Several system stored procedures are designed to help you work with SQL Server Agent.

I list a few of the several dozen stored procedures here:

- ✔ sp_add_alert
- ✔ sp_add_job
- ✔ sp_add_jobstep
- ✔ sp_add_schedule

Detailed consideration of how to use the full range of stored procedures to work with SQL Agent is beyond the scope of this chapter. To reference information, use SQL Server Books Online, which you can access by choosing Start⇨ All Programs⇨Microsoft SQL Server 2005⇨Documentation and Tutorials⇨ SQL Server Books Online.

# Using the Maintenance Plan Wizard

The Maintenance Plan Wizard is a tool that assists you in setting up automated maintenance tasks. Undercover, the Maintenance Plan Wizard creates SQL Server Agent jobs appropriate to what you want to do.

Use the Maintenance Plan Wizard to automate tasks such as the following:

- ✔ Reorganize data on data and index pages
- ✔ Compress data files and remove empty database pages
- ✔ Perform internal consistency checks on the data

To access the Maintenance Plan Wizard, you must have Agent extended procedures turned on. I show you how to do that earlier in this chapter (in the aptly named section, "Enabling SQL Agent extended stored procedures").

To access the Maintenance Plan Wizard, follow these steps:

1. **Open SQL Server Management Studio. Select a SQL Server Instance in Registered Servers. Right-click the desired instance and choose Connect⇨Object Explorer from the context menu.**

   The desired instance displays in the Object Explorer.

2. **Expand the Management node.**

3. **Select the Maintenance Plan node and right-click it. Select the New Maintenance Plan option from the context menu.**

   The New Maintenance Plan dialog box opens, which contains a text box so that you can specify a name for the maintenance plan that you're about to create.

4. **Enter a name.**

   A Toolbox containing several maintenance tasks displays with a large pane where you can define aspects of the maintenance plan. Depending on how you've configured SQL Server Management Studio, you see an appearance similar to Figure 16-22.

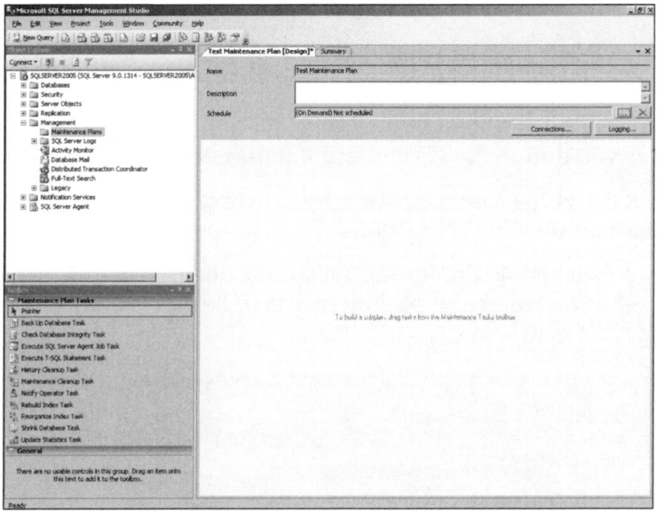

**Figure 16-22:** The initial appearance when running the Maintenance Plan Wizard.

You have a very large number of options available so that you can customize a maintenance plan. The next steps indicate the steps necessary to back up a database.

5. **To add a Backup Database Task, drag it to the design pane.**

6. **You need to define a connection for the Backup Database Task. To do that, double-click it the task.**

   The Backup Database Task dialog box opens.

7. **In the Back Up Database Task dialog box, specify which server you want to back up and which databases.**

   The appearance is similar to Figure 16-23.

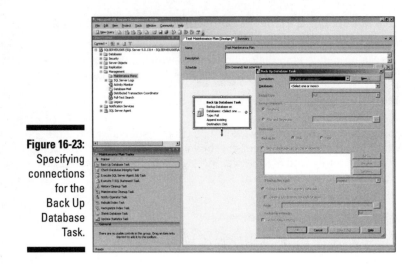

**Figure 16-23:**
Specifying
connections
for the
Back Up
Database
Task.

8. **After you define the server and databases to be backed up, click OK.**

9. **Click the ellipsis next to the Schedule text box (see the position of the mouse pointer in Figure 16-24).**

   The Job Schedule Properties dialog box opens, where you specify the schedule on which the backup task is to be carried out.

**Figure 16-24:**
The Job
Schedule
Properties
dialog box.

You build up a maintenance plan by using steps such as those described. The wizard is sufficiently powerful to allow you to fairly easily create complex maintenance plans.

I describe the use of the Maintenance Plan Wizard further in Chapter 18.

# Chapter 17

# Sending Information Using Notification Services

● ● ● ● ● ● ● ● ● ● ● ● ● ● ● ● ● ● ● ● ● ● ● ● ● ● ● ● ● ● ● ● ● ● ● ● ● ● ● ● ● ● ● ● ● ●

## In This Chapter

▶ Sending notifications and setting up events

▶ Creating a Notification Services application

● ● ● ● ● ● ● ● ● ● ● ● ● ● ● ● ● ● ● ● ● ● ● ● ● ● ● ● ● ● ● ● ● ● ● ● ● ● ● ● ● ● ● ● ● ●

**C**ommunication is a key to any successful business or successful life in the modern world. You need to be aware of what is going on. In various contexts, you need to know that something is happening, has happened, has changed, or whatever. And it's also very useful to be able to choose when you are informed about events that interest you. Some things you want to know about immediately; other events are less urgent. Notification Services in SQL Server 2005 is one approach to informing you of events to which you have subscribed.

One issue that any communication system must deal with is to target relevant information. The world is full of a deluge of information, only some of which is relevant to you. In Notification Services applications, you make a choice to opt in to subscriptions that interest you. You may not want to know that the stock price that you pinned your future hopes on has crashed, but it's certainly important to know if and when it happens. That kind of information is something that you need to know about straightaway, because you need to take action based on what has happened. For other information, being informed of events or situations on a scheduled basis, perhaps daily or even on the hour, is suitable.

You can use Notification Services to send notifications to thousands, even millions, of subscribers. To do that, you likely need to make use, as appropriate, of the scalability and availability features of SQL Server 2005 to ensure that your solution can cope with peak loadings and be available to subscribers globally throughout each 24-hour period.

# The Notification Services Approach

Notification Services is a platform, which is part of SQL Server 2005, and that can be used to build applications that produce and send notifications to subscribers. A *notification* is a message or piece of information that can be sent to a range of devices. A *subscriber* is a person who has expressed an interest in being notified of a specified range of events.

You can have notifications sent to a range of devices or media, depending on whether subscribers are mobile or are always logged on to a network. Examples include

- ✔ E-mail
- ✔ Mobile phone
- ✔ Personal Digital Assistant (PDA)
- ✔ Windows Messenger

## The basic steps

From the viewpoint of the persons subscribing to a SQL Server Notification Services application, the process appears like this:

- ✔ Users subscribe to one or more notifications offered to them, specifying the criteria of events that interest them and they also specify how and when they want to be notified.
- ✔ In response to chosen events, or at specified times, the subscribers are notified by using the medium (such as e-mail or mobile phone text messaging) selected when subscribing.

Your application collects events. *Events* can consist of individual pieces of information, perhaps delivered as XML files, relational data, or some aspect of business performance as measured by SQL Server 2005 Analysis Services.

Notification Services attempts to match events and subscriptions. When it finds a match, Notification Services generates a *notification*. The choice of delivery method made by a subscriber determines how the notification is formatted for delivery.

# New notification features in SQL Server 2005

Notification Services was added to SQL Server 2000 after the original release. Several features are new in Notification Services in SQL Server 2005:

✔ Installation of Notification Services is integrated into SQL Server 2005 setup.

✔ Management is integrated into SQL Server Management Studio.

✔ Subscribers can influence some queries through new functionality called *condition actions*.

✔ Notification Services applications can use an existing database.

✔ A new API, Notification Services Management Objects (NMO), allows you to create and manage Notification Services applications. It uses the `Microsoft.SqlServer.Management.Nmo` namespace.

✔ A new Analysis Services event provider (which I describe in the "Working with events" section).

✔ You can host the Notification Services engine in your own applications.

In the SQL Server Management Studio Object Explorer, you can carry out many tasks on Notification Services instances that previously could only be carried out from the command line. You can also use SQL Server Management Studio as an XML editor and T-SQL editor.

# How Notification Services works

You, or a developer colleague, create a notification application by using either of the two approaches described in the next paragraph. Notification Services hosts that application. The data and metadata for the application is hosted in SQL Server 2005.

You can create a Notification Services application in two ways:

✔ **Use two XML files:** An Application Definition file and an Instance Configuration file to specify the properties of the application.

These files provide Notification Services with the information it needs to respond appropriately to events, to construct notifications appropriately, and to distribute those notifications in the appropriate way that subscribers chose. See the "Application Definition and Instance Configuration Files" section, later in this chapter, for more information.

✔ **Create an application programmatically:** Using Notification Services Management Objects, NMO. I don't describe the use of NMO further in this book.

The internals of Notification Services consist of three parts:

✔ **Event provider:** This component responds to selected data events, which I describe in the next section.

✔ **Generator:** This component matches events with subscribers and subscriptions. Raw notifications are passed to the distributor.

✔ **Distributor:** The distributor converts and styles the raw notifications for the chosen output methods and distributes these final notifications to the relevant subscribers.

## *Working with events*

Notification Services has several standard *event providers*. Alternatively, you can create a custom event provider if the standard event providers don't provide the functionality you need. You use an event provider to detect whether or not an event of interest has occurred or not.

The standard event providers are the following:

✔ **File System Watcher:** This event provider watches a specified directory for the addition of an XML file to it. The XML file must have an .xml file extension. File System Watcher ignores non-XML files. You can define how locked XML files are handled. If a new XML file's security settings prevent the event provider from immediately accessing it, Notification Services monitors the file until it can be accessed.

The File System Watcher Event Provider can queue files when your application starts. This prevents files being missed due to the relevant buffer being full. It can also add a file to the queue if processing of the file fails. Before passing the XML to your application, it's validated against a W3C XML Schema document. After an XML file is processed, a .done extension and timing information is concatenated (or appended) to the original filename.

✔ **SQL Server:** Uses a T-SQL query to get data from a SQL Server database.

✔ **Analysis Services:** Uses an MDX (MultiDimensional Expression) query to retrieve data from an Analysis Services cube.

The Analysis Services Event Provider monitors an Analysis Services cube, in a way similar to the monitoring of a folder by the File System

Watcher Event Provider. Changes in the parts of the cube relevant to the MDX query are treated as events and notifications are generated.

The result set of an MDX query used in the Analysis Services Event Provider can have multiple dimensions. However, Notification Services can process only a flat rowset. You are responsible for ensuring that Notification Services can process the result of the query.

Whichever standard event provider you use, information is written to the events table.

# Application Definition and Instance Configuration Files

The Application Definition file and Instance Configuration files allow you to define key aspects of a Notification Services application. Each of these files is an XML file that allows you to declaratively create a Notification Services application.

As the names suggest, the Application Definition file contains the information that defines a Notification Services application and the Instance Configuration file contains information about how to configure a Notification Services instance.

## The Application Definition file

The Application Definition file allows you to define the following properties of a Notification Services application:

- ✔ Application version and history
- ✔ Definition of the application database (optional)
- ✔ Event class properties, such as names, schemas, and indexes
- ✔ Subscription class properties, such as names, schemas, rules, and indexes
- ✔ Notification class properties, such as names, schemas, content formatters, protocols, and delivery options
- ✔ Event provider properties
- ✔ Generator properties
- ✔ Distributor properties
- ✔ Operational settings

The application properties are specified by adding XML elements to the Application Definition file corresponding to these properties. The comments in the following skeletal Application Definition file indicate where to add elements, as you create a functioning Notification Services application.

```xml
<?xml version="1.0" encoding="utf-8" ?>
<Application xmlns:xsd="http://www.w3.org/2001/XMLSchema"
xmlns:xsi="http://www.w3.org/2001/XMLSchema-instance"
xmlns="http://www.microsoft.com/MicrosoftNotificationServices/ApplicationDefinit
          ionFileSchema">

  <!-- Version -->
  <!-- History -->
  <!-- Database Definition -->
  <!-- Event Classes -->

  <!-- Subscription Classes -->
  <SubscriptionClasses></SubscriptionClasses>

  <!-- Notification Classes -->
  <NotificationClasses></NotificationClasses>

  <!-- Event Providers -->

  <!-- Generator Settings -->
  <Generator>
    <SystemName>%SystemName%</SystemName>
  </Generator>

  <!-- Distributor Settings -->
  <Distributors>
    <Distributor>
      <SystemName>%SystemName%</SystemName>
    </Distributor>
  </Distributors>

  <!-- Application Execution Settings -->
  <!-- Important: At minimum, you should define
   a vacuuming schedule and turn off some or all
   distributor logging. -->

</Application>
```

To specify properties of the application database, you provide information inside the following XML structure:

```xml
<Database>
    <DatabaseName></DatabaseName>
    <SchemaName></SchemaName>
    <!--Multiple NamedFileGroup Elements are Allowed-->
    <NamedFileGroup>
        <FileGroupName></FileGroupName>
        <FileSpec>
```

```
            <LogicalName></LogicalName>
            <FileName></FileName>
            <Size></Size>
            <MaxSize></MaxSize>
            <GrowthIncrement></GrowthIncrement>
        </FileSpec>
    </NamedFileGroup>
    <LogFile>
        <LogicalName></LogicalName>
        <FileName></FileName>
        <Size></Size>
        <MaxSize></MaxSize>
        <GrowthIncrement></GrowthIncrement>
    </LogFile>
    <DefaultFileGroup></DefaultFileGroup>
    <CollationName></CollationName>
</Database>
```

You can add similar XML structures to an Application Definition file to specify the properties listed in the earlier bulleted list. Microsoft provides a template for a complete Application Definition file in the SQL Server Books Online.

## The Instance Configuration file

You use the Instance Configuration file to configure a Notification Services instance.

```
<?xml version="1.0" encoding="utf-8"?>
<NotificationServicesInstance
xmlns:xsd="http://www.w3.org/2001/XMLSchema"
xmlns:xsi="http://www.w3.org/2001/XMLSchema-instance"
xmlns="http://www.microsoft.com/MicrosoftNotificationServices/ConfigurationFileS
            chema">

<!-- Notification Services Instance Name -->
<InstanceName></InstanceName>

<!-- Database Engine Instance -->
<SqlServerSystem></SqlServerSystem>

<!-- Applications -->
<Applications>
 <Application>
  <ApplicationName></ApplicationName>
    <BaseDirectoryPath></BaseDirectoryPath>
   <ApplicationDefinitionFilePath></ApplicationDefinitionFilePath>
 </Application>
</Applications>

<!-- Delivery Channels -->
```

```
<DeliveryChannels>
 <DeliveryChannel>
  <DeliveryChannelName></DeliveryChannelName>
  <ProtocolName></ProtocolName>
 </DeliveryChannel>
</DeliveryChannels>

</NotificationServicesInstance>
```

The SQL Server 2005 Books Online gives details of the permitted values allowed in the XML structure.

# Chapter 18

# Maintaining a SQL Server System

*A*fter you set up a working SQL Server 2005 installation, your work is not over. As time passes, you need to carry out various maintenance tasks. How often you carry out tasks and which tasks you carry out depends on the situation in which you are running SQL Server 2005. Your needs are very different on a development machine from a production server on which your business depends.

One crucial task is the backing up of databases and log files. If you're running an Enterprise Edition database with large numbers of transactions on which your business crucially depends, you must be very sure that you are making frequent backups (as well as taking steps to ensure high availability).

## Using Maintenance Plans

SQL Server 2005 provides a visual way to carry out common maintenance tasks using SQL Server Management Studio. The visual designer (which is a limited version of the SQL Server Integration Services functionality discussed in Chapter 20) supports these tasks:

- ✔ Back up databases
- ✔ Check database integrity
- ✔ Execute SQL Server Agent jobs
- ✔ Execute T-SQL statements

✔ Clean up history

✔ Clean up maintenance

✔ Notify operators

✔ Rebuild indexes

✔ Reorganize indexes

✔ Shrink databases

✔ Update statistics

You can combine these tasks visually using the designer inside SQL Server Management Studio. You also have an option to extend maintenance plans inside the Business Intelligence Development Studio inside a SQL Server Integration Services package. However, if you extend a maintenance plan in that way, you can no longer modify it inside SQL Server Management Studio.

## Backing up

Making backups and being able to restore *successfully* from backups is one of the most important tasks that a database administrator has to carry out. Imagine a scenario where your company has thousands of employees who cannot access crucial data because your backups are corrupted (so that parts of the business grind to a halt) or where thousands of customer orders have been lost. If you allow yourself to get into that situation, you have a high chance of becoming a former employee. If you really foul up, the company could even stand a chance of becoming a former company. Impossible? Imagine you lost a week's orders because of corrupt backup tapes. The loss of cash flow and the costs of putting things right could sink some companies.

 If you're now feeling nervous about the whole issue of backing up and restoring, that's a good thing. Treat the whole activity with respect and treat it as important. Don't cut corners. Take time to get it right. Take time, also, to ensure that you can restore from backups. Regularly check that you can restore the backups on a test server. It's the only way to be absolutely sure!

You can back up by using T-SQL or you can use either the Maintenance Plan Wizard or the New Maintenance Plan options from the Object Explorer in SQL Server Management Studio.

To back up the `Chapter16` database, using the New Maintenance Plan option in the Object Explorer, follow these steps:

1. **Open SQL Server Management Studio. In the Registered Servers pane, select the desired SQL Server instance, right-click, and choose Connect➪ Object Explorer.**

   A node for the SQL Server instance displays in the Object Explorer.

2. **Expand the node for the desired SQL Server instance, expand the Management node, and then right-click the Maintenance Plans node and select New Maintenance Plan from the context menu.**

   The New Maintenance Plan dialog box displays, as shown in Figure 18-1.

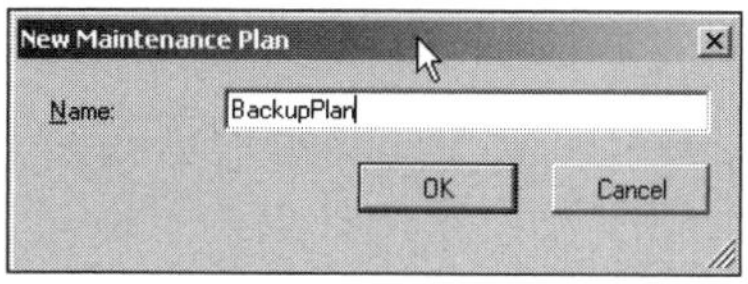

**Figure 18-1:**
Supply
a name for
the new
mainte-
nance plan.

3. **Supply a name for the plan, such as BackupPlan, and click OK.**

   The New Maintenance Plan dialog box closes.

4. **Supply a description for the BackupPlan maintenance plan.**

   Figure 18-2 shows the BackupPlan in SQL Server Management Studio. Notice the Toolbox on the left side of SQL Server Management Studio.

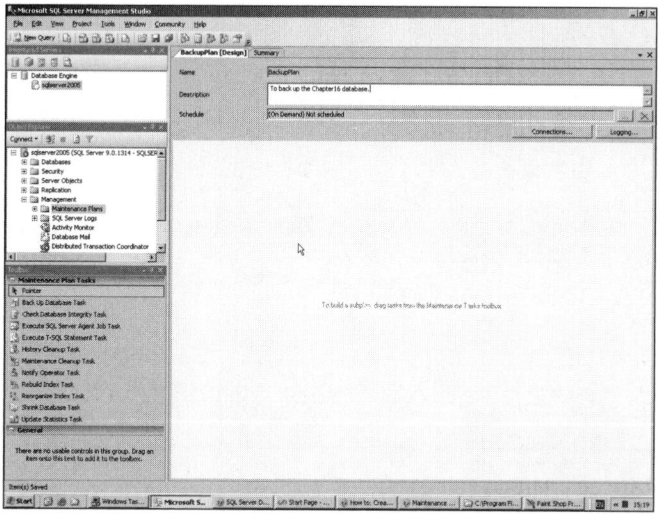

**Figure 18-2:**
Creating a
new mainte-
nance plan.

5. **Drag the Back Up Database Task shape from the Toolbox to the design surface.**

6. **Right-click the Back Up Database Task shape and select Rename from the context menu. Enter a name, such as Backup Chapter16 Database. Click outside the shape to confirm the edit of the name.**

7. **Right-click the Backup Chapter16 Database and select Autosize.**

   The appearance is similar to Figure 18-3. Notice the red X on the right indicating that configuration of the shape is not complete.

**Figure 18-3:**
The Backup
Chapter16
Database
shape after
renaming
and
autosizing.

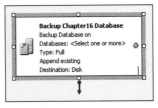

**Backup Chapter16 Database**
Backup Database on
Databases: <Select one or more>
Type: Full
Append existing
Destination: Disk

8. **Right-click the Backup Chapter16 Database shape and select Edit.**

   The Back Up Database Task dialog box opens, as shown in Figure 18-4.

**Back Up Database Task**

| | |
|---|---|
| Connection: | Local server connection | New... |
| Databases: | <Select one or more> |

Backup type: Full

Back up component
- ● Database
- ○ Files and filegroups:

Destination

Back up to: ● Disk   ○ Tape

○ Back up databases across one or more files:

Add...
Remove
Contents

If backup files exist: Append

● Create a backup file for every database
☐ Create a sub-directory for each database
Folder:
Backup file extension: bak
☐ Verify backup integrity

OK   Cancel   View T-SQL   Help

**Figure 18-4:**
The
Back Up
Database
Task
dialog box.

9. **Select an existing connection from the Connection drop-down menu to connect to a SQL Server instance.**

   If the desired connection is available from the drop-down menu, skip ahead to Step 13.

10. **Alternatively, you can click the New button to create a new connection.**

11. **In the New Connection dialog box that opens (shown in Figure 18-5), name the connection, specify the SQL Server instance name, and whether you connect with Windows Authentication or SQL Server Authentication, and then click OK after you have made the relevant choices.**

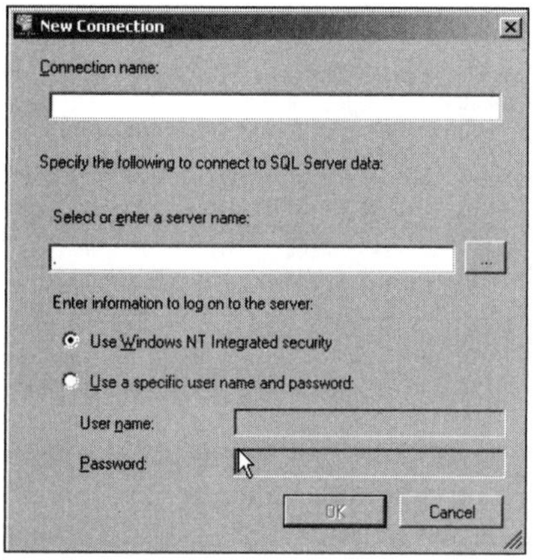

**Figure 18-5:**
The New
Connection
dialog box.

12. **After returning to the Back Up Database Task dialog box, select a SQL Server instance to connect to from the Connection drop-down menu.**

13. **In the Back Up Database Task dialog box, choose which database or databases you want to back up. See Figure 18-6.**

   Your choices are

   - All databases
   - System databases (`master`, `msdb`, and `model`)
   - All user databases
   - Specified databases

   In this example, select the `Chapter16` database to back up.

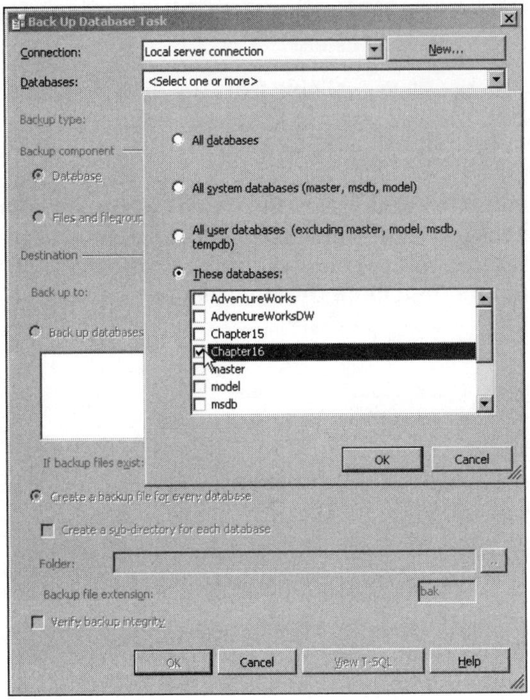

Figure 18-6:
Select one
or more
databases
to back up.

14. **Choose which type of backup you want to make. You have three options (Full, Differential, and Transaction Log), but choose Full for this occasion.**

    I discuss the backup options in the next section, "Different types of backup."

15. **Select if you want to back up to disk or tape. On this occasion, select Disk.**

16. **Select the Create a Backup File for Every Database radio button.**

17. **Click the Verify Backup Integrity check box.**

18. **To view the T-SQL that your choices created, click the View T-SQL button.**

    The Transact-SQL (Task Generated) dialog box opens (see Figure 18-7).

19. **Click Close in the Transact-SQL (Task Generated) dialog box. Click OK in the Back Up Database Task dialog box.**

    You are back on the design surface. The red X that indicated that the task wasn't fully configured should now be absent.

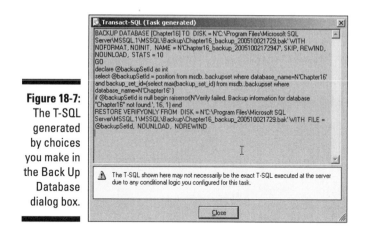

**Figure 18-7:**
The T-SQL
generated
by choices
you make in
the Back Up
Database
dialog box.

**20. Right-click the tab for Backup Plan and select Save Selected Items from the context menu to save the modified maintenance plan.**

You've created a maintenance plan. Now you need to create a schedule to run it on.

**21. Click the ellipsis (...) button to the right of the Schedule drop-down menu (which is currently grayed out).**

Note the position of the cursor in Figure 18-8.

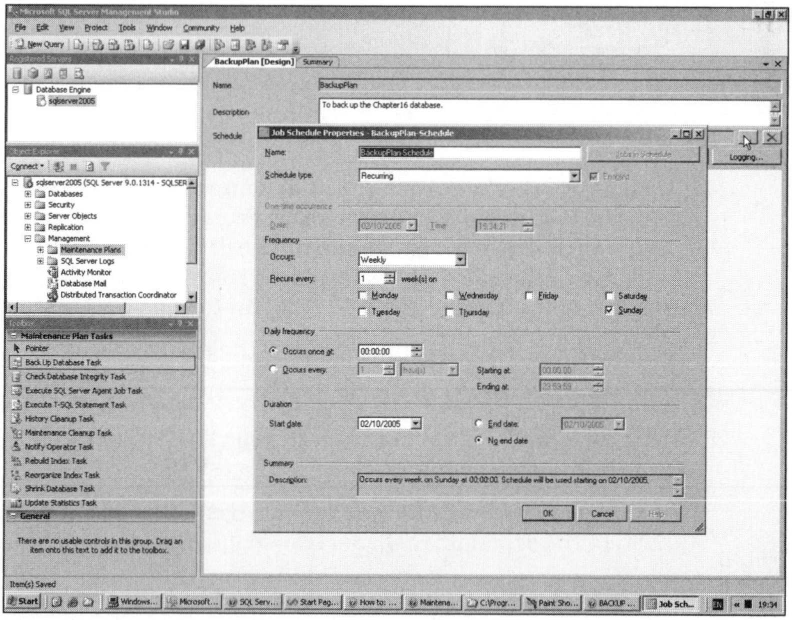

**Figure 18-8:**
The Job
Schedule
Properties -
BackupPlan
- Schedule
dialog box.

22. **You can modify the name of the schedule to aid easy identification, if you want.**

23. **Select how the schedule runs.**

    You have the following options (as shown in Figure 18-9):

    - Start automatically when SQL Server Agent starts
    - Start whenever the CPUs become idle
    - Recurring
    - One time

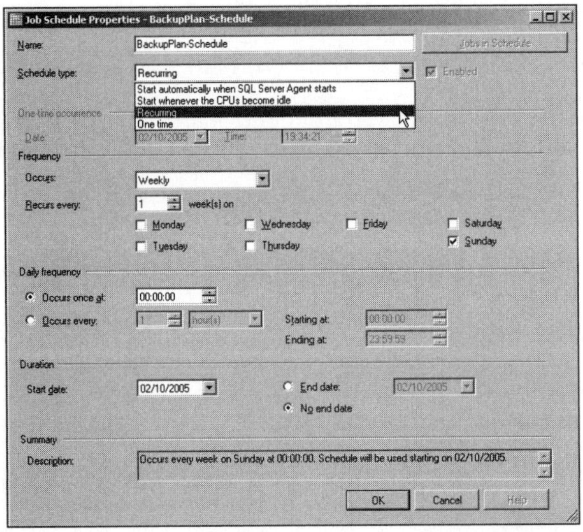

**Figure 18-9:**
Selecting when the SQL Server agent job runs.

24. **To create a schedule that runs at five minutes to midnight on Monday, Tuesday, Wednesday, Thursday, and Friday, select Weekly from the Occurs drop-down menu, and then check the check boxes for Monday, Tuesday, Wednesday, Thursday, and Friday. Finally, to specify the time that the job runs, enter 23:55:00 in the Occurs Once At control.**

    See Figure 18-10 for the appearance at the end of this step.

25. **Click OK to finish creating a schedule.**

26. **Right-click the BackupPlan tab and select Save Selected Items to save the maintenance plan together with its schedule.**

    If you expand the node for SQL Server Agent, you see that BackupPlan is added to the scheduled SQL Server Agent jobs, as shown in Figure 18-11.

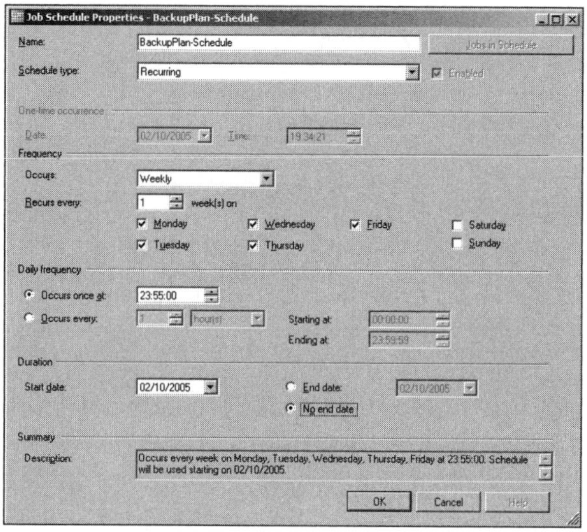

**Figure 18-10:** Specifying a schedule to run on five days each week.

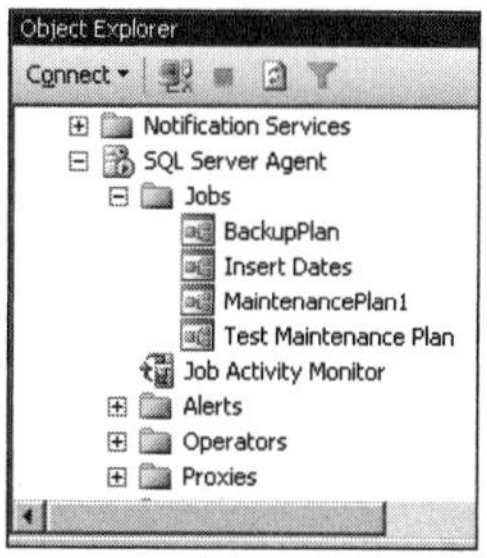

**Figure 18-11:** The Backup Plan maintenance plan added to SQL Server Agent jobs.

The BackupPlan maintenance plan is a very simple example. You would likely combine it with other maintenance tasks. To do that, simply drag the relevant tasks from the Toolbox to the design surface and connect the shapes by using the *precedence constraints* (blue or green lines) to show the order (precedence) in which to execute the tasks.

**REMEMBER**

The purpose of making backups is so that you can successfully restore data from them. Think about worst-case scenarios, such as a fire in the room or building where you run your SQL Server machine and also store the backups. Result? No live data and no backups either! Make sure that you have a plan to cope with these worst-case scenarios. Why? Because worst-case scenarios happen eventually to someone. If you're the unfortunate someone, be sure that you have a routine in place that lets you efficiently get the data up and running again.

## Different types of backup

In this section, I describe the types of backup you might consider using. There are three broad types of backup available to you:

- ✔ **Full:** Backs up the entire database together with the part of the transaction log that allows the database to be restored corresponding to the point in time that the full backup is made. A full backup can take up a lot of space on your storage media and takes longer than a full differential backup. Typically, a full backup is carried out on a regular schedule.

- ✔ **Full differential (often just called Differential):** Backs up data that has changed since the last full backup. A full differential backup takes up less media space than a full backup and is faster. A full differential backup is based on a full backup termed the *base backup*. When restoring from a full differential backup, you must restore its base backup first.

- ✔ **Transaction log:** Backs up the transaction log only. A transaction log backup uses less media space than a full backup and is also faster. When restoring from transaction log backups, you need a full backup as base and then the chain of transaction log backups in order to restore to a point of time or point of failure.

## Restoring from backups

It is a *major* disaster if you omit testing of the restore procedure, and then find that the backups are corrupt for the past week or two when a hard drive goes down on the live server.

 After you make a backup, or series of backups, make time to routinely test whether you can restore the data to a test server. It may not be practical with frequent backups to check every backup, but think through the consequences of going a day or week without detecting a fault in your backup tapes.

## Checking Error Logs

The maintenance plans described in the preceding section allow you to automate tasks that need to be carried out routinely. Part of your task in maintaining a SQL Server installation is to check for the occurrences of errors in log files.

To view SQL Server log files, follow these steps:

1. **Open SQL Server Management Studio and select the desired SQL Server instance in the Registered Servers pane. Right-click and choose Connect⇨Object Explorer.**

2. **Expand the Management node in the Object Explorer and expand the SQL Server Logs node.**

3. **Right-click the SQL Server Logs node and choose View⇨SQL Server Log, as shown in Figure 18-12.**

   Notice that you can choose to view SQL Server log files and Windows log files together.

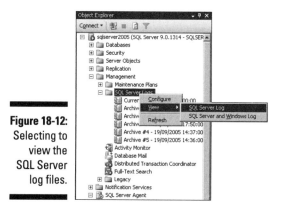

**Figure 18-12:**
Selecting to
view the
SQL Server
log files.

The Log File Viewer opens, as shown in Figure 18-13. By default, only the content of the current log displays.

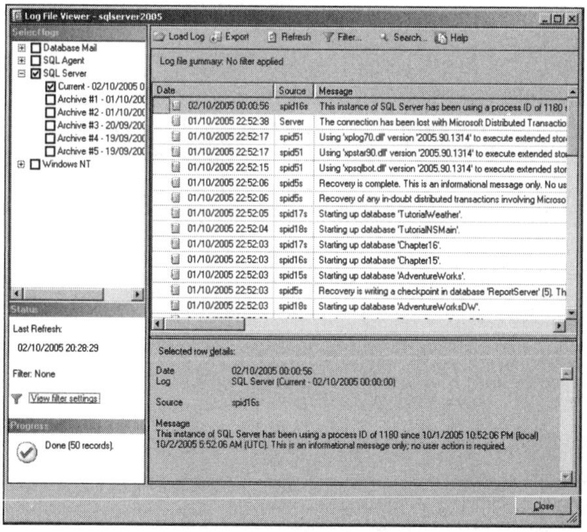

**Figure 18-13:**
The Log File
Viewer.

In a production server, the number of entries in a SQL Server log file can soon become enormous. Therefore, you need to filter the display to look for more serious events that may require some sort of intervention.

4. **To increase the number of entries in a development machine, select all logs. To filter the display, click the Filter button in the Log File Viewer window.**

   The Filter Settings dialog box opens (see Figure 18-14). You can filter by several criteria.

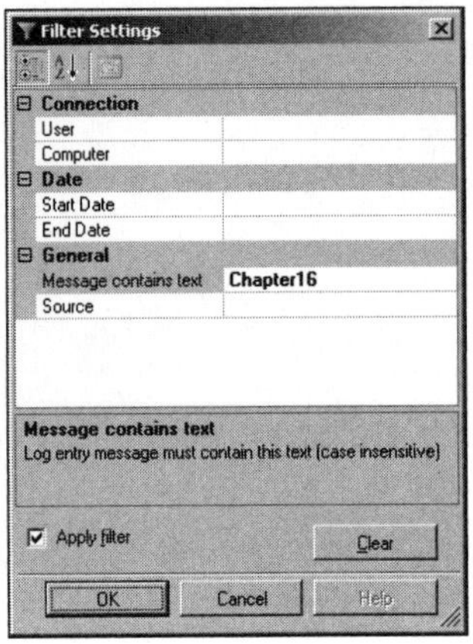

**Figure 18-14:**
The Filter
Settings
dialog box.

5. **To view all events for the Chapter16 database, enter** Chapter16 **(no spaces) in the Message Contains Text box.**

6. **Check the Apply Filter check box to apply the filter, and then click OK.**

   The filtered messages appear in the Log File Viewer, as shown in Figure 18-15.

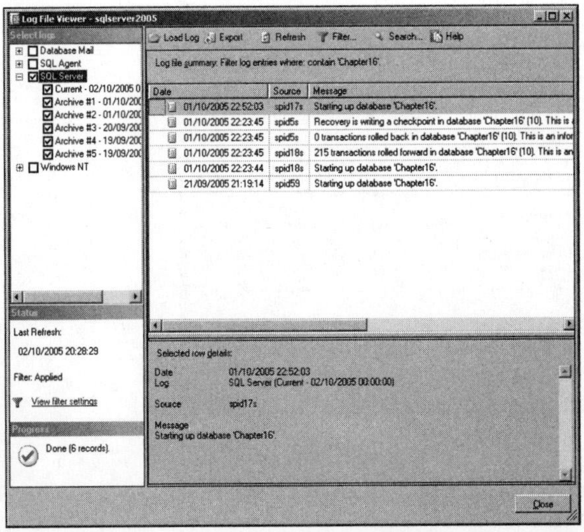

**Figure 18-15:**
Events
filtered for
Chapter16.

In real life, you would often be particularly interested in terms such as "error", "failure", or "severity".

7. **To filter for log entries containing the word "severity", click the Filter button; in the Filter Settings dialog box, edit the text in the Message Contains Text box to "severity", ensure that the Apply Filter check box is checked, and click OK.**

Figure 18-16 shows the results.

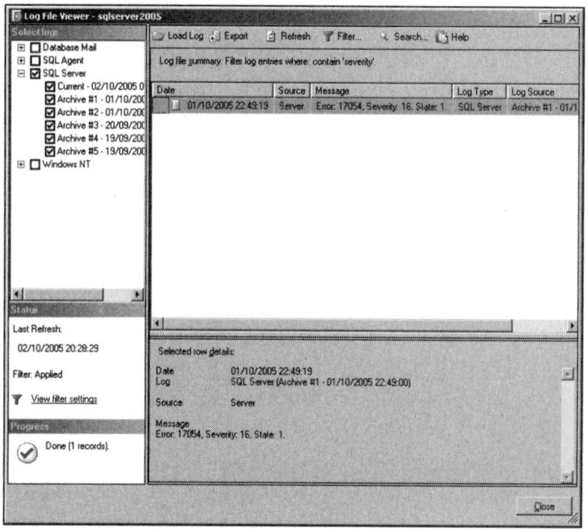

**Figure 18-16:** Entries filtered for the text severity.

8. **To export log files, click the Export button; in the dialog box that opens (shown in Figure 18-17), navigate to a directory where you want to save SQL Server log files, enter an appropriate name for the log file you want to export, and click Save.**

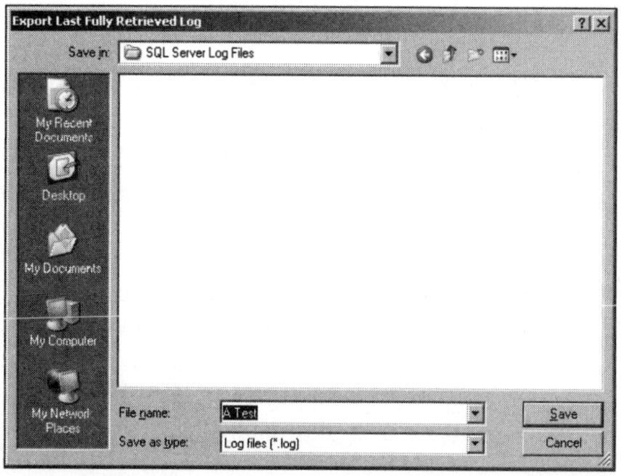

**Figure 18-17:** Selecting a location to export SQL Server log files to.

# Working with Indexes

An index in a database management system provides a way to access desired data, similar to the principles used in the index of a book. Apart from situations where the quantity of data is small, using an index is often an efficient way to find out where to look for a particular piece of information. A *database index*, similarly, contains information to assist the rapid retrieval of data by specifying the location of a desired row.

Designing indexes involves a number of trade-offs. In essence, you trade off speed of inserting data versus speed of retrieving data. The more indexes you add, the longer each INSERT or UPDATE statement takes to run because, when a row of data is inserted or changed, the corresponding index(es) also must be changed.

Over time, the changes made automatically to indexes by SQL Server when you insert, update, or delete rows can cause the indexes to become fragmented. A fragmented index performs less well. The need to defragment indexes means that, periodically, you need to rebuild or reorganize indexes to restore optimum performance.

You can find out how fragmented the indexes for a particular table are by following these steps:

1. **Open SQL Server Management Studio. Click the New Query button.**

2. **Create two variables to hold values representing the ID of the database and table that you are interested in.**

   ```
   DECLARE @db_id SMALLINT;
   DECLARE @object_id INT;
   ```

3. **Specify the database and table of interest:**

   ```
   SET @db_id = DB_ID(N'AdventureWorks');
   SET @object_id = OBJECT_ID(N'AdventureWorks.Person.
        Contact');
   ```

4. **Specify that you want to see the avg_fragmentation_in_percent column of sys.dm_db_index_physical_stats.**

   ```
   SELECT avg_fragmentation_in_percent
   FROM sys.dm_db_index_physical_stats (@db_id,
        @object_id, DEFAULT, DEFAULT, N'Detailed')
   ```

Figure 18-18 shows the percentage of fragmentation in the indexes for the Person.Contact table of the AdventureWorks database.

As you can see in Figure 18-18, these indexes have minimal fragmentation, so you don't need to rebuild or reorganize them.

To rebuild or reorganize the indexes for the `Person.Contact` table of the `Adventureworks` database in a maintenance plan, follow these steps:

1. **Open SQL Server Management Studio. Select the desired SQL Server instance in the Registered Servers pane. Right-click and choose Connect⇨Object Explorer.**

2. **Expand the Management node. Right-click Maintenance Plans and select New Maintenance Plan.**

3. **Give the maintenance plan the name `Reorganize_AdventureWorks_ Person_Contact_Index`.**

   You cannot use a space character or a period in the name.

4. **Drag a Reorganize Index Task to the design surface.**

5. **Right-click the Reorganize Index Task shape and select Edit from the context menu.**

   The Reorganize Index Task dialog box opens.

6. **Click the Databases drop-down menu. Select the These Databases radio button, and then select the Adventureworks check box, and then click OK.**

7. **From the Object drop-down menu, select Table.**

8. From the Selection drop-down menu, select the These Objects radio button, check the `Person.Contact` table (as shown in Figure 18-19), and then click OK.

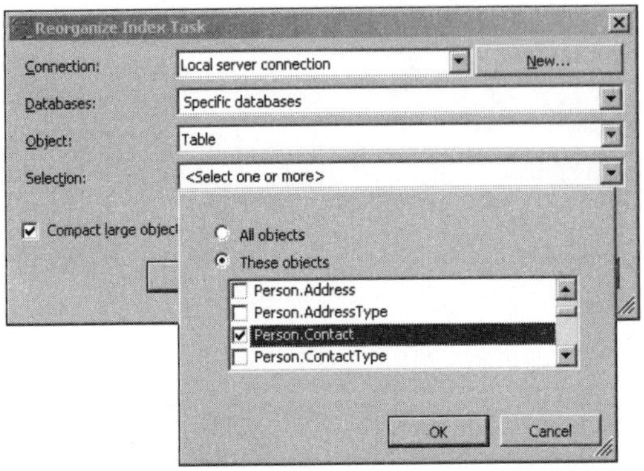

Figure 18-19:
Specify the
Person.
Contact
table.

9. In the Reorganize Index Task dialog box, click the View T-SQL button.

You see a dialog box with the following code:

```
USE [AdventureWorks]
GO
ALTER INDEX [AK_Contact_rowguid] ON [Person].[Contact]
      REORGANIZE WITH ( LOB_COMPACTION = ON )
GO
USE [AdventureWorks]
GO
ALTER INDEX [IX_Contact_EmailAddress] ON
      [Person].[Contact] REORGANIZE WITH (
      LOB_COMPACTION = ON )
GO
USE [AdventureWorks]
GO
ALTER INDEX [PK_Contact_ContactID] ON
      [Person].[Contact] REORGANIZE WITH (
      LOB_COMPACTION = ON )
GO
USE [AdventureWorks]
GO
ALTER INDEX [PXML_Contact_AddContact] ON
      [Person].[Contact] REORGANIZE WITH (
      LOB_COMPACTION = ON )
```

10. Close the dialog box that displays the T-SQL code. Click OK.

11. Optionally, you can create a schedule to run the maintenance plan on a regular schedule.

I show you how to create a schedule as part of backing up a database in the earlier section, "Backing up."

# *Halting Runaway Queries with the Dedicated Administrator Connection*

The Dedicated Administrator Connection is a new feature in SQL Server 2005. It is intended to allow a database administrator to be able to stop a SQL Server query that would in earlier versions of SQL Server require a restart of SQL Server. The Dedicated Administrator Connection is a reserved connection that is still available to an administrator even when CPU usage is maxing out.

The following example demonstrates how you can use the Dedicated Administrator Connection to terminate a runaway script:

```
DECLARE @myVariable int;
SET @myVariable = 1;
WHILE (@myVariable=1)
 BEGIN
 SELECT *
 FROM sys.databases
 -- Do nothing
 END
GO
```

It has a `WHILE` loop that continues endlessly querying for the databases on that SQL Server instance.

1. **Run the `WhileLoop.sql` script by using the SQLCMD utility, entering a command like the following at the command line (depending on where you have saved the T-SQL script):**

   ```
   sqlcmd -i "\\machinename\shareddocs\Chapter 18\
           WhileLoop.sql"
   ```

   The path to the script goes in the paired quotes.

2. **Press Enter and the script runs.**

   CPU usage rises to about 99 percent.

3. **To create a query by using the Dedicated Administrator Connection, click the Database Engine Query on the SQL Server Management Studio toolbar.**

4. **In the Connection dialog box, enter the following to connect to serverName:**

   ```
   ADMIN:serverName
   ```

   A query pane using the Dedicated Administrator Connection opens.

5. **Run the following query to find out which request is using up CPU time:**

```
SELECT session_id, cpu_time
FROM sys.dm_exec_requests
```

Figure 18-20 shows that a process with `session_id` equal to `61` is using a lot of CPU time. When you run the code, the `session_id` may be different.

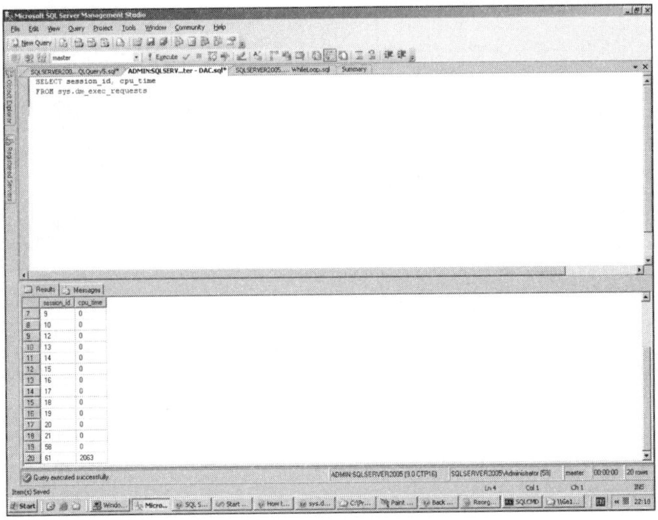

**Figure 18-20:**
Finding the session with high CPU usage.

6. **To kill the runaway process, run the following code from the Dedicated Administrator Connection query window:**

```
KILL 61
```

Using the Dedicated Administrator Connection in a similar way allows you to kill a runaway process or processes and avoid having to restart the SQL Server instance.

# Looking under the Covers with Profiler

SQL Server Profiler is a tool that allows you to examine the performance of a SQL Server instance.

To create a new *trace* (a record of events that take place in a SQL Server instance) and examine the characteristics of the endless loop script used in the preceding section, follow these steps.

1. **Open SQL Server Profiler by choosing Start⇨All Programs⇨Microsoft SQL Server 2005⇨Performance Tools⇨SQL Server Profiler.**

2. **Choose File⇨New Trace.**

3. **In the Connect to Server dialog box that opens, specify the desired SQL Server instance and authentication method.**

   The Trace Properties dialog box opens.

4. **On the General tab, specify a name for the trace and select a template from the Use the Template drop-down menu (as shown in Figure 18-21).**

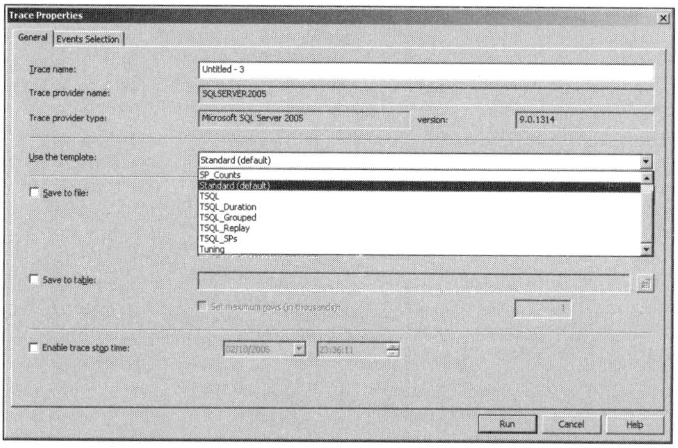

**Figure 18-21:** The General tab of the Trace Properties dialog box.

5. **On the Events Selection tab of the Trace Properties dialog box, shown in Figure 18-22, select which events to monitor in the trace you are creating.**

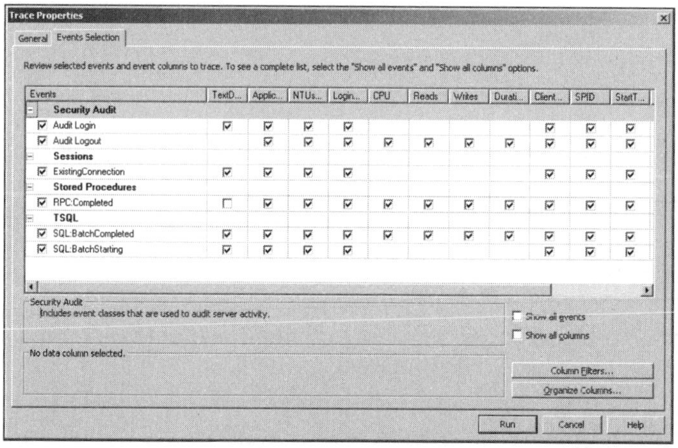

**Figure 18-22:** The Events Selection tab of the Trace Properties dialog box.

6. **Click Run to start running the trace.**

7. **Start the SQLCMD script (as described in the preceding section), and allow it to run for several seconds.**

8. **Stop the SQLCMD script (also described in the preceding section) by using the Dedicated Administrator Connection (or pressing Ctrl+C in the command window).**

9. **Click the Stop button in SQL Server Profiler to stop the trace.**

10. **Look for a line showing SQLCMD in the `ApplicationName` column (as shown in Figure 18-23).**

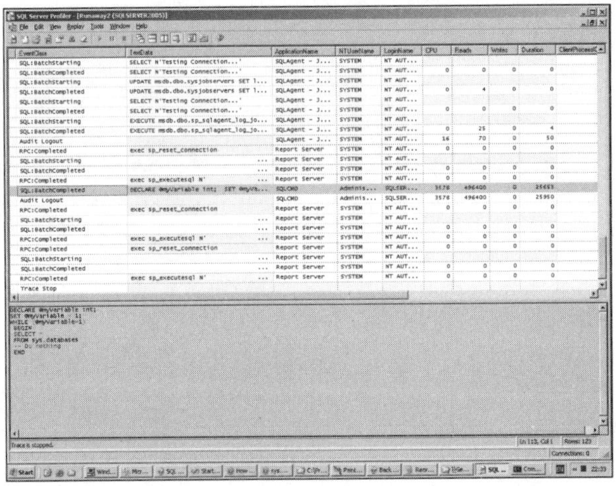

Figure 18-23:
The
SQLCMD
script's
characteris-
tics shown
in SQL
Server
Profiler.

11. **Examine the values in the CPU, Reads, and Duration columns.**

    As you can see in Figure 18-23, the SQLCMD script, as you already knew, consumed a lot of CPU time.

You can save traces to disk or load traces with specified characteristics to run for particular purposes.

# Using the Database Engine Tuning Advisor

The Database Engine Tuning Advisor, a new tool in SQL Server 2005, allows you to test the effect on performance of loads applied to a database. It replaces the Index Tuning Wizard that was in SQL Server 2000. The function-ality of the Database Tuning Advisor goes beyond the capabilities of the Index Tuning Wizard.

To start the Database Engine Tuning Advisor and connect to a selected instance of SQL Server, follow these steps:

1. **Choose Start➪All Programs➪Microsoft SQL Server 2005➪ Performance Tools➪Database Engine Tuning Advisor.**

2. **In the Connect to Server dialog box, enter the name of the desired SQL Server instance and specify the appropriate means of authentication.**

   Figure 18-24 shows the appearance when Database Engine Tuning Advisor opens.

You can select databases whose response to workload you want to examine.

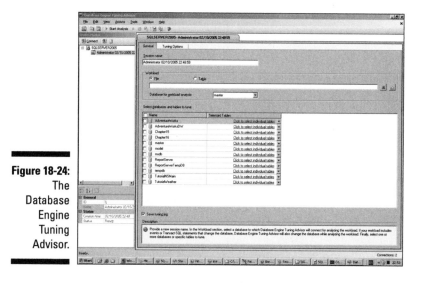

**Figure 18-24:**
The
Database
Engine
Tuning
Advisor.

# Chapter 19

# Working with Multiple Servers

*I*n this chapter, I introduce two topics — replication and SQL Server 2005 Service Broker — that you'll often use in a scenario where you have multiple instances of SQL Server. Each feature of SQL Server 2005 allows you to send information between instances of SQL Server. How and when you use these features differ significantly, as I show you in this chapter.

Replication is important in many business scenarios where you and colleagues need to work with multiple copies of the same information. For simple situations where data is not changing fast and/or the volumes of data are small, you might simply choose to send a copy of the database between business sites. In many real-life business situations, however, such an approach isn't fast enough, granular enough, or reliable enough. So you need a better way to keep different copies of your company's data up to date and synchronized. Replication is one solution.

Service Broker is designed so that you can build a new type of messaging application that allows asynchronous communication from inside a SQL Server instance. Asynchronous processing of messages inside multiple instances of SQL Server 2005 means that processing may be deferred until, for example, CPU utilization is low and also allows communication when one instance is not available at the time of initially sending a message. Asynchronous messaging avoids slowing response times in the SQL Server instance at times when load is higher. If synchronous processing of messages takes place at times of high CPU load, then the whole server can slow down. You can look at asynchronous processing as a way of making better use of CPU cycles over a day.

# Replication Overview

A common business scenario is that you need to have information available at multiple sites. For example, the head office may replicate business data to several regional offices. Or a regional office may want to replicate data to sales personnel in the field who use SQL Server Mobile Edition.

It is important that the various copies of the data say the same thing. The problem is how to keep the copies saying the same thing. More precisely, for them to differ slightly at some points in time is acceptable, but at other points you need to know that the copies of the data are consistent with each other.

## Replication jargon

A lot of jargon is used in relation to the process of replication. The following list contains definitions of some commonly used terms:

- **Article**: A database object that you replicate.
- **Distributor:** The server that contains the distribution database. In a production setting, snapshots are typically stored on the distributor.
- **Filtering:** The process of limiting what data is sent to a subscriber.
- **Publisher:** The server that contains the data to be replicated. Each publisher has only one associated distributor.
- **Subscriber:** A principal to which data is replicated. You can use SQL Server 2005 Express Edition or SQL Server Mobile Edition as a subscriber.

SQL Server 2005 supports the following types of replication:

- **Merge:** Typically used for bidirectional replication. Subscribers often need to change data and merge it back, when online, to the publisher.
- **Snapshot:** Distributes data at specified moments in time. Does not monitor the data for updates. At synchronization, the entire snapshot is sent to subscribers.
- **Transactional:** After initial synchronization, using a snapshot, data changes at the publisher are distributed to the subscribers in close to real time.

# Replication enhancements in SQL Server 2005

SQL Server 2005 provides you with many enhancements in several categories, some of which I list here:

✔ **Security:** Security is more granular; you no longer need to run replication under the context of SQL Server Agent. If you change a password, you can now do it in one place. To make use of the new security features replication scripts, you must upgrade from SQL Server 2000 and SQL Server 7.0.

✔ **Manageability:** You can manage replication from SQL Server Management Studio. There is a new Replication Monitor.

✔ **Availability:** The ability to make schema changes to published tables. Peer-to-peer transactional replication.

✔ **Programmability:** Replication Management Objects (RMO) provide a new managed code programming model.

✔ **Mobility:** Merge replication can be carried out over HTTPS.

✔ **Scalability and performance:** Performance is improved and solutions are more scalable.

✔ **Updatable transactional subscription:** Can now handle updates to large data types at a subscriber.

✔ **Heterogeneous data:** You can publish data by using transactional and snapshot replication from an Oracle publisher.

# Security for replication

Because the reason for using replication is, typically, to share important business data, you need to fully secure the replication process in your company. Replication security builds on existing Windows security and SQL Server security.

To implement a fully secure replication configuration, you must give careful thought to the following aspects of security:

✔ **Authentication:** Verify that a principal is who or what it claims to be.

✔ **Authorization:** Control access of an authenticated principal to resources such as a table in a database.

   ✔ **Encryption:** Convert data to a form that can be read only by the intended recipient, often decoded by means of a key.

   ✔ **Filtering:** Filter the data available to a subscriber.

Authentication and authorization are used to control access to servers that participate in a replication process and to control access to replicated database objects. Appropriate authentication and authorization rely on the following aspects of security:

   ✔ **Agent security:** Use the replication agent security model appropriately.

   ✔ **Administration roles**: Use the appropriate server and database roles for setup, maintenance, and processing of replication.

   ✔ **Publication Access List (PAL):** Grants access to a replication publication. The PAL is an access control list for replication.

Replication does not directly encrypt data held in tables or sent across a network. To encrypt data during replication, use a transport layer encryption process — for example, Virtual Private Network (VPN), Secure Sockets Layer (SSL), or IP Security (IPSEC).

Appropriate filtering also forms part of a well-thought-out security configuration for replication. SQL Server 2005 supports two types of filtering: row and column. For example, if you replicate sales information to a field salesperson, you would likely omit data from other sales representatives or territories. Similarly, if you're replicating human resources information to a branch office, you might include contact information but omit sensitive information about salary and other contract terms. If you replicate information to a partner company, you might explicitly share only information that has a value of Yes in a `SharedInformation` column.

# Replicating Your Data

In this section, I show you some aspects of the process of replicating data. In the space available for the topic, I can describe some key information only.

## Setting up a publisher and distributor

A publisher is a computer on which you publish data that is to be replicated.

To set up a computer as a publisher, follow these steps:

1. **Open SQL Server Management Studio. Select the desired SQL Server 2005 instance in the Registered Servers pane. Right-click and choose Connect⇨Object Explorer.**

2. **Right-click the Replication node. Select Configure Distribution from the context menu.**

   Despite the name suggesting that you can configure distribution only, you can use the Configure Distribution Wizard for the following purposes (as shown in Figure 19-1):

   - Configure the server as a distributor.

   - Configure the server as a publisher with the distributor on the same server.

   - Configure the server as a publisher with the distributor on another server.

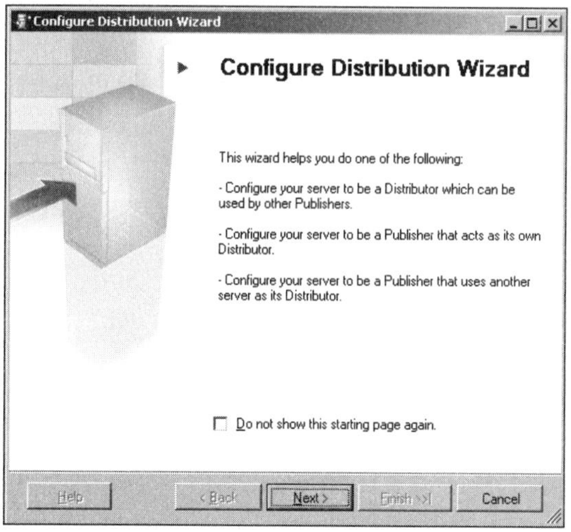

**Figure 19-1:**
The opening
screen
of the
Configure
Distribution
Wizard.

3. **Click Next.**

   On the following screen, you have two options. The first is to configure the current server as distributor. The second is to specify that the current server is to be a publisher only and use an already configured distributor. See Figure 19-2.

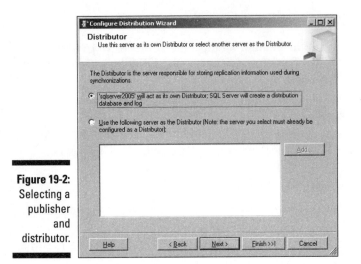

**Figure 19-2:**
Selecting a
publisher
and
distributor.

4. **Select the option where the current server is distributor. Click Next.**

5. **On the Snapshot Folder screen (see Figure 19-3), specify the location to store snapshots. Specify a network location and click Next.**

   I have chosen a shared folder on a machine whose name is SQLServer2005.

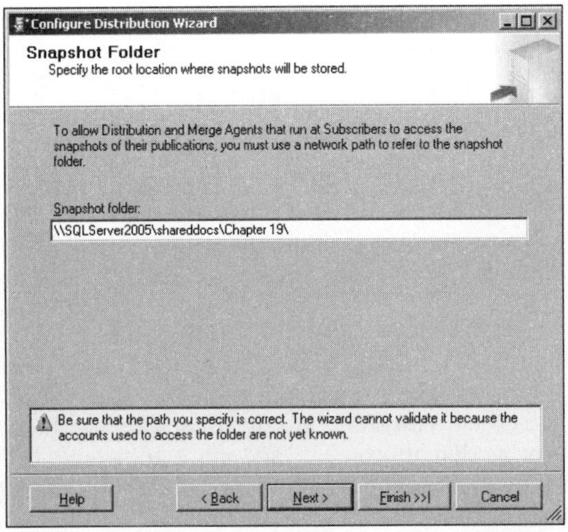

**Figure 19-3:**
Specifying
a location
where
snapshots
are stored.

6. **On the Distribution Database screen, specify the name of the distribution database, the location of the distribution database file, and the distribution database log file, and then click Next.**

In this case, I have accepted the default values. See Figure 19-4. A distribution database stores changes until they can be replicated to subscribers.

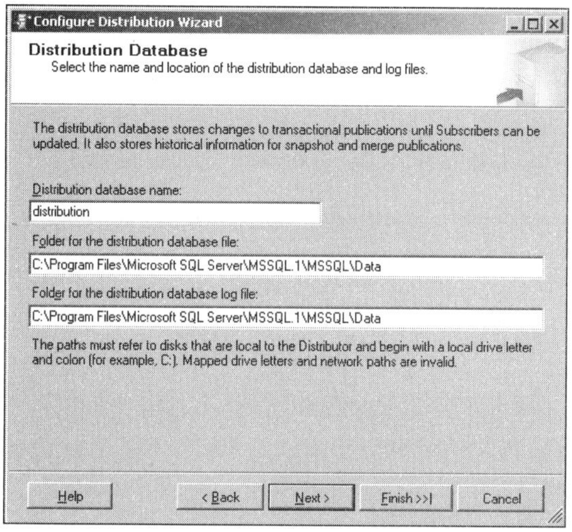

**Figure 19-4:**
Naming the
distribution
database
and
selecting its
location.

On the Publishers screen, which appears next, you can add other publishers that can use the distribution database.

**7. To add other publishers, click the Add button, as shown in Figure 19-5.**

You can add a SQL Server publisher or an Oracle publisher. In this example, I did not add another publisher.

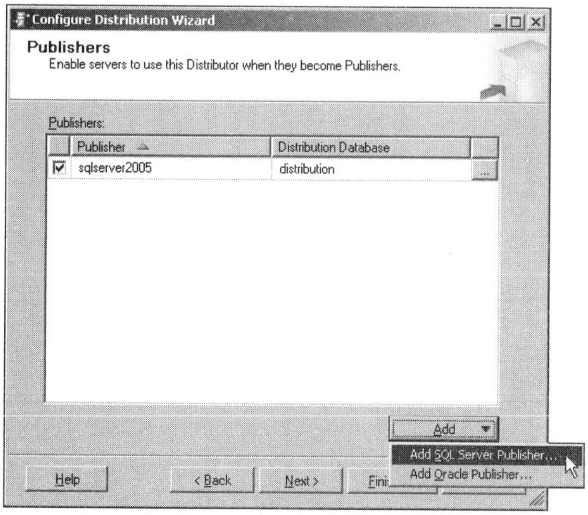

**Figure 19-5:**
Adding an
additional
publisher
to use the
distribution
database.

8. **Click Next to move to the Wizard Actions screen; leave the Configure Distribution check box checked (see Figure 19-6), and then click Next.**

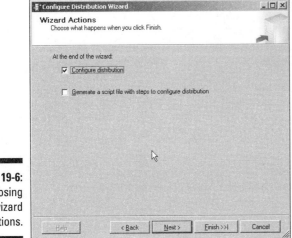

**Figure 19-6:**
Choosing
the wizard
actions.

9. **On the Complete the Wizard screen, review the choices you have made (see Figure 19-7).**

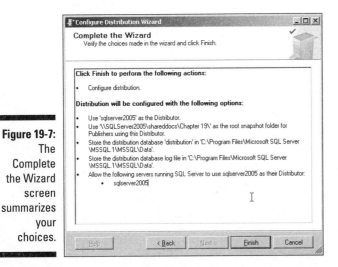

**Figure 19-7:**
The
Complete
the Wizard
screen
summarizes
your
choices.

10. **If you need to modify some aspect of the wizard, click Back; if you're satisfied that the wizard will do what you intended, click Finish.**

When you click Finish, the wizard proceeds to configure the distributor and the publisher. When completed, you see an appearance like Figure 19-8.

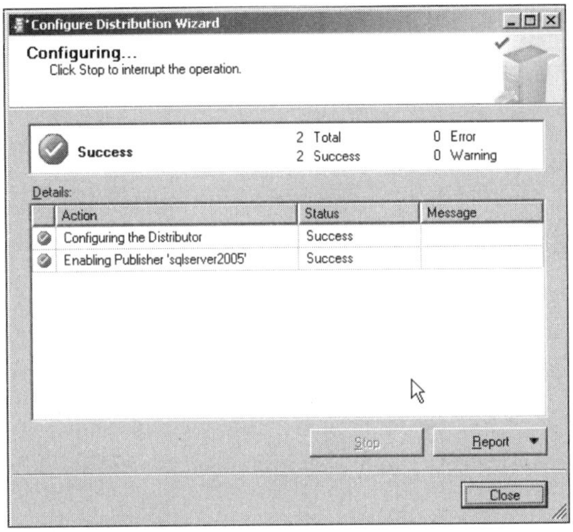

**Figure 19-8:**
A suc-
cessfully
configured
distributor
and
publisher.

**11. Click Close.**

Now that you've configured the publisher and distributor, new options are available to you on the context menu when you right-click the Replication node in the Object Explorer (see Figure 19-9).

**Figure 19-9:**
The context
menu for a
configured
publisher
and
distributor.

**12. From the context menu, select Launch Replication Monitor.**

The Replication Monitor opens. See Figure 19-10.

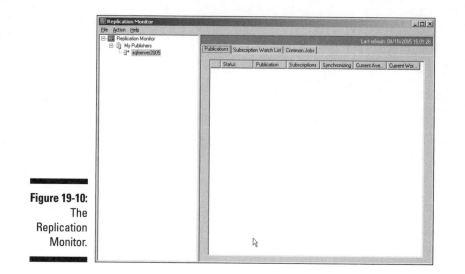

**Figure 19-10:**
The
Replication
Monitor.

Now you need to create a database to be replicated. To create a database called Chapter19ForReplication, follow these steps:

1. **Click the Database Engine Query button in SQL Server Management Studio.**

2. **Create a new database, Chapter19ForReplication.**

   ```
   CREATE DATABASE Chapter19ForReplication
   ```

3. **Create a Messages table and insert some sample data into it.**

   ```
   USE Chapter19ForReplication
   CREATE TABLE Messages
   (MessageID timestamp,
     Message varchar(1000))

   INSERT INTO Messages (Message)
    VALUES ('Hello World!')
   INSERT INTO Messages (Message)
    VALUES ('This is a second message.')
   ```

4. **Confirm that the sample data can be retrieved.**

   ```
   SELECT *
   FROM Messages
   ```

To create a matching database on another machine (the database that you're replicating data into), follow these steps:

1. **Create a new query in SQL Server Management Studio, ensuring that you're connecting to the SQL Server instance that you want to replicate data to.**

2. **Create a database, `Chapter19AsSubscriber`.**

```
CREATE DATABASE Chapter19AsSubscriber
```

3. **In that database, create a `Messages` table.**

```
USE Chapter19AsSubscriber
CREATE TABLE Messages
  (MessageID timestamp,
   Message varchar(1000))
```

4. **Confirm that the `Messages` table on that machine is empty.**

```
SELECT *
FROM Messages
```

## Creating a new publication

Now that the publisher is configured and you have a database to replicate and a database to replicate into, you create a new publication. Follow these steps:

1. **In the Object Explorer, expand the Replication node.**

2. **Right-click the Local Publications node and select New Publication from the context menu.**

   The New Publication Wizard opens. Figure 19-11 shows the options available to you.

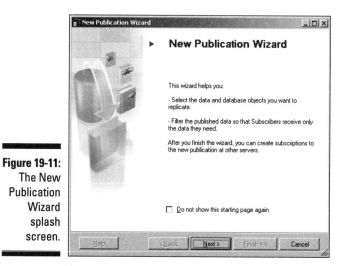

**Figure 19-11:** The New Publication Wizard splash screen.

3. **Click Next. On the Publication Database screen, select the `Chapter19ForReplication` database, as shown in Figure 19-12.**

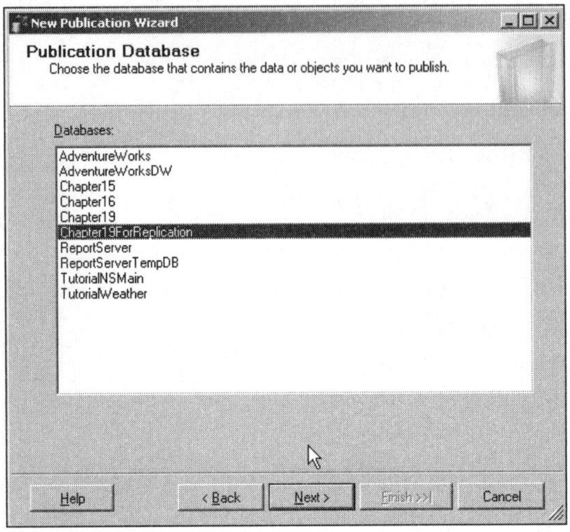

**Figure 19-12:**
Selecting
a database
to be
published.

4. **Click Next. On the Publication Type screen, select Snapshot Publication, as shown in Figure 19-13.**

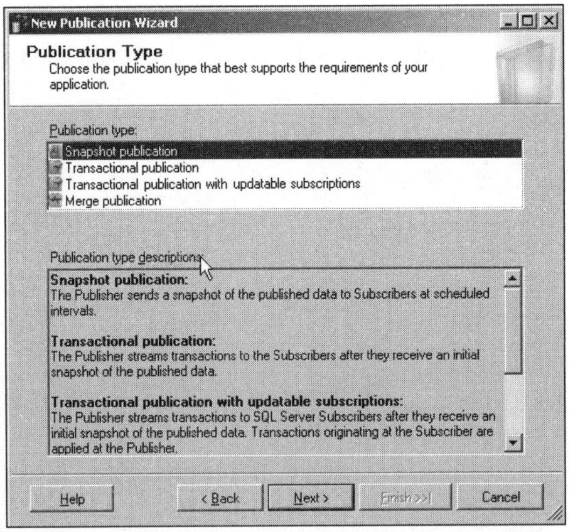

**Figure 19-13:**
Selecting
the type of
replication
to use in the
publication.

5. **Click Next. On the Articles screen, expand the Tables node and check the Messages table, as shown in Figure 19-14.**

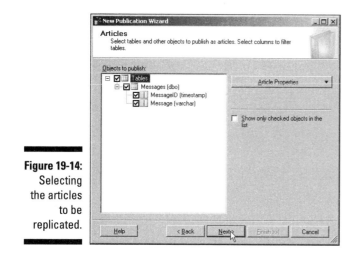

**Figure 19-14:**
Selecting
the articles
to be
replicated.

6. **Click Next. You are shown the Filter Table Rows screen. In this example you don't need to filter rows, so click Next.**

7. **On the Snapshot Agent screen, check the Create a Snapshot Immediately option, as shown in Figure 19-15.**

   Creating a snapshot allows you to replicate straightaway. If you don't create a snapshot in this step, you have to wait until a schedule snapshot is created.

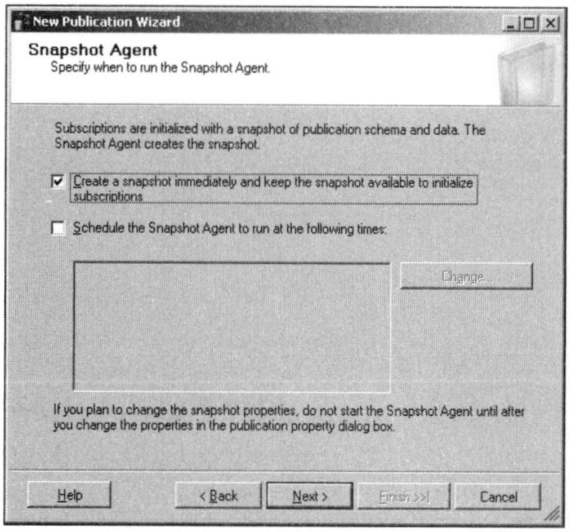

**Figure 19-15:**
Creating a
snapshot
of the
`Chapter`
`19For`
`Repli-`
`cation`
database.

8. **Click Next. On the Agent Security screen, click the Security Settings button.**

   The Snapshot Agent Security dialog box opens (as shown in Figure 19-16).

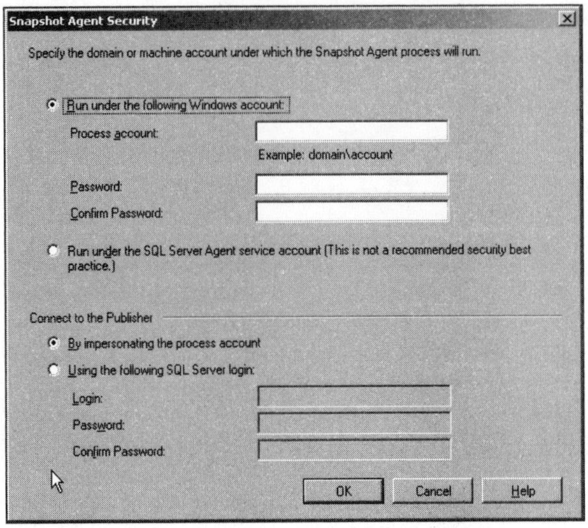

**Figure 19-16:**
Choosing an
account to
use with the
publication.

9. **For simplicity in running this example, choose the SQL Server Agent Account. Click OK. When you return to the Agent Security screen, click Next.**

10. **On the Wizard Actions screen, ensure that the Create the Publication check box is checked and click Next.**

11. **On the Complete the Wizard screen, name the publication A Test Publication and click Finish.**

    The Creating Publication screen shows the steps in creating the publication. When each has succeeded, you see an appearance similar to Figure 19-17.

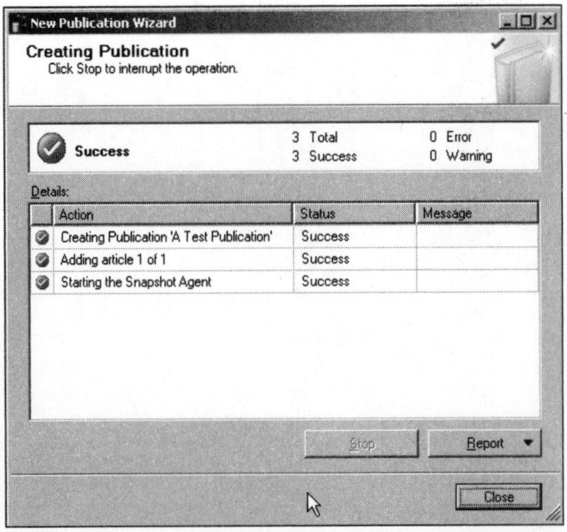

**Figure 19-17:**
Success
creating the
A Test
Publication
publication.

12. **Click Close.**

13. **In the Object Explorer, if necessary, expand the Local Publications node.**

    Notice that a new publication has been created, as shown in Figure 19-18.

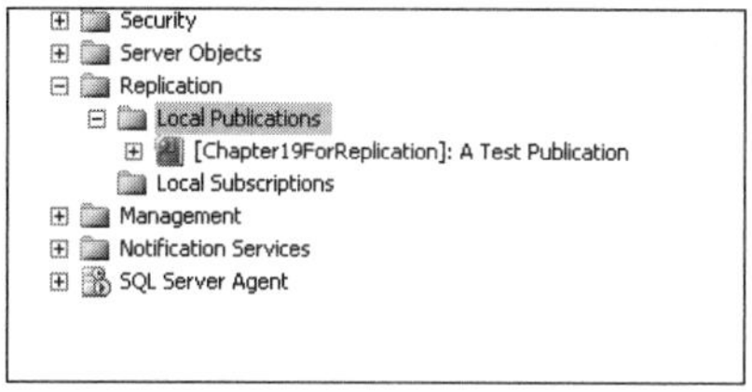

**Figure 19-18:**
A new
publication
has been
added in the
Object
Explorer.

In Replication Monitor, the newly created publication displays.

Now that you have created a publication, you can subscribe to it.

## Creating a subscription

To create a subscription, you would normally do so on another machine. Follow these steps.

1. **Open SQL Server Management Studio. In the Registered Servers pane, select another SQL Server 2005 instance. Right-click and choose Connect➪Object Explorer.**

   Alternatively, you can switch to the other machine and run SQL Server Management Studio there. That is the approach I take in the following steps.

2. **In the Object Explorer, expand the Replication node. Right-click on the Local Subscriptions node and select New Subscriptions from the context menu.**

   The New Subscription Wizard opens, as shown in Figure 19-19.

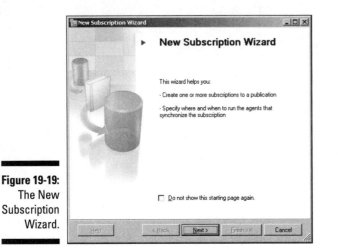

**Figure 19-19:**
The New
Subscription
Wizard.

**3. Click Next.**

The Publication screen opens, as shown in Figure 19-20. Because the machine has no publications, an error message displays on the Publication screen.

**Figure 19-20:**
An error
displays
if there are
no local
publications.

**4. In the Publisher drop-down menu, select <Find SQL Server Publisher> if you have no other publications of which the instance of SQL Server is aware. Type the name of the server that is the publisher — in my case, the machine name is SQLServer2005. Click Connect.**

You return to the Publication screen, but now you can choose a publication, as shown in Figure 19-21. You can see A Test Publication that you created earlier.

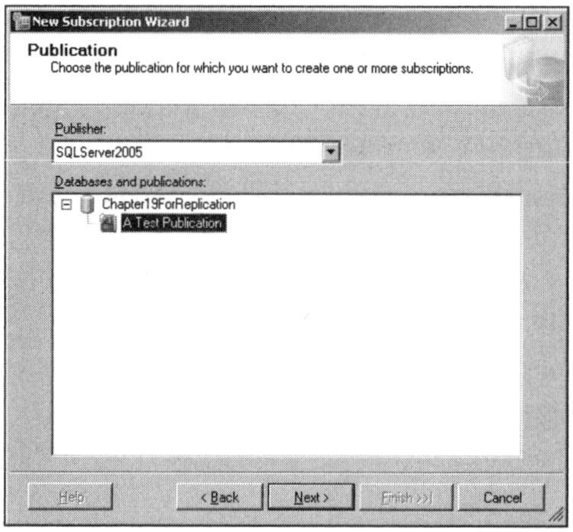

**Figure 19-21:**
You can now choose a publication on the Publication screen.

5. **Be sure A Test Publication is highlighted, and then click Next.**

6. **On the Distribution Agent Location screen that's displayed, select the Pull Subscription option and click Next.**

   The distribution agent can run on the subscriber or distributor. In this case, it runs on the subscriber and generates a pull subscription. If it runs on the distributor it generates a push subscription.

7. **On the Subscribers screen, select the `Chapter19AsSubscriber` database from the Subscription Database drop-down menu, as shown in Figure 19-22, and click Next.**

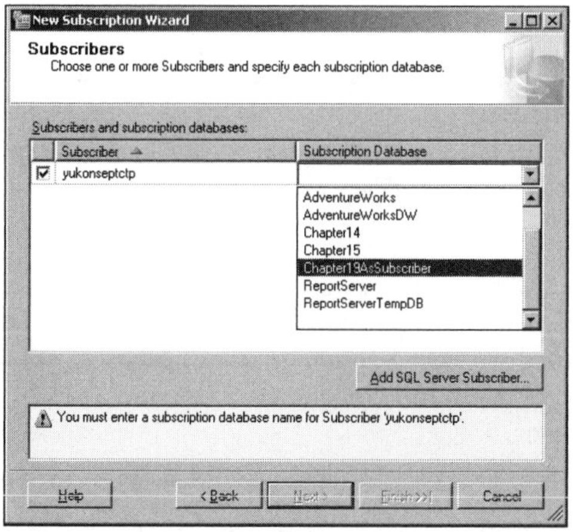

**Figure 19-22:**
Selecting the subscription database, `Chapter 19AsSubscriber`.

8. **On the Distribution Agent Security screen, click the ellipsis button and select to run as SQL Server Agent (not recommended in a production setting). Click Next.**

9. **On the Synchronization Schedule screen, select Run on Demand Only from the Agent Schedule drop-down menu. Click Next.**

10. **On the Initialize Subscriptions screen, select Immediately from the Initialize When drop-down menu. Click Next.**

11. **On the Wizard Actions screen, ensure that the Create Subscription(s) check box is checked. Click Next.**

12. **Review your choices on the Complete the Wizard screen (shown in Figure 19-23), and then click Finish.**

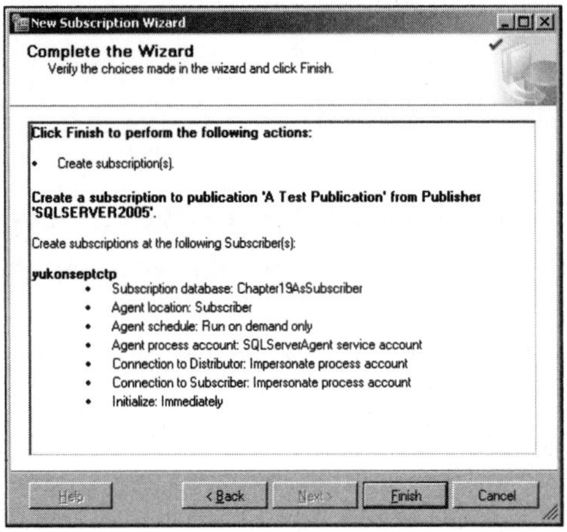

**Figure 19-23:** Review the choices you made about the new subscription.

The Creating Subscription(s) dialog box shows success, as shown in Figure 19-24.

If you see an error at this point, one possible cause is that you omitted to create a snapshot.

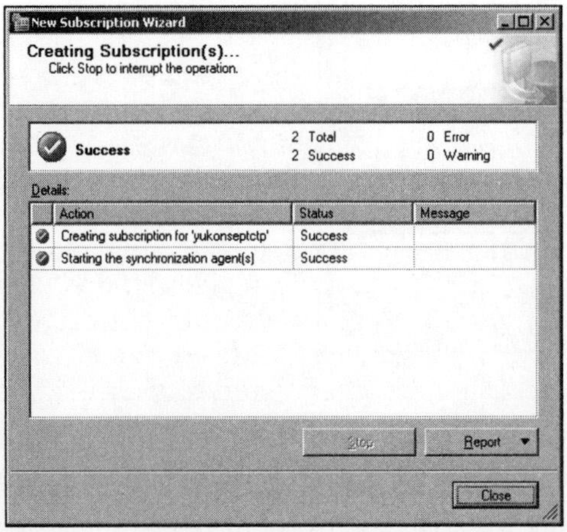

**Figure 19-24:** A new subscription created successfully.

13. **On the publisher machine, confirm that Replication Monitor recognizes the subscription, as shown in Figure 19-25.**

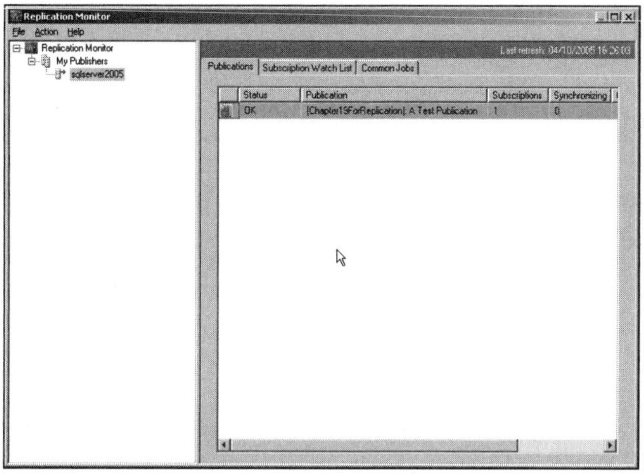

**Figure 19-25:**
The new subscription recognized in the Replication Monitor on the publisher machine.

14. **Run the following code on the subscriber machine to show the data replicated to the subscriber machine.**

```
USE Chapter19AsSubscriber
SELECT *
FROM Messages
```

You now see the two sample rows from the publisher displayed in the Chapter19AsSubscriber database.

# Introducing Service Broker

SQL Server 2005 Service Broker is a new feature in SQL Server 2005. Service Broker is a platform for building asynchronous queued distributed database applications. Service Broker is intended to allow you to create a new type of messaging application that is based on an instance of SQL Server 2005. Service Broker allows you to create transaction-based messaging applications.

What kind of things is Service Broker useful for? Imagine a situation where you have an order entry application that uses SQL Server 2005 and a shipping application that also uses SQL Server 2005. Messages have to pass reliably between the applications. High reliability is crucial because you don't want a scenario where a customer places an order, you acknowledge the items are ordered, but they're never shipped. Asynchronous communication may be acceptable in at least some scenarios, because you don't necessarily need to ship instantly. And of course, in some situations, you can't possibly ship immediately — such as when you're out of stock.

Service Broker is part of the SQL Server 2005 database engine. You can look at a normal SQL Server table as a type of queue — some applications add a row or rows to the table, one or more other applications can take data from the table. As I hope you can see, a message queue has similarities.

Service Broker, because it is in the SQL Server 2005 database engine, has the same benefits as the operations of SQL Server itself. It has high availability and high scalability. Service Broker transactions are written to the SQL Server transaction logs, so you have minimal chance of losing data. If you use database mirroring, when a SQL Server goes down, your data and messages are processed on the mirroring server as if nothing had happened (after a short pause).

When you back up a SQL Server instance that hosts a Service Broker application, then the data and messages relating to Service Broker back up, too.

## Queues

Queues, if they are well managed, can help get things done. But not all queues are equally well managed. Compare a supermarket with multiple queues (and you don't know which is best to process) and an airport queue with a single queue for all passengers who are waiting to check in. A properly ordered queue is important in order to process messages efficiently and reliably.

Related messages also need to be processed appropriately. For example, two different queue readers simultaneously processing two messages from the same conversation could lead to data corruption. Service Broker removes that risk by taking a lock on a group of messages (called a *dialog group* or *conversation group*). All messages in that dialog group are pulled from the queue by one queue reader and processed appropriately as a group.

In Service Broker, you typically have multiple reader queues. This is important in order to achieve good scalability. The dialog group locks help ensure that related messages are processed in the correct order.

Queues are first-class database objects in SQL Server 2005. In addition, new extensions to T-SQL in SQL Server 2005 allow you to manipulate queues from T-SQL.

## Messages

Service Broker is based on messages and offers advantages over some traditional messaging approaches.

When delivering messages, it can be necessary to retry delivery. Similarly, the route that a message takes can vary. This means that messages may enter a queue at the receiving end in a different order from which they were sent out. Service Broker can preserve the ordering of messages so that messages that are sent out first are *processed* first. Service Broker guarantees correct processing order in the following situations:

- ✔ Across transactions
- ✔ Across sending threads
- ✔ Across receiving threads

Service Broker does that by using dialogs. Dialogs in Service Broker have these characteristics:

- ✔ Guaranteed delivery.
- ✔ Support one-way or two-way dialogs.
- ✔ Sent so messages are received exactly once. Service Broker keeps retrying until the message is received once.
- ✔ Messages are processed in order.
- ✔ Dialogs are persistent. A dialog can survive the restarting of one of the servers taking part in the dialog.
- ✔ A dialog is a logical connection process rather than a physical connection process.

## Behind the scenes

So far, I have described Service Broker in terms of the functionality that you see as a database developer. In this section, I briefly describe what happens in Service Broker to achieve that functionality.

A dialog between two instances of Service Broker has dialogs with this set of *logical* characteristics:

- ✔ Exactly once delivery
- ✔ In order delivery
- ✔ Uses encryption and authentication

However, in reality, two instances of Service Broker have no direct physical network connection. The underlying transport protocol has these characteristics:

- ✔ Efficient binary message format
- ✔ Built on TCP/IP
- ✔ Bidirectional and multiplexed (multiple dialogs going across a single connection), best efforts protocol

In ways analogous to how the Internet is "reliable" despite the possibility that any packet of data can be lost, so Service Broker ensures reliability at a logical level while the underlying transport protocol can, for practical reasons, only have a best-efforts aim.

Another assumption in Service Broker is that an application is running that is able to process messages in a queue. Server Broker uses a process called *activation* to ensure that messages that arrive in a queue (essentially a table in a SQL Server database) are then processed. For example, if messages from a queue are processed by a particular stored procedure, Service Broker checks whether the stored procedure is running. If it's not running, then Service Broker starts the relevant stored procedure and the message is processed.

Another aspect of activation in Service Broker is that the performance of a stored procedure is measured against the number of messages arriving in the relevant queue. If too many messages are arriving too fast for a single copy of the stored procedure to keep up, then an additional copy of the stored procedure is started. In principle, the number of copies of the stored procedure that are running is adjusted upwards to cope with the number of messages arriving in the queue. However, you can specify a maximum number of copies of the stored procedure to run.

## Security

Because Service Broker communicates asynchronously, you can't use connection-oriented security. After all, the two applications at the two ends of a dialog may never run at the same time. The approach used in Service Broker is a private key/public key pair.

In test situations you can turn encryption off, with the following clause:

```
WITH ENCRYPTION = OFF
```

# Part VI

# Using SQL Server Business Intelligence (BI) Services

The 5th Wave    By Rich Tennant

I told Russell he should data model before we go any further.

Miss Claudia Schiffer, please.

## In this part . . .

1 introduce you to the Integrate, Analyze, Report paradigm that allows you to combine data from various
sources, analyze it and report on it with one SQL Server
2005 solution.

I show you how to use the Business Intelligence Development Studio to create projects using SQL Server Integration Services, Analysis Services, and Reporting Services.

# Chapter 20

# SQL Server Integration Services

- - - - - - - - - - - - - - - - - - - - - - - - - - - - - - - - - - - - - - - - - - - - - - - - - - -

## In This Chapter

▶ Finding out about business intelligence

▶ Using an ETL approach with Integration Services

▶ Exploring the Business Intelligence Development Studio

▶ Going through the Import/Export Wizard

▶ Creating an Integration Services project

▶ Deploying an Integration Services project

- - - - - - - - - - - - - - - - - - - - - - - - - - - - - - - - - - - - - - - - - - - - - - - - - - -

*B*usiness intelligence is one of the key new emphases of SQL Server 2005. One of the aims of any installation of SQL Server 2005 is to provide information that is relevant to the financial and other operations and performance of a business. At one level, you can use T-SQL queries or applications built on T-SQL or the CLR (Common Language Runtime) to process data in an almost infinite number of ways. In SQL Server 2005, Microsoft has put a lot of effort into supporting developers in manipulating and displaying information in ways that are particularly relevant to overall business activity and performance. *Business intelligence* refers to the processing of data in these ways to create information that relates to business performance.

In this chapter, I introduce you to SQL Server 2005 Integration Services, one of the three aspects of Microsoft's Business Intelligence paradigm:

✔ Integrate (SQL Server Integration Services — the topic of this chapter)

✔ Analyse (SQL Server Analysis Services — Chapter 21)

✔ Report (SQL Server Reporting Services — Chapter 22)

Business intelligence, based on SQL Server 2005 business intelligence functionality, is a significant focus of the upcoming Office 12 product suite. However, because Office 12 is at an early stage of development at the time of this writing, I don't cover integrating Office with SQL Server 2005 Business Intelligence applications in this book.

# Overview of Business Intelligence

SQL Server 2005 has made huge improvements in the support for Business Intelligence compared to SQL Server 2000. The all-new, more scalable and powerful SQL Service Integration Services replaces Data Transformation Services from SQL Server 2000. A new programming model in SQL Server 2005 Analysis Services enables you to make improvements in how you process data in Analysis Services cubes. New functionality has been added to that available in SQL Server 2000 Reporting Services.

You can view the SQL Server 2005 business intelligence workflow as the following sequence:

- **Integrate:** Bringing relevant data together with Integration Services.
- **Analyze:** Analyzing the content of data, using Online Analytical Processing (OLAP) or Data Mining with Analysis Services.
- **Report:** Presenting to end users the data that may have been integrated by using Integration Services and analyzed by using Analysis Services.

## Business intelligence tools

In SQL Server 2005, most development work is done in the Business Intelligence Development Studio. You have the option to install the Business Intelligence Development Studio when you install SQL Server 2005. If you install an edition of Visual Studio 2005, the business intelligence design functionality is automatically integrated inside Visual Studio 2005.

In SQL Server Management Studio, you have tools to manage Integration Services, Analysis Services, and Reporting Services servers. The buttons in the Registered Servers pane of SQL Server Management Studio allow you to view and select servers in any of the preceding categories.

## Data warehouses

Many companies aggregate data in specifically tuned databases called *data warehouses*. A data warehouse may contain data aggregated from many sources. For historical reasons, perhaps because of different systems being used in individual subsidiaries, the data to be aggregated may be held in varied formats. To store that data together, you must structure that data in a standard way in the data warehouse. Integration Services is an ideal tool to restructure and clean data before placing it in a data warehouse.

Data warehouses may contain enormous amounts of data. To get optimal performance, you can use the partitioning of tables introduced in SQL Server 2005.

Analysis of the data in data warehouses is a typical use of SQL Server 2005 Analysis Services. SQL Server 2005 Reporting Services is an ideal Enterprise grade reporting tool.

# Integration Services Overview

Integration Services is an *ETL* (Extract, Transform, and Load) tool. Integration Services can *extract* data from various sources, *transform* the loaded data into a different structure, and *load* that altered structure into, for example, a SQL Server 2005 database.

The ETL approach allows you to handle many real-life business problems. Examples of scenarios where you would consider using Integration Services are the following:

- ✔ A store chain where sales data is collected at each store and needs to be aggregated centrally for analysis.
- ✔ Scenarios where two companies share human resources data for security reasons but hold the data in different formats. This need may occur at an airport where individual airlines would inform the airport of staffing changes.
- ✔ Aggregating and filtering data from Weblogs (or *blogs*).
- ✔ Process financial transactions and split off transactions according to specified criteria to identify outliers and process them for further human examination — for example, to identify fraud or human error.

SQL Server Integration Services can accept data from many sources, including the following database and enterprise planning products:

- ✔ SQL Server
- ✔ Oracle
- ✔ IBM DB2
- ✔ SAP

Integration Services is based on *packages*. In the next section, I tell you a little about the process of creating an Integration Services package. Later in the chapter, I show you step by step how to create a package.

## Creating an Integration Services package

Broadly, an Integration Services package consists of sources, transformations, and destinations. A *source* is where you get data that you want to transform. A *transformation* is how you restructure data to make sure it is clean and compatible with the destination's table structure. A *destination* is where you send transformed data.

You create an Integration Services package by selecting *tasks* from the Toolbox and dragging those tasks, as appropriate, to the Control Flow tab design surface or the Data Flow tab design surface. See Figure 20-1.

You set the properties of each task. After you do so, you join the tasks together by using precedence constraints. I show you the process in more detail in the later section, "Creating an Integration Services Project," after I summarize the wide range of tasks that are available to you in Integration Services.

On the Control Flow tab, you specify the overall logic of the package. In the Data Flow tab, you specify the way data is processed in an Integration Services *pipeline*.

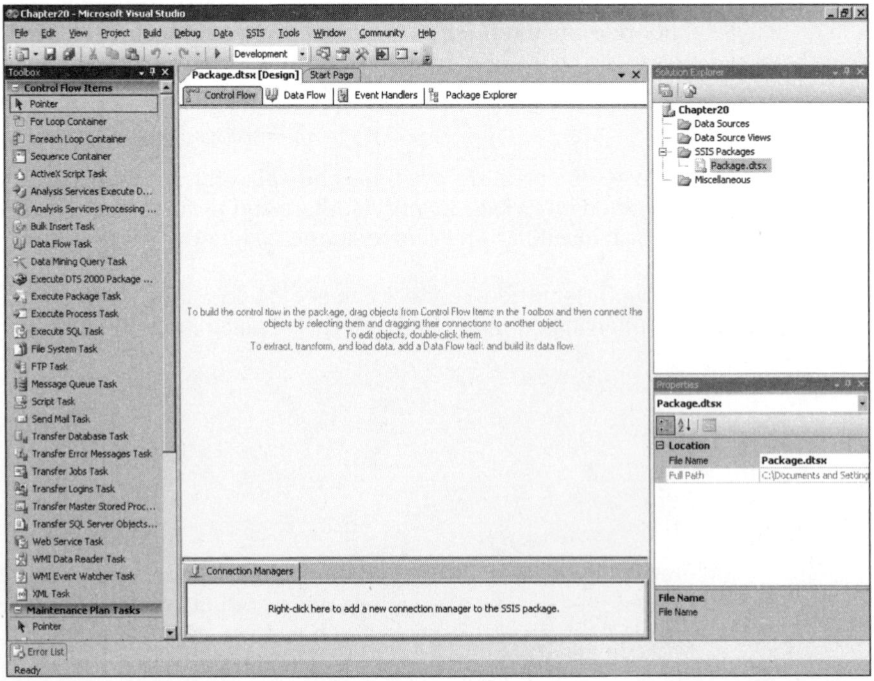

**Figure 20-1:**
An empty
Integration
Services
project
showing
the Control
Flow tab.

# *Sources*

SQL Server Integration Services supports a useful number of sources for data. Select the Data Flow tab to use shapes representing data sources. You configure a *connection manager* that you associate with each data source.

The sources supported in SQL Server 2005 are the following:

- **DataReader:** A datareader source consumes data from a .NET data provider. Typically, it uses an ADO.NET connection manager.
- **Excel:** An Excel source retrieves data from a worksheet or a range in an Excel workbook.
- **Flat File:** A Flat File source retrieves data from a text file that can contain delimited (such as comma delimited), fixed width, or mixed data.
- **OLE DB:** An OLE DB source retrieves data from an OLE DB-enabled database, such as Access or SQL Server.
- **Raw File:** Reads a file where the data is stored in Integration Services's native format. Typically, the Raw file is saved from an Integration Services Raw File destination. The Raw File source does not need a connection manager.
- **XML:** Reads an XML file. An XSD schema file is needed, either as a separate file or inline, to allow Integration Services to create an appropriate tabular structure from the hierarchical XML data.

The types of connection manager supported in SQL Server 2005 Integration Services are the following:

- **ADO:** Connect to an *ActiveX Data Object* (ADO), or a data source, such as a recordset.
- **ADO .NET:** Connect a package to data by means of a .NET provider.
- **EXCEL:** Use with an Excel source.
- **FILE** Allow a source to reference a single existing file or folder.
- **FLATFILE:** Use with the Flat File source. The connection manager allows you to specify how Integration Services should parse the source text file.
- **FTP:** Enable an Integration Services package to connect to a FTP server.
- **HTTP:** Enable a package to retrieve files from a Web server with HTTP.
- **MSMQ:** Connect to a Microsoft Message Queue (MSMQ) message queue.
- **MSOLAP90:** Allow a package to connect to an Analysis Services server to retrieve data from an Analysis Services database or project.

✓ **MULTIFILE:** Allow a source to reference multiple files or folders.

✓ **MULTIFLATFILE:** Allow a source to reference multiple text files.

✓ **ODBC:** Connect to a database management system by using Open Database Connectivity (ODBC).

✓ **OLE DB:** Use with the OLE DB source.

✓ **SMOServer:** Used with the Transfer Logins task (which I describe later in this chapter).

✓ **SMTP:** Enable a package to connect to a *Simple Mail Transfer Protocol* (SMTP) server.

✓ **SQLMOBILE:** Enable a package to connect to a SQL Server Mobile database.

✓ **WMI:** Enables a package to use Window Management Instrumentation.

The Connection Managers tab is shown in the lower part of Figure 20-1. Right-clicking in that area allows you to select which type of connection manager to create. To view the full list of connection managers, select New Connection in the context menu.

The preceding lists of data sources and connection managers show you how flexible SQL Server Integration Services is in accepting data from diverse data sources.

## Transformations

After you retrieve (loaded) information in the Extract, Transform, Load paradigm, you then transform it. SQL Server Integration Services supports many types of data transformation.

Select the Data Flow tab to access SQL Server Integration Services from the Toolbox. The following transforms are part of Integration Services:

✓ **Aggregate:** Calculates aggregates. Functionality includes sum, average, count, minimum, and maximum.

✓ **Audit:** Enables an Integration Services package to have access to information about the environment in which it is running.

✓ **Character Map:** Enables functions to be applied to character data; for example, conversion to uppercase or lowercase.

✓ **Conditional Split:** Enables data to route separately depending on specified values in the data.

✓ **Copy Column:** Creates a copy of an input column. The original column and the copy column can then be processed in different ways later.

- ✔ **Data Conversion:** Converts data in an input column to a different datatype.

- ✔ **Data Mining Query:** Enables you to create a Data Mining Extensions (DMX) query.

- ✔ **Derived Column:** Enables you to manipulate data in an input column to create a different value in an output column. For example, you can convert pounds to kilograms.

- ✔ **Export Column:** Enables you to read data in a data flow and export it to a file.

- ✔ **Fuzzy Grouping:** Cleans data and increases standardization.

- ✔ **Fuzzy Lookup**: Similar to the Lookup transformation, except that it uses fuzzy matching and assists increasing standardization of data.

- ✔ **Import Column:** Reads data from files and inserts the data into columns in a data flow.

- ✔ **Lookup:** Joins data in a reference dataset with data in a column in a data flow.

- ✔ **Merge:** Combines two sorted datasets into one dataset.

- ✔ **Merge Join:** This join takes place in the Integration Services pipeline. The Merge join doesn't take place in a SQL Server database.

- ✔ **Multicast:** Enables data to be sent to two or more outputs. Each row in the input is sent to every output.

- ✔ **OLE DB Command:** Enables you to run a T-SQL statement for each row in a data flow.

- ✔ **Percentage Sampling:** Enables you to randomly sample the data in the data flow. The number of rows sampled depends on the percentage chosen.

- ✔ **Pivot:** Enables you to manipulate data in a data flow similarly to the Excel pivot operation.

- ✔ **Row Count:** Counts the rows that pass through a data flow and stores the count in a variable.

- ✔ **Row Sampling:** Enables you to randomly sample the rows passing through a data flow.

- ✔ **Script Component:** Enables you to create custom code in Visual Basic. NET, using the Visual Studio for Applications development environment.

- ✔ **Slowly Changing Dimension:** Coordinates the updating of dimension tables in a data warehouse.

- ✔ **Sort:** Enables you to sort input data. You can apply multiple sorts in a Sort transformation.

- ✔ **Term Extraction:** Enables you to extract terms from input columns.

- **Term Lookup:** Enables you to match terms in input against a reference dataset.

- **Union All:** Combines multiple inputs into one output.

- **Unpivot:** Carries out the opposite operation from the Pivot transformation.

When you use this extensive range of transformations, particularly in combination, you have a very powerful and flexible tool to manipulate input data in a huge number of useful ways. If the built-in transformations don't already do exactly what you need, the Script component allows you to construct custom transformations in Visual Basic.NET.

## Destinations

After you transform your data in the way(s) that you want, you then have several choices of where you can output the data. In Integration Services terminology, you output data in *destinations*.

In many scenarios, you're loading transformed data into SQL Server 2005 databases or data warehouses. However, Integration Services supports a broad range of destinations:

- **Data Mining Model Training:** Use output data to train a data mining model in SQL Server 2005 Analysis Services.

- **DataReader:** Expose the output data, using an ADO.NET DataReader interface. The data can be used as the basis of a SQL Server 2005 Reporting Services report.

- **Dimension Processing:** Use the output data as input to a SQL Server 2005 Analysis Services dimension.

- **Excel:** Load output data into an Excel workbook.

- **Flat File:** Write data to a text file in a specified format — for example, a comma-delimited file.

- **OLE DB:** Load data into an OLE DB compliant database.

- **Partition Processing:** Load data into a SQL Server 2005 Analysis Services partition.

- **Raw File:** Save data in SQL Server Integration Services's native data format.

- **Recordset:** Create and populate an ADO recordset.

- **SQL Server:** Load data into a SQL Server table or view.

- **SQL Server Mobile:** Load data into a SQL Server Mobile database.

# Task flows

In SQL Server Integration Services, ETL tasks are contained in *task flows*. Task flows allow you to specify the order in which tasks take place, using *precedence constraints*.

You use precedence constraints to define the order in which tasks are executed.

# Error flows

When you process potentially huge volumes of data, often from multiple sources, some errors almost inevitably occur. It therefore makes sense to expect errors during the execution of a SQL Server Integration Services package and handle errors in a way that does not prevent a package executing. In Integration Services, error flows handle errors. You can create an error flow on any task in an Integration Services package. You can save the output in an error flow — for example, in an Error table in SQL Server for manual review or to process automatically in some appropriate way.

In addition to error flows, Integration Services supports *data viewers*. You use data viewers to review data at one or more points in the execution of an Integration Services package. Visually checking the data can provide an assessment of how well, or not, a transformation is handling data.

# Event handling

Tasks and containers in an Integration Services package raise events as they execute. You can write code to create custom event handlers to add functionality. For example, you could e-mail a staff member if an error occurs during the execution of a package.

# Logging options

You can log runtime events during the execution of an Integration Services package. You can configure logging for the following destinations:

- ✔ SQL Server
- ✔ SQL Server Profiler
- ✔ Text file

✔ Windows Event Log

✔ XML file

You can enable logging on a task, a container, or a package.

## Package restart

When large packages run, they can hit problems. When processing potentially many millions of rows of data, you can save significant amounts of time if the package doesn't have to run again from the beginning. If a problem happens, and you have defined one or more checkpoints in the package, you can restart the package from the checkpoint.

## Digital signing

The tasks that Integration Services packages carry out can be crucial to the functioning of a business. It therefore makes sense in some scenarios to be sure that the packages that you run are trustworthy. You can have Integration Services packages digitally signed.

# Business Intelligence Development Studio

The Business Intelligence Development Studio (BIDS) is a Visual Studio-like programming environment that allows you to create business intelligence projects. During SQL Server 2005 setup, you need to install the Business Intelligence Development Studio.

If you install BIDS and Visual Studio on the same development machine, the two pieces of software are merged. When you create a project, both business intelligence projects and conventional Visual Studio projects are offered in the same Visual Studio development environment.

These types of business intelligence projects are supported in BIDS:

✔ Analysis Services project (see Chapter 21)

✔ Import Analysis Services 9.0 database (see Chapter 21)

✔ Integration Services project (in the "Creating an Integration Services Project" section, later in this chapter)

✔ Report Model project (see Chapter 22)

> ✔ Report project (see Chapter 22)
> ✔ Report Project Wizard (see Chapter 22)

The Integration Services Designer has these tabs:

 ✔ **Control Flow:** One of the visual design surfaces in BIDS. You drag shapes from the Toolbox to the design surface and connect the shapes to specify the order of execution of tasks.

 ✔ **Data Flow:** The second visual design surface in BIDS. You drag shapes that represent data sources, transformations, and destinations to the design surface.

 ✔ **Event Handlers:** The third visual design surface in BIDS. You choose an Integration Services event and drag a shape representing the action to be taken when the event fires. For example, you may use the Send Mail task to send e-mail to an administrator if an error occurs during package execution.

 ✔ **Package Explorer:** Visually displays the structure of a package.

 ✔ **Progress:** This is not visible when you first create the package. It displays when you run the package in debug mode. After you complete debug mode, the label of the tab changes to Execution Results.

## *The Control Flow tab*

On the Control Flow tab, you design the logic of your package.

When you're on the Control Flow tab, you have access to a large number of tasks that you can drag to the design surface. You can group tasks in containers.

The shapes available from the Toolbox are the following:

 ✔ **For Loop container:** Iterate a specified number of times. Similar in effect to a `for` loop in a programming language.

 ✔ **Foreach Loop container:** Iterate through a set of data; for example, all the files in a directory.

 ✔ **Sequence container:** Group other control flow tasks. This is useful — for example, during debugging — when a group of tasks in a Sequence container can easily be disabled.

 ✔ **ActiveX Script:** Create custom code written in Visual Basic.NET.

 ✔ **Analysis Services Execute DDL:** Execute DDL (Data Definition Language) statements on data mining models or Analysis Services cubes.

 ✔ **SQL Server Analysis Services Processing:** Process Analysis Services objects; for example, cubes and data mining models.

- **Bulk Insert:** Quickly copy large amounts of data into SQL Server 2005.

- **Data Flow:** A data flow task can have data sources, transformations, and destinations as I describe earlier in this chapter.

- **Data Mining Query:** Run DMX prediction queries based on Analysis Services data mining models.

- **Execute DTS 2000 Package:** Run a SQL Server 2000 Data Transformation Services package.

- **Execute Package:** Run another SQL Server 2005 Integration Services package.

- **Execute Process:** Run a Windows application or a batch file.

- **Execute SQL:** Run T-SQL statements or stored procedures.

- **File System:** Set attributes on files and folders or move, create, or delete them.

- **FTP:** Upload or download files and manage directories on an FTP server.

- **Message Queue:** Enables you to use Microsoft Message Queuing (MSMQ) to send and receive messages.

- **Script:** Add custom functionality by using code written in Visual Basic.NET.

- **Send Mail:** Send an e-mail message. A common use is to inform an administrator of the result of package execution.

- **Transfer Database:** Transfer a database between two SQL Server instances.

- **Transfer Error Messages:** Transfer user-defined error messages between SQL Server instances.

- **Transfer Jobs:** Transfer SQL Server Agent jobs between SQL Server instances.

- **Transfer Logins:** Transfer logins between SQL Server instances.

- **Transfer Master Stored Procedures:** Transfer user-defined stored procedures between the `master` databases on two SQL Server instances.

- **Web Service:** Execute a Web service method.

- **WMI Data Reader:** Retrieve data from Windows Management Instrumentation (WMI).

- **WMI Event Watcher:** Monitor for the occurrence of a Windows Management Instrumentation (WMI) event.

- **XML:** Retrieve or manipulate XML documents.

In addition to what you could call the general Integration Services tasks, the Toolbox also contains several tasks that you can use to write or extend Maintenance Plans.

The Maintenance Plan tasks are

- ✔ **Back Up Database:** Carry out SQL Server database backups.
- ✔ **Check Database Integrity:** Check the structural integrity of one or more databases.
- ✔ **Execute SQL Server Agent Job:** Execute a SQL Server Agent job.
- ✔ **Execute T-SQL Statement:** Execute a T-SQL statement.
- ✔ **History Cleanup:** Delete history information in the msdb database.
- ✔ **Maintenance Cleanup:** Remove old files related to maintenance plans.
- ✔ **Notify Operator:** Send messages to SQL Server Agent operators.
- ✔ **Rebuild Index:** Rebuild SQL Server indexes.
- ✔ **Reorganize Index:** Reorganize SQL Server indexes.
- ✔ **Shrink Database:** Shrink the size of SQL Server database and log files.
- ✔ **Update Statistics:** Update information about key values in one or multiple statistics groups in a table or indexed view.

The preceding tasks are adequate for many straightforward maintenance plans. If the functionality available from the Maintenance Plan Wizard (see Chapter 18) is inadequate, you can extend the functionality by adding additional Integration Services tasks. After you add other Integration Services tasks, you must modify the package in Business Intelligence Development Studio. You can no longer use SQL Server Management Studio to modify the maintenance plan.

# The Data Flow tab

The Data Flow tab is a way of looking inside a Data Flow task. Alternatively, you can look on it as the place where you design the functionality of a Data Flow task.

You specify the components of the Data Flow task by dragging sources, transformations, and destinations from the Toolbox, specifying their properties and joining them by using precedence constraints to specify the order in which the code executes.

# The Event Handlers tab

The Event Handlers tab allows you to design functionality to execute in response to specified Integration Services events.

You can design an event handler with these events:

- ✔ **OnError:** Raised when an error occurs.
- ✔ **OnExecStatusChanged:** Raised when the status of an executable — for example, a container — changes.
- ✔ **OnInformation:** Raised during the validation and execution of an executable.
- ✔ **OnPostExecute:** Raised by an executable immediately after it executes.
- ✔ **OnPostValidate:** Raised when validation of an executable is complete.
- ✔ **OnPreExecute:** Raised by an executable immediately before execution begins.
- ✔ **OnPreValidate:** Raised by an executable immediately before validation begins.
- ✔ **OnProgress:** Raised by an executable when progress is made.
- ✔ **OnQueryCancel:** Raised by an executable to specify when it should stop.
- ✔ **OnTaskFailed:** Raised by a task when it fails.
- ✔ **OnVariableValueChanged:** Raised by an executable when the value of a variable changes.
- ✔ **OnWarning:** Raised when a warning occurs.

## The Package Explorer tab

The Package Explorer tab allows you to explore the structure of a package. Figure 20-2 shows the appearance in the Package Explorer tab when debugging the example package I create later in the chapter.

**Figure 20-2:**
The
Package
Explorer tab.

## The Toolbox

The Toolbox contains the shapes available to you to design functionality in an Integration Services package. The contents of the Toolbox depend on which tab you select.

## The Solution Explorer

The Solution Explorer gives a visual display of the components of an Integration Services package (solution). Figure 20-3 shows the appearance after I created the example package later in this chapter.

# Import/Export Wizard

One of the easiest ways to use Integration Services is to use the Import/Export Wizard. The Import/Export Wizard allows you to connect to the following data sources:

- ✔ Access
- ✔ ADO.NET
- ✔ Excel
- ✔ Flat files
- ✔ OLE DB
- ✔ SQL Server

The Import/Export Wizard has very limited transformation capabilities compared to a full Integration Services project.

In the following example, I import data from the `Northwind` database that is a sample database that comes with recent versions of Microsoft Access. If you don't have a copy of the database file, select an alternate data source in Steps 7 and 8.

To create an Integration Services Project with the Import/Export Wizard, follow these steps:

1. **Open the Business Intelligence Development Studio.**

2. **Choose File⇨New⇨Project.**

3. **In the New Project dialog box, select the Integration Services Project option and name the project** Import Export Wizard Example **(see Figure 20-4). Then click OK.**

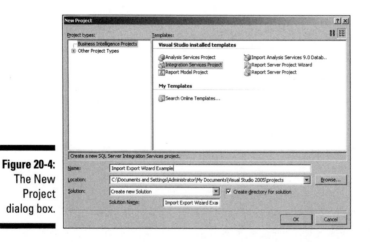

**Figure 20-4:**
The New
Project
dialog box.

After a pause, the blank project opens. See Figure 20-5. Notice the Solution Explorer in the upper right of the screen.

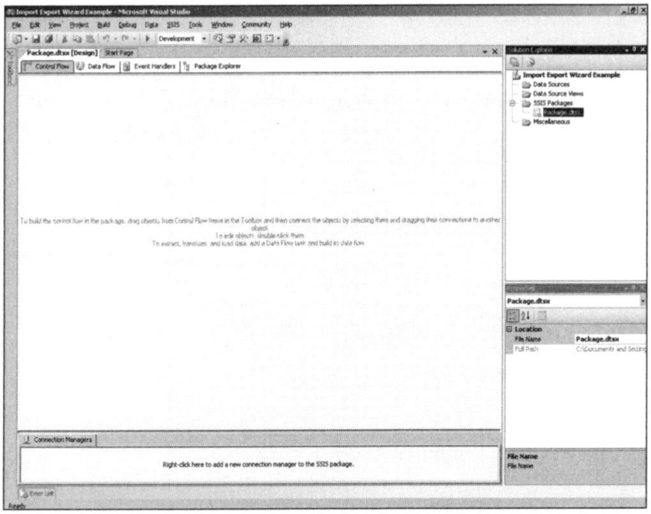

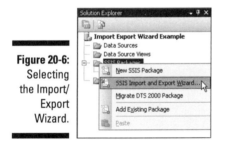

**Figure 20-5:**
A new
Integration
Services
project.

4. **In the Solution Explorer, right-click the SSIS Packages node and select SSIS Import and Export Wizard, as shown in Figure 20-6.**

**Figure 20-6:**
Selecting
the Import/
Export
Wizard.

5. **On the first screen of the Import/Export Wizard screen, click Next.**

   The Choose a Data Source screen opens.

6. **From the Data source drop-down menu, select Microsoft Access (see Figure 20-7, which also shows several of the other options for a data source).**

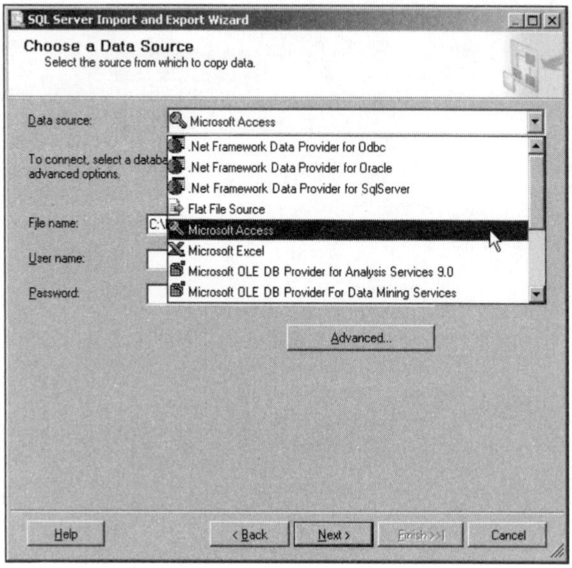

**Figure 20-7:**
Selecting a
Microsoft
Access data
source.

7. **In the File Name text box, enter a path to the Northwind.mdb file or use the Browse button to browse to an appropriate location, and then click Next.**

The Choose a Destination screen opens (see Figure 20-8).

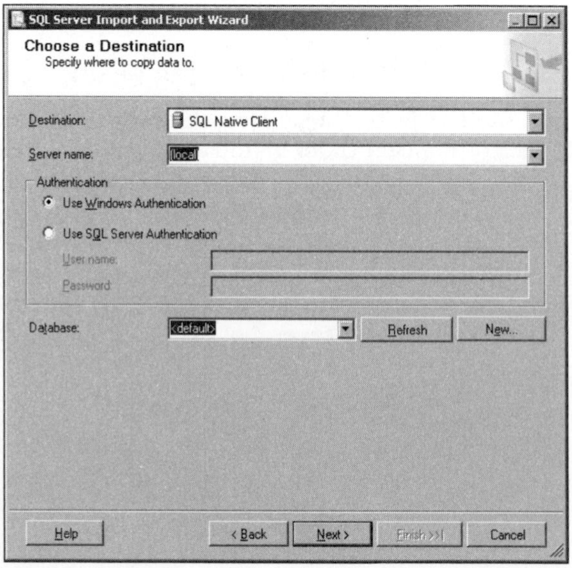

**Figure 20-8:**
Specify a
location for
the source
Access
database
file.

8. **Select SQL Native Client from the Destination drop-down menu. If connecting locally, leave the Servername as (local).**

9. **To create a new table in the desired SQL Server instance, click the New button to the right of the Database drop-down menu.**

   The Create Database dialog box opens.

10. **Name the database** NorthwindImport **(see Figure 20-9) and click OK.**

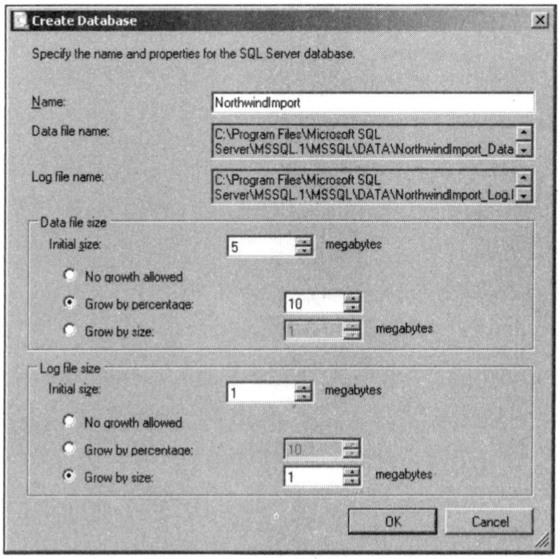

**Figure 20-9:** Naming a database to hold the imported data.

11. **Back in the Choose a Destination screen, click Next.**

12. **In the Specify Table Copy or Query area, select the Write a Query to Specify the Data to Transfer radio button and then click Next.**

    The Provide a Source Query opens.

13. **Enter the following SQL statement (see Figure 20-10) and click Next:**

```
SELECT *
FROM Employees
```

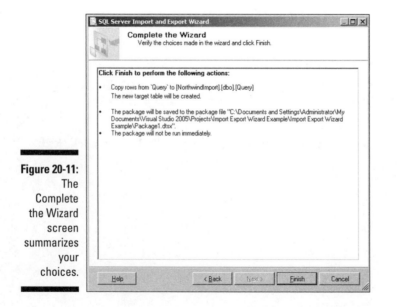

**Figure 20-10:**
Specifying
the data to
import.

14. **On the Select Source Tables and Views screen, click Next.**

15. **On the Complete the Wizard screen (see Figure 20-11), review the actions you have chosen. If you're satisfied with the description, click Finish.**

**Figure 20-11:**
The
Complete
the Wizard
screen
summarizes
your
choices.

If the wizard created the package successfully, you see an appearance similar to Figure 20-12.

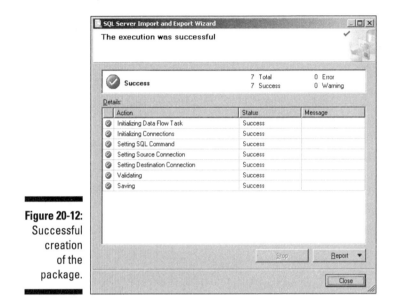

**Figure 20-12:**
Successful
creation
of the
package.

16. **Click Close.**

You return to the Business Intelligence Development Studio. The Control Flow tab looks like Figure 20-13. You're now ready to run the package you created with the wizard.

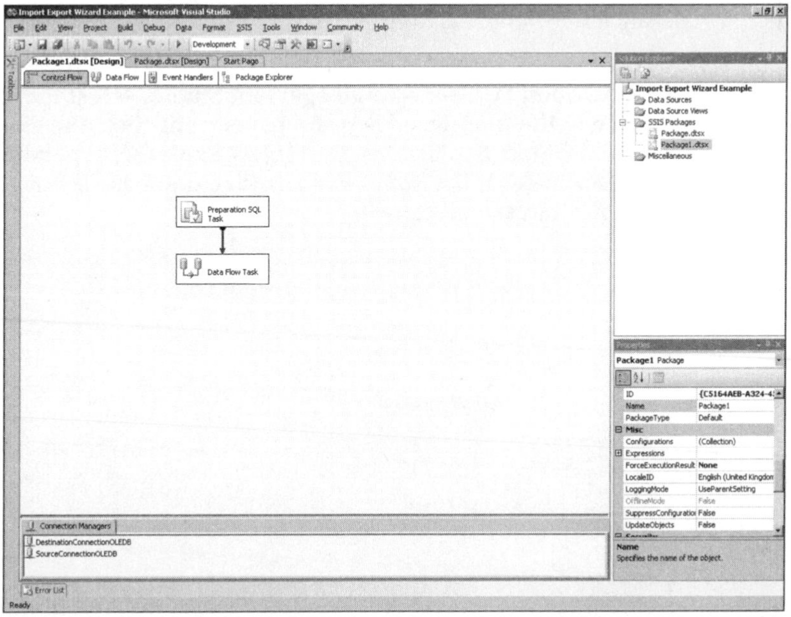

**Figure 20-13:**
The Control
Flow tab
with the
needed
shapes.

**17. To run in debug mode, press F5.**

After a pause, the window layout changes significantly as BIDS enters debug mode. If the package runs successfully, each shape changes appearance from its original appearance of yellow to green. After successfully running the package, the appearance is similar to Figure 20-14.

**Figure 20-14:**
Appearance after successfully running the package.

**18. To be able to create the package in the next example, you need to exit debug mode, so press Shift+F5 to stop debugging.**

**19. To confirm that the table is created in the desired SQL Server instance, open SQL Server Management Studio, select the desired instance in the Registered Servers pane, right-click and choose Connect⇨Object Explorer. In the Object Explorer, expand the Databases node. If the `NorthwindImport` database is not visible, right-click and select Refresh.**

The content of the Databases node shows the database created by the Integration Services package, as shown in Figure 20-15.

**Figure 20-15:**
The
`Northwind`
`Import`
database
visible in the
Object
Explorer.

20. **To view the data you imported, expand the NorthwindImport node, expand the Tables node, right-click dbo.Query (the name given by the package) and select Open Table.**

    The names from the Access database appear in the right pane of SQL Server Management Studio.

# Creating an Integration Services Project

In this section, I show you how to create a simple Integration Services project. First, you create a simple source file that contains comma-separated data. The content of the source file, `Patients.txt`, is shown here:

```
LastName,FirstName,Diagnosis,DateOfBirth
Smith,James,lymphoma,1955-11-20
Schmidt,Peter,acne,1943-10-03
Carlton,Sheila,breast carcinoma,1965-03-28
Nutten,Patrick,gangrene,1933-02-19
Craven,Alicia,cirrhosis,1955-10-23
```

Notice that the columns are delimited by commas and that the first line contains the names for the columns.

Also, you need to create a database in the desired SQL Server instance to put the data into by running this code:

```
USE master
CREATE DATABASE Chapter20
```

Then create a table to hold the data:

```
USE Chapter20
CREATE TABLE PatientData
  (LastName nvarchar(25),
  FirstName nvarchar(25),
  Diagnosis nvarchar(50),
  DateOfBirth datetime)
```

To create an Integration Services project, follow these steps:

1. **Open Business Intelligence Development Studio. Choose File⇨ New⇨Project.**

   The New Project dialog box opens.

2. **Highlight the Business Intelligence Projects option in the left pane of the New Project dialog box.**

3. **Click the Integration Services Project option in the right pane.**

4. **Click in the Name text box, delete the default name and type the project name:** Chapter20.

5. **Edit the location to save the solution if you don't want to accept the default location.**

6. **Make sure that the Create Directory for Solution check box is checked and then click the OK button.**

   The Integration Services Designer displays. You need to create a connection manager for the source of the data.

7. **Right-click in the Connection Manager tray on the Control Flow tab and select the New Flat File Connection option from the context menu.**

8. **In the Flat File Connection Manager Editor dialog box that opens, supply a name for the connection:** Retrieve Patient Data.

9. **Add a description such as** Retrieves file containing information on new patients.

10. **Click the Browse button to the right of the File Name text box and navigate to the location of the `Patients.txt` file. Select `Patients.txt` and click Open.**

11. **Because `Patients.txt` has titles for columns in the first row, check the Column Names in First Data Row check box.**

12. **Click Columns in the left pane of the Flat File Connection Manager Editor.**

    The appearance is similar to that shown in Figure 20-16.

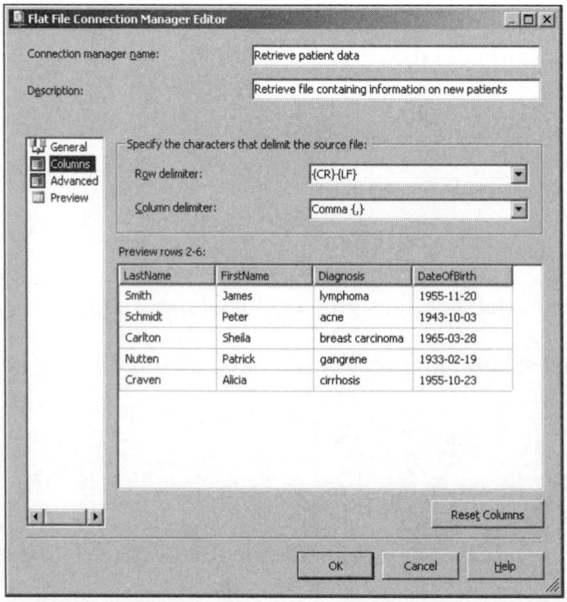

**Figure 20-16:**
The Flat File Connection Manager Editor displaying the source data.

13. **Click Advanced in the left pane.**

    The name of each column in the source file displays. In the right part of the dialog box, the properties of the LastName column display. A width of 50 characters for a last name is excessive.

14. **Edit the value of the OutputColumnWidth property to 25 and change the datatype to Unicode String.**

15. **Click on FirstName. Edit the value of its OutputColumnWidth property to 25 and change the datatype to Unicode String.**

16. **Don't change the length of the Diagnosis column because that could be up to 50 characters, but change its datatype to Unicode String.**

17. **Click on DateOfBirth. Click the drop-down menu for the DataType property and select the Database Timestamp option.**

    You need to scroll up to see it. See Figure 20-17.

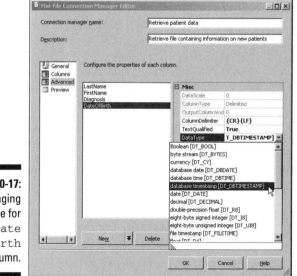

**Figure 20-17:** Changing datatype for the Date OfBirth column.

18. **Click the Preview button in the left column and review the data to ensure that it is not being truncated. Click OK.**

    You have created a connection manager. It appears in the Connection Managers tray in the lower part of the BIDS designer.

19. **To create a data flow, switch to the Data Flow tab and click the text in the middle of the design surface.**

    After a pause, its color changes to cream, indicating that you can use it as a design surface.

At this point, you have specified that the project consists of a single Data Flow task. You now need to define what the Data Flow Task consists of.

20. **Drag a Flat File source from the Toolbox onto the Data Flow design surface.**

    The Flat File source has a red X on it, indicating that it isn't connected correctly.

21. **Right-click the Flat File Source icon and select Edit.**

    The Flat File Source Editor opens, as shown in Figure 20-18.

    The Connection Manager is highlighted in the left pane of the Flat File Source Editor. The `Retrieve Patient Data` connection manager is selected by default, because there is only one available connection manager in the package.

22. **Click Columns in the left pane of the Flat File Source Editor to confirm that the external columns (those in `Patients.txt`) match the columns in the output columns. See Figure 20-19.**

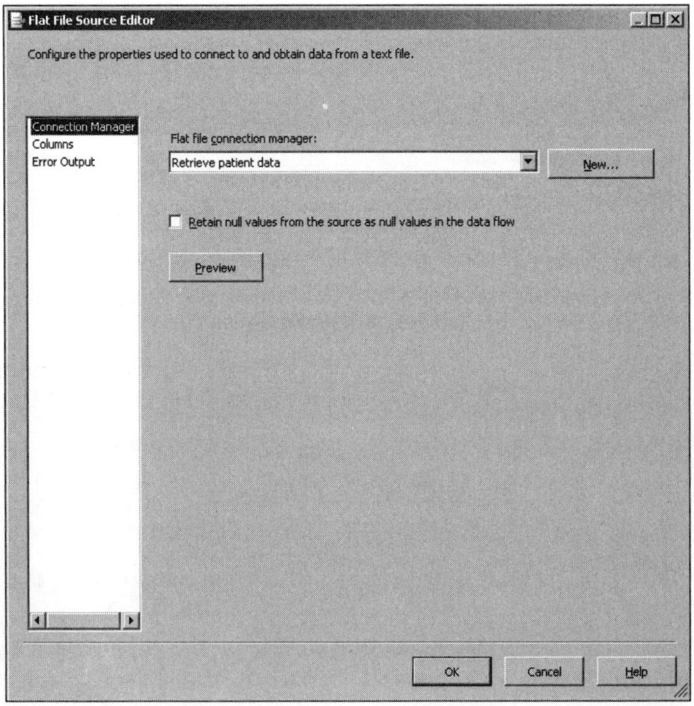

**Figure 20-18:**
The Flat File
Source
Editor.

23. **If you want to omit some input columns, uncheck the relevant check box. If you want to rename an output column, click in its name and edit it. In this case, accept the defaults and click OK.**

    The Flat File source no longer displays the red X you saw earlier. You now know that the information necessary to retrieve the flat file data is defined.

24. **Right-click the Flat File Source icon and select Rename from the context menu. Rename the Flat File source as** Retrieve Patient Data.

25. **Right-click and select Autosize on the context menu.**

    Now you define a destination for the data.

26. **In the Connection Managers tray, right-click and select New OLE DB Connection.**

27. **In the Configure OLE DB Connection, click New.**

28. **In the Connection Manager dialog box, select . (a period character) as the server name and Chapter20 as the database name. Click OK.**

29. **Drag an OLE DB Destination from the Toolbox to the design surface. (It has a red X indicating that it is not yet fully configured.) Click the**

Retrieve Patient Data shape and drag the green line (a precedence constraint) so that it joins to the new OLE DB Destination shape.

30. **Right-click the OLE DB Destination shape and select Edit. You may receive a warning. Click OK.**

    The OLE DB Destination Editor dialog box opens. See Figure 20-20.

    Because one appropriate connection manager is defined, it's selected by default.

31. **Click the Name of The Table or The View drop-down menu. After a pause, confirm that the `PatientData` table (the only option in the `Chapter20` database) displays in the menu.**

32. **Click Mappings in the left pane of the OLE DB Destination dialog box.**

    You see an appearance similar to Figure 20-21, indicating that the input columns nicely match the output columns.

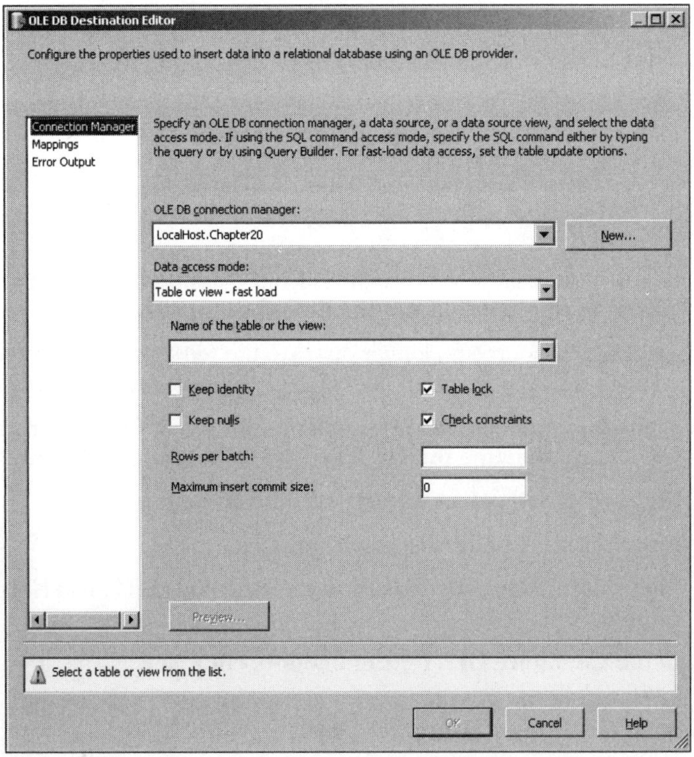

**Figure 20-20:**
The OLE DB
Destination
Editor
dialog box.

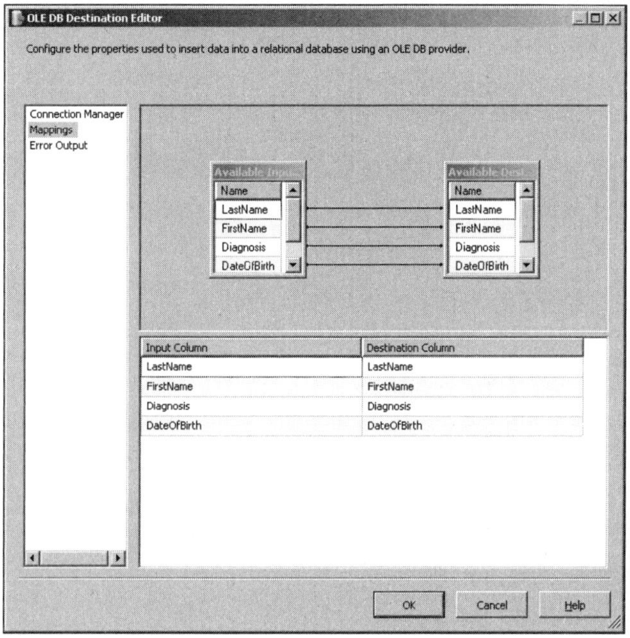

**Figure 20-21:**
The Map-
pings in the
OLE DB
Destination
Editor
dialog box.

The OLE DB Destination shape no longer has a red X visible.

**33. To run the package, press F5.**

The shapes successively turn yellow and then green, indicating successful running of the package.

**34. Review package progress by clicking the Progress tab. See Figure 20-22.**

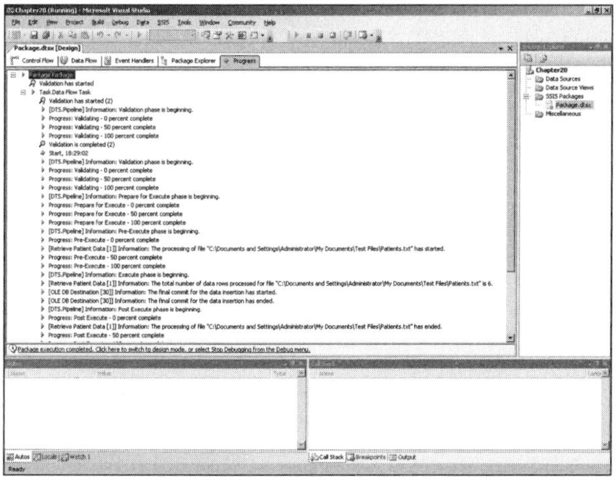

**Figure 20-22:**
The
Progress
tab.

35. **Press Shift+F5 to exit debug mode.**

36. **Choose File⇨Save to save the package.**

You can use SQL Server Integration Services to create much more complex packages than the example shown in this section. However, I have shown you several of the key techniques that you use to create complex Integration Services packages.

# Deploying an Integration Services Project

You have two options to deploy an Integration Services project. You can deploy it to the `msdb` database inside SQL Server 2005, or you can deploy it to the file system.

Before deployment, you create a package configuration. For deployment to SQL Server 2005, you create a configuration in the `msdb` database. For file system deployment, you have several options — including using an XML configuration file.

To enable a package for deployment, right-click the package in the Solution Explorer and select Properties. The Property Pages dialog box opens. You have options to specify that a deployment utility is created when the package is built (see Figure 20-23). You also specify the location for the deployment folder. After you specify the deployment information, rebuild the package.

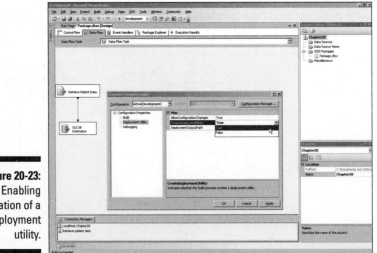

**Figure 20-23:**
Enabling creation of a deployment utility.

# Chapter 21

# Analysis Services

• • • • • • • • • • • • • • • • • • • • • • • • • • • • • • • • • • • • • • • • • • • • • •

• • • • • • • • • • • • • • • • • • • • • • • • • • • • • • • • • • • • • • • • • • • • • •

SQL Server Analysis Services is the second component of the Integrate, Analyze, Report paradigm that underlies business intelligence in SQL Server 2005. You use SQL Server Integration Services to gather data from possibly heterogeneous sources. You use Analysis Services to analyze the data. You use Reporting Services to create reports for other colleagues to use.

Analysis Services allows you to analyze data by using Online Analytical Processing (OLAP) or Data Mining techniques. To use Online Analytical Processing, you create multidimensional structures that contain data aggregated from several sources. To use Data Mining functionality, you create data mining models.

Unfortunately, in the space available, I can introduce only a small part of the huge range of features in SQL Server 2005 Analysis Services. For further information, see *Professional SQL Server Analysis Services 2005 with MDX,* by Sivakumar Harinath and Stephen R. Quinn (Wiley).

## Introducing Analysis Services

Analysis Services helps you find out what is happening in your business. You can view Analysis Services as a way to make sense out of the huge volumes of data that many modern businesses accumulate.

Analysis Services consists of two main types of processing: OLAP (Online Analytical Processing) and Data Mining

Analysis Services consists of both client-based and server-based components. The server components consist of one or more instances of SQL Server 2005 Analysis Services server. Clients communicate with Analysis Services by using XML for Analysis (XMLA). XMLA is a SOAP-based protocol, exposed as a Web service that supports sending requests and receiving responses.

The server components of Analysis Services undertake the following tasks:

- Parsing statements received from client applications
- Handling transactions
- Executing calculations
- Storing dimension data
- Creating aggregations
- Scheduling queries
- Managing server resources
- Managing metadata

You can write Analysis Service queries in any of the following languages:

- T-SQL
- Multi Dimensional Expressions (MDX)
- Data Mining Extensions (DMX)

The Analysis Services server returns client components process data. They also allow the user to specify what analyses they want carried out.

You can manage Analysis Services objects directly by using Analysis Services Scripting Language (ASSL). Often you can use other applications to conceal ASSL. For example, both SQL Server Management Studio and Business Intelligence Studio use ASSL to interact with Analysis Services. ASSL consists of two components:

- A Data Definition Language (DDL)
- A command language

## *New features in Analysis Services 2005*

The following features are new or enhanced in Analysis Services in SQL Server 2005:

- Business Intelligence Development Studio as a development environment
- SQL Server Management Studio as a management tool.

- ✔ Unified Dimensional Model as a single way to model or view your data.
- ✔ Proactive caching supports great performance as underlying data updates.
- ✔ Key Performance Indicators (KPI) summarize key measures of business performance.
- ✔ Translations provide access to metadata in multiple languages for easier use of Analysis Services analyses internationally.
- ✔ Multiple instances of Analysis Services.
- ✔ Failover clustering of Analysis Services.
- ✔ XML for Analysis support.
- ✔ Multiple fact tables are supported in a cube.
- ✔ Perspectives are predefined subsets of a cube that allow specified aspects of the business data to be viewed more clearly.
- ✔ Attributes allow more meaningful navigation of the information in a dimension.
- ✔ Multiple hierarchies are now supported in a dimension.
- ✔ Now only two dimension types — standard and linked (compare to four in Analysis Services 2000).
- ✔ Support for SQL Server 2005 Integration Services.
- ✔ Business intelligence wizards carry out complex tasks.

# Key Performance Indicators

A Key Performance Indicator (KPI) allows you to display summary data for information workers and executives in a way that is meaningful for them to compare performance to business goals.

A KPI allows you to compare business performance, as judged by a selected measure, against actual performance. Threshold values are defined and the display graphically summarizes actual performance versus target performance.

A Key Performance Indicator includes the following components. However, you may choose to display or use only some of these in individual settings:

- ✔ A business goal for performance
- ✔ An actual performance
- ✔ Compare actual performance to the target performance
- ✔ Assess the change in status over time
- ✔ Visually display status

    ✔ Visually display trend

    ✔ Attach an importance to individual KPIs

## Managing Analysis Services

SQL Server Management Studio is the tool you use to carry out many management tasks on a SQL Server 2005 Analysis Services instance.

To register an Analysis Services instance and view its properties by using SQL Server Management Studio, follow these steps:

1. **Open SQL Server Management Studio. If the Registered Servers pane is not visible, choose View➪Registered Servers.**

2. **In the Registered Servers pane, click the Analysis Services button at the top of the pane.**

   The Analysis Services button is second from the left in Figure 21-1.

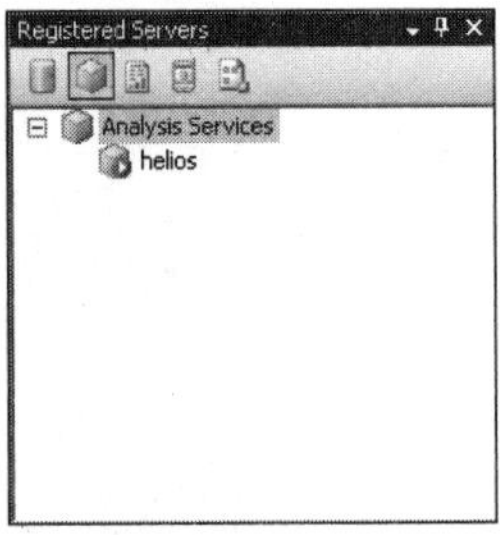

**Figure 21-1:**
The
Registered
Servers
pane in SQL
Server
Manageme
nt Studio.

3. **Right-click in the Registered Servers pane and choose New➪Server Registration.**

   The New Server Registration dialog box opens.

4. **Supply a server name and, optionally, an instance name in the Server name text box. Click Test to test the connection. Click Save.**

   An Analysis Services instance is added to the Registered Servers pane.

5. **To view the properties of an Analysis Services instance, right-click the desired instance of Analysis Services and choose Connect➪Object Explorer.**

   The Object Explorer opens with an appearance similar to Figure 21-2.

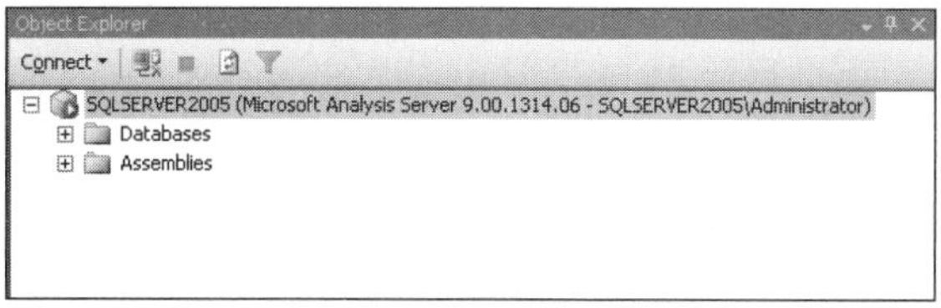

**Figure 21-2:**
An Analysis
Services
instance in
the Object
Explorer.

**6. Expand the Databases and Assemblies nodes.**

If you just installed Analysis Server, the Databases node is empty. Figure 21-3 shows the Assemblies node.

**Figure 21-3:**
Viewing the
Assemblies
node in an
Analysis
Server
instance in
the Object
Explorer.

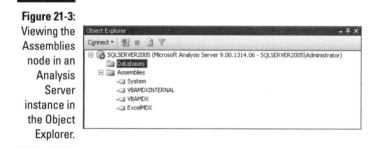

# *Business Intelligence Development Studio and Analysis Services*

You use the Business Intelligence Development Studio to create Analysis Services solutions, similar to how you create Integration Services solutions (see Chapter 20). However, the designer for Analysis Services 2005 solutions has many differences from Integration Services as I show you later in this chapter.

When you use an Analysis Services project, you use several objects repeatedly in the Business Intelligence Development Studio:

- **Data Sources:** A *data source* is a representation of a connection to a source of data. Often you use a data source that is a relational database, as in the example later in the chapter. However, you can also use XML, Excel files, Active Directory, and so on, as a data source.

  You specify the SQL Server instance, the database, tables, and columns you want to use.

✔ **Data Source Views:** A *data source view* is a view on to the tables that make up a data source. Just as you can have views in ordinary relational databases, you can have views in Analysis Services. Views allow developers, for example, to create calculated columns that exist only in the data source view. The user may not have permissions to access the underlying tables to add any additional columns.

✔ **Cubes:** A cube is a multidimensional model of business data. Each dimension expresses an aspect of the business data. In Analysis Services 2005, each cube can have multiple dimensions.

✔ **Dimensions:** Each dimension represents one dimension in the multi-dimensional cube.

✔ **Mining Structures:** The Data Mining tools in SQL Server 2005 allow you to explore your data to find patterns in it. I describe the supported algorithms in Analysis Services 2005 Data Mining later in this chapter.

✔ **Roles:** Roles are used to manage security for Analysis Services objects and models.

In this chapter, I describe how to create an Analysis Services solution by using the Business Intelligence Development Studio. You can also programmatically create Analysis Services solutions, using Analysis Management Objects (AMO) in projects created in Visual Studio 2005. Details of using Analysis Management Objects are beyond the scope of this chapter.

# Creating an Analysis Services Project

In this section, I describe one approach to creating an Analysis Services solution with the Business Intelligence Development Studio.

To create an Analysis Services solution, follow these steps:

1. **Open the Business Intelligence Development Studio.**

2. **Choose File➪New➪Project.**

   The New Project dialog box opens.

3. **In the New Project dialog box, select Business Intelligence Projects in the left pane. Then select Analysis Services Project in the right pane. Name the project** Chapter21.

   The New Project dialog box looks similar to Figure 21-4.

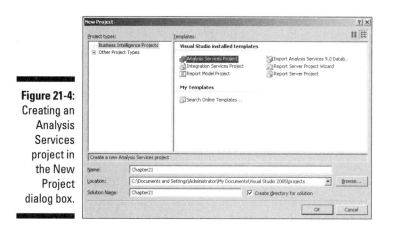

**Figure 21-4:**
Creating an
Analysis
Services
project in
the New
Project
dialog box.

Notice in Figure 21-4 that the New Project dialog box includes an additional option to import an Analysis Services 9.0 database project. If you have an existing Analysis Services 2005 database, you can use that option.

**4. Click OK.**

After a pause, you see the initial appearance, similar to that shown in Figure 21-5. If you use the Start Page, you see that as a background.

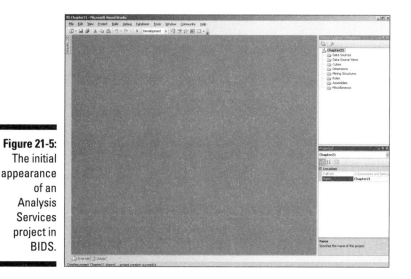

**Figure 21-5:**
The initial
appearance
of an
Analysis
Services
project in
BIDS.

Notice the folders contained in the Solution Explorer, towards the upper right of Figure 21-5.

First, you need to define where the data is to come from. You do that by creating a data source for the solution.

5. **Right-click the Data Sources folder in the Solution Explorer. Select New Data Source from the context menu.**

6. **When the Data Source Wizard opens, click Next.**

7. **On the Select How to Define a Connection screen, click the New button to create a connection.**

   The Connection Manager dialog box opens.

8. **In the Server Name text box, enter a single period if you're connecting to a local instance of SQL Server. If you're connecting to a remote SQL Server instance, enter the information in the form _machineName\instanceName_ when connecting to a named instance or _machineName_ when connecting to a default instance. Select the AdventureWorksDW database from the Select or Enter a Database drop-down menu, as shown in Figure 21-6.**

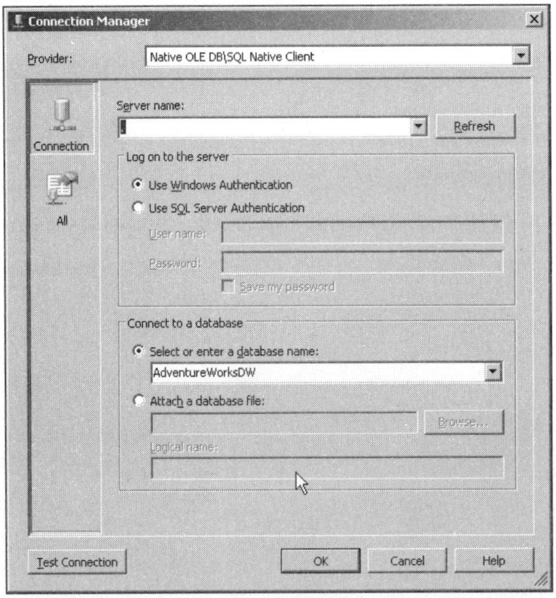

**Figure 21-6:** Selecting a server and database to connect to.

9. **Click the Test Connection button to confirm that a connection can be made and then click OK.**

   If a connection cannot be made, check that you haven't mistyped the server or instance name. If no obvious error is there, check that the desired instance of SQL Server is running and that the network connection is intact.

10. **Click OK in the Connection Manager dialog box.**

   You return to the Select How to Define the Connection screen (see Figure 21-7).

11. **Click Next.**

   The Impersonation Information screen opens.

12. **Select the Use the Service Account radio button (see Figure 21-8), and then click Next.**

The Completing the Wizard screen displays.

13. **Name the data source** AdventureWorksDW Source **(see Figure 21-9). Inspect the connection information. Click Finish.**

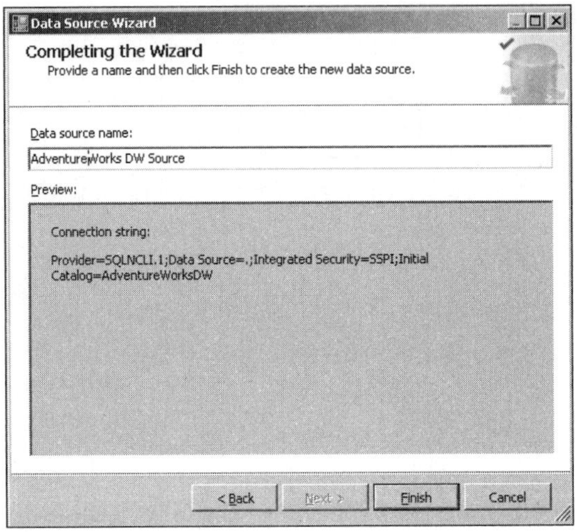

**Figure 21-9:**
Naming the
data source.

The newly created data source is added to the Data Sources folder in the Solution Explorer (see Figure 21-10).

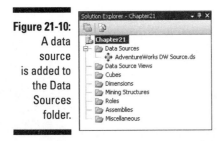

**Figure 21-10:**
A data
source
is added to
the Data
Sources
folder.

Next you create a data source view. The data source has access to all the data in the AdventureWorksDW database. When you define a data source view, you specify which parts of that data you want to make use of in the project you're creating.

14. **Right-click the Data Source Views folder and select New Data Source View.**

After a pause, the Data Source View Wizard opens (see Figure 21-11).

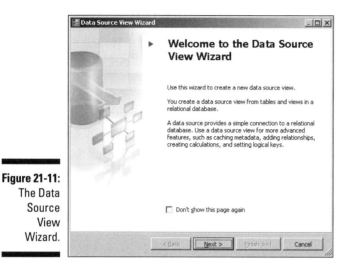

**Figure 21-11:**
The Data
Source
View
Wizard.

15. **Click Next.**

    The Select a Data Source screen opens.

16. **Select a data source to use in the data source view you are creating.**

    If you've created only the data source specified earlier in this example, you see the appearance shown in Figure 21-12.

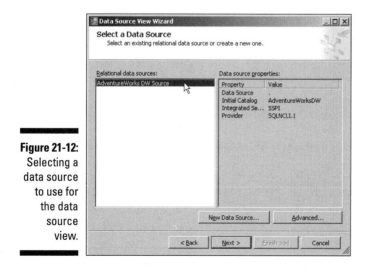

**Figure 21-12:**
Selecting a
data source
to use for
the data
source
view.

17. **When you have chosen a data source, click Next.**

    After a pause, the Select Tables and Views screen displays.

    You now choose which tables and/or views in the `AdventureWorksDW` database you want to include in the data source view that you're creating.

18. **To make it easier to see the available choices, resize the Select Tables and Views screen, as shown in Figure 21-13. Also uncheck the Show System Objects check box.**

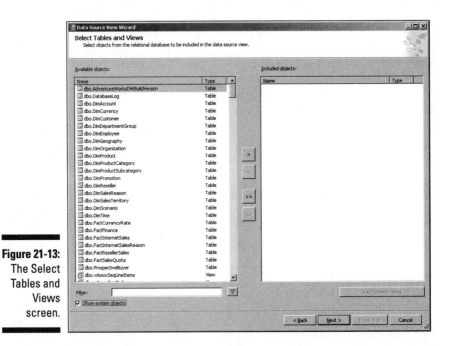

**Figure 21-13:** The Select Tables and Views screen.

19. **Notice in the names of the tables that some are dimension tables and some are fact tables. Select the following tables so that you can examine the sales data for customer, geographical locality, product, and time:**

    - DimCustomer
    - DimGeography
    - DimProduct

- DimTime
- FactInternetSales

Make sure at this stage that you always select at least one fact table.

You have now selected some tables with information relevant to what you want. However, to create the desired data source view, you need information from associated tables, too. The wizard can help you find related tables.

20. **With all the listed tables selected, as shown in Figure 21-14, click the Add Related Tables button.**

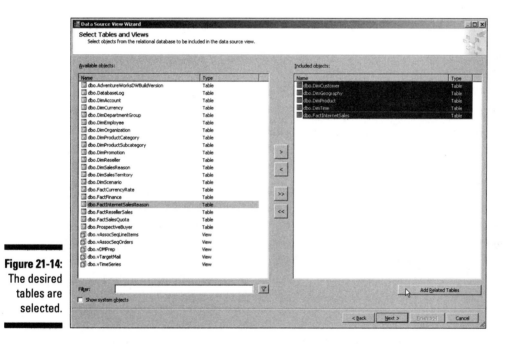

**Figure 21-14:** The desired tables are selected.

Several more tables are added to the right pane of the Select Tables and Views screen, as shown in Figure 21-15. The tables that the wizard added for you are shown with a gray background.

21. **Click Next.**

22. **On the Completing the Wizard screen that opens, name the data source view** AdventureWorksDW Data Source View. **Inspect the components of the data source view in the lower pane. Click Finish.**

    The appearance of the Business Intelligence Development Studio changes markedly, as shown in Figure 21-16.

23. **In the Solution Explorer, confirm that the data source view you created has been added to the Data Source Views folder.**

24. **Navigate around the data source view design surface.**

    For reasons of space, accept the data source view as created by the wizard. You have options to, for example, add additional columns.

    You now create a cube from the data source view.

25. **In the Solution Explorer, right-click the Cubes folder and choose New Cube.**

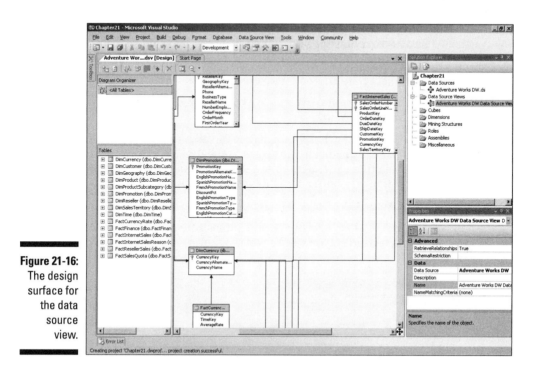

**Figure 21-16:**
The design
surface for
the data
source
view.

26. **When the Cube Wizard opens, click Next.**

The Select Build Method screen opens (see Figure 21-17).

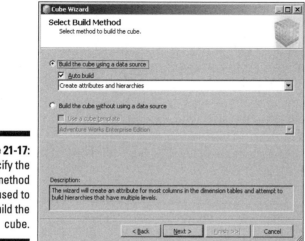

**Figure 21-17:**
Specify the
method
used to
build the
cube.

**27. Accept the default choices on the screen (which creates *attributes* and *hierarchies* for you), leave the Auto Build check box checked, and then click Next.**

The Select Data Source View screen opens.

**28. Select the AdventureWorksDW Data Source View that you created earlier and click Next.**

The Detecting Fact and Dimension Tables screen displays. The wizard automatically inspects the tables in the data source view and attempts to assign them as a fact table, a dimension table or, occasionally, a table that it thinks is both a fact table and a dimension table.

**29. Click Next.**

The Identify Fact and Dimension Tables screen displays (see Figure 21-18 that is resized so you can see all the tables).

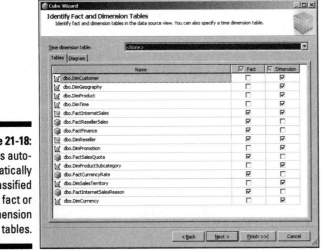

**Figure 21-18:** Tables automatically classified as fact or dimension tables.

**30. Select the DimTime table from the Time Dimension Table drop-down menu.**

On the Diagram tab, the graphical relationship between tables is shown in Figure 21-19.

**31. Click Next.**

The Select Time Periods screen opens.

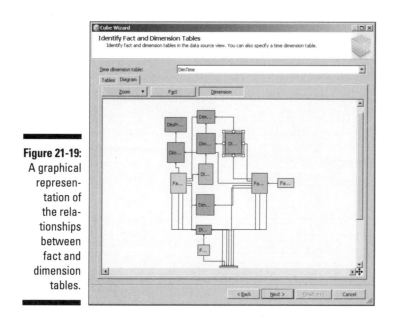

**Figure 21-19:**
A graphical
represen-
tation of
the rela-
tionships
between
fact and
dimension
tables.

32. **Map properties in the left column to column names in the right
column of the screen, as shown in Figure 21-20, and then click Next.**

| Time Property Name | Time Table Columns |
| --- | --- |
| Year | CalendarYear |
| Half Year | CalendarSemester |
| Quarter | CalendarQuarter |
| Trimester | |
| Month | EnglishMonthName |
| Date | FullDateAlternateKey |
| Ten Days | |
| Week | |
| Hour | |
| Minute | |
| Second | |
| Undefined Time | |
| Is Holiday | |
| Is Weekday | |
| Is Working Day | |
| Day of Week | |
| Day of Ten Days | |
| Day of Month | |
| Day of Quarter | |
| Day of Trimester | |
| Day of Half Year | |
| Day of Year | |

**Figure 21-20:**
Mapping
time
properties
to columns
in the
DimTime
table.

The Select Measures screen displays (see Figure 21-21).

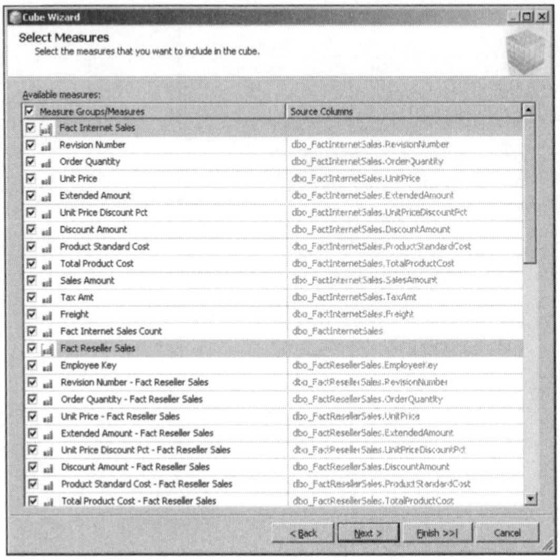

**Figure 21-21:**
You can
choose
which
measures to
select and
deselect.

33. **On this screen, you would typically select and deselect measures. For simplicity, leave all the measures checked and click Next.**

    The Detecting Hierarchies screen displays. The wizard detects hierarchies in the cube you're creating.

34. **Click Next when you see the message that detecting hierarchies is complete.**

    The Review New Dimensions screen displays. Explore the hierarchies that have been created, as shown in Figure 21-22.

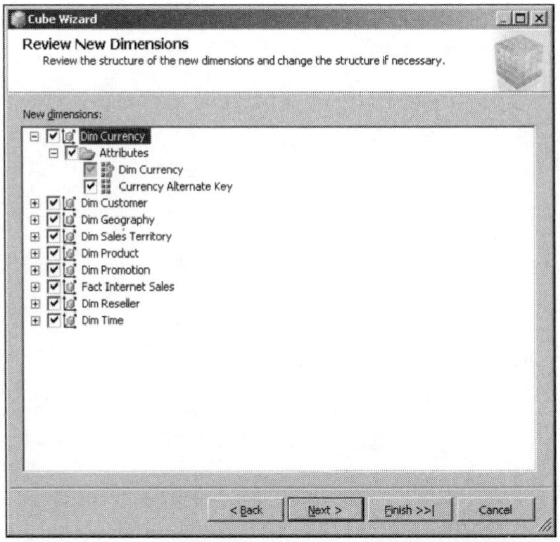

**Figure 21-22:**
Inspect the
dimension
hierarchies.

**35. Click Next. In the Completing the Wizard screen that appears, name the cube** AdventureWorksDW Cube. **Click Finish.**

After a pause, the design surface changes again, as shown in Figure 21-23.

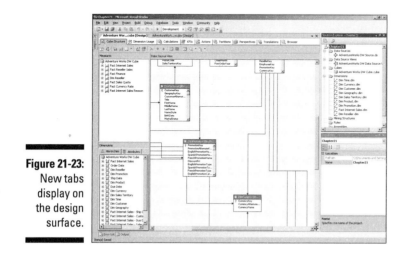

**Figure 21-23:** New tabs display on the design surface.

**36. Save the solution by choosing File⇨Save All.**

Notice that several new tabs display:

- ✔ Cube Structure
- ✔ Dimension Usage
- ✔ Calculations
- ✔ KPIs
- ✔ Actions
- ✔ Partitions
- ✔ Perspectives
- ✔ Translations
- ✔ Browser

Each of the preceding tabs has an associated designer. I suggest you click on each tab and inspect its appearance and functionality.

Notice too that a cube has been added to the Cubes folder and several dimensions have been added to the Dimensions folder in the Solution Explorer.

Typically, you would explore and modify aspects of the project you have created. For reasons of space, I show you how to deploy the project.

To deploy the project you created, follow these steps:

1. **In the Solution Explorer, right-click the project name, Chapter21, and choose Properties.**

   The Property Pages dialog box opens.

2. **Select Deployment in the left pane of the Property Pages dialog box (see Figure 21-24).**

3. **Modify the properties as appropriate to your deployment scenario. Click OK to confirm any changes.**

   If you intend to deploy on the local machine, leave the properties unchanged.

To deploy an Analysis Services project, follow these steps:

1. **In Solution Explorer, right-click the project name and choose Deploy from the context menu.**

   After a significant pause, the Deployment Progress pane appears.

2. **Monitor progress in that pane until a message indicating success (as shown in Figure 21-25) or failure displays.**

3. **After the project is successfully deployed, click the Browser tab.**

   Figure 21-26 shows the appearance.

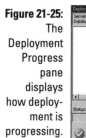

**Figure 21-25:**
The
Deployment
Progress
pane
displays
how deploy-
ment is
progressing.

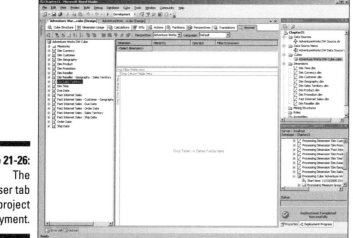

**Figure 21-26:**
The
Browser tab
after project
deployment.

4. **You can drag items from the left pane to the design surface.**

The designer gives you visual cues as to where you can drop items.

To create a simple display of sales by year by territory, follow these steps:

1. **Expand the Measures node in the left (metadata) pane.**
2. **Drag Sales Amount to the Drop Totals or Details Fields Here area.**
3. **Expand the DimSalesTerritory node.**
4. **Drag SalesTerritory Country to the Drop Row Fields Here area.**
5. **Expand the Dim Time and the DimTime.CalendarYear nodes.**
6. **Drag Calendar Year to the Drag Column Fields Here area.**

Figure 21-27 shows the appearance of the simple display of data.

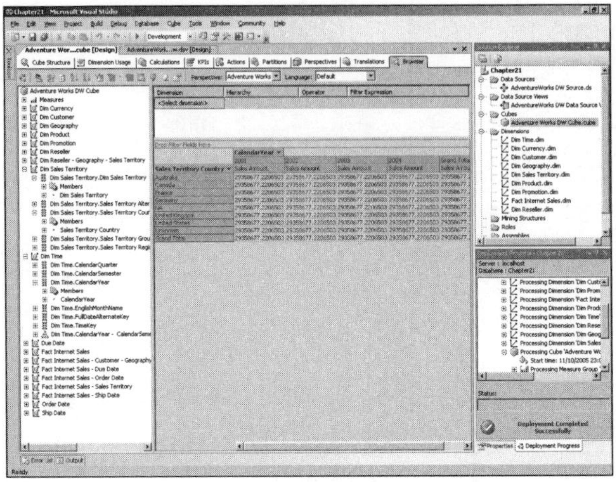

**Figure 21-27:**
A simple
analysis
created with
Analysis
Services.

In a real project, you would tidy formatting and so on. But this example gives you an impression of what you can do with Analysis Services projects.

# Data Mining

Data mining allows you to predict what is going to happen. For example, you can estimate which target group you can best send a product mailing to. You can also predict sales or other business performance by analyzing relationships between factors in your existing data.

Data mining in SQL Server 2005 supports the use of several complex mathematical algorithms. SQL Server 2005 Data Mining supports the following algorithms:

- ✔ Association
- ✔ Clustering
- ✔ Decision Trees
- ✔ Linear Regression
- ✔ Logistic Regression
- ✔ Naive Bayes
- ✔ Neural Network
- ✔ Sequence Clustering
- ✔ Time Series

Details of data mining and how to use the wizards that support it is beyond the scope of this chapter.

# Chapter 22

# Building Business Reports with Reporting Services

. . . . . . . . . . . . . . . . . . . . . . . . . . . . . . . . . . . . . . . . . . . . . . . .

## In This Chapter

▶ Finding out what you can do with Reporting Services

▶ Creating reports

▶ Viewing reports

▶ Managing reports

▶ Distributing reports to others

▶ Viewing reports with Report Builder

. . . . . . . . . . . . . . . . . . . . . . . . . . . . . . . . . . . . . . . . . . . . . . . .

*T*he third component of SQL Server 2005's Integrate, Analyze, Report paradigm is SQL Server 2005 Reporting Services. SQL Server 2005 Reporting Services builds on the functionality in SQL Server 2000 Reporting Services that was released in January 2004.

One of the key aims of business reporting is to make available to users up-to-date, relevant business information in a form that can be delivered or accessed in a convenient way. Some users need text (numeric) data. Others want graphical presentation of data. SQL Server Reporting Services can meet both needs.

SQL Server 2005 Reporting Services allows you, as a developer, to create business reports for end users such as managers, departmental heads, and individual information workers. You have a choice of delivery mechanism for reports that I discuss later in this chapter.

Used in that way, SQL Server 2005 has many similarities to SQL Server 2000 Reporting Services. However, SQL Server 2005 has a new tool, Report Builder, which is intended to allow end users to create their own ad hoc business reports. A developer needs to create the underlying report model by using the Business Intelligence Development Studio. The end user then creates, from the model, ad hoc reports.

# Overview of Reporting Services

SQL Server 2005 Reporting Services is a server-based product designed to produce a range of business reports.

SQL Server Reporting Services supports the following activities:

- ✔ **Report authoring:** Report Designer (part of Business Intelligence Development Studio), Report Model Designer (also part of BIDS) and Report Builder (an end user report design tool).

- ✔ **Report Deployment:** Report Designer and Report Model Builder (both part of Business Intelligence Development Studio).

- ✔ **Report management:** Report Manager (a browser-based management tool), SQL Server Management Studio.

- ✔ **Report delivery:** You can schedule the delivery of reports and can deliver reports by e-mail or to a fileshare.

You use Reporting Services to produce the following types of report:

- ✔ Tabular
- ✔ Matrix
- ✔ Chart
- ✔ Free-form

You can create reports by using the following types of data source:

- ✔ SQL Server data
- ✔ Other relational data, for example, Oracle
- ✔ XML data
- ✔ Multidimensional data from an Analysis Services cube

You have options to present reports in the following formats:

- ✔ HTML
- ✔ Excel
- ✔ PDF
- ✔ XML

Installing Reporting Services can be a complex process. To minimize problems, I suggest that, for testing, you set up Reporting Services on the same development machine as SQL Server 2005. Be sure to check the default configuration option for Reporting Services.

You must install Internet Information Services (IIS) before you install Reporting Services. During the System Configuration Check before installing SQL Server and Reporting Services, you're warned if IIS is missing, but you are allowed to continue with the SQL Server install.

You can register a Reporting Services server in the Registered Servers pane of SQL Server Management Studio. You can view information about the report server by right-clicking the report server in the Registered Servers pane and choosing Connect⇨Object Explorer.

A report server contains the metadata that define reports and how and when to deliver them. It also holds credentials for connecting to data sources used in reports.

## Replicating to a Report Server

You can replicate data to the Reporting Services server so that creating reports does not add load to your main server. The Report Server accesses data on the server containing replicated data and leaves resources on the main server uninterrupted by the sometimes heavy needs of retrieving data for Reporting Services reports.

## Database mirroring and database views

Another approach to creating a Reporting Services server is to use database mirroring to create a server that has a copy of the transaction database that is up-to-date almost to the second. You cannot report directly against a database mirror but you can create a database view on the database mirror and create reports against the database view. A *database view* is a read-only copy of a database at a specific point in time.

Combining a database mirror and database view provides a good way to have a reporting server that is not likely to be heavily loaded. If you anticipate that the Reporting Services server will be heavily loaded, you must consider how to cope with the occasional and temporary increased load on the machine when the original primary server fails and the database mirror server takes over that transaction load.

# Creating Reports

If you install only SQL Server 2005 on a development machine, Business Intelligence Development Studio (BIDS) is the tool you use to create Reporting Services reports. If you also install Visual Studio 2005, then the

Visual Studio 2005 shell incorporates BIDS and you can also create Reporting Services reports there too.

I show you how to use Business Intelligence Development Studio. The process is almost identical in Visual Studio 2005, assuming that SQL Server 2005 is installed on the same machine.

You can design a report in two ways: with the Report Wizard or from a blank report.

To create a Reporting Services report with the Report Wizard, follow these steps:

1. **Open Business Intelligence Development Studio (or Visual Studio 2005).**

2. **Choose File⇨New⇨Project.**

   The New Project dialog box opens.

3. **Select Business Intelligence Projects in the left pane. In the right pane, select Report Server Project Wizard (see Figure 22-1).**

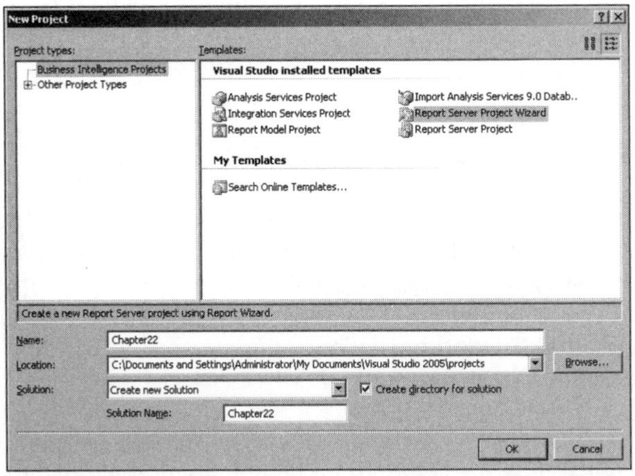

Figure 22-1:
Create a
Report
Project
Wizard
project and
name it.

Notice in the right pane the options for a Report Server Project. If you want to create a blank report project, choose that option.

4. **Click OK.**

   After a pause, the Welcome to the Report Wizard screen displays (see Figure 22-2). It lists the steps you follow when using the wizard.

5. **Click Next.**

   The Select the Data Source screen opens. You now need to create a data source.

**Figure 22-2:**
The
Welcome
screen for
the Report
Wizard.

6. **In the Name text box, enter** Using Adventureworks **as the name of the data source.**

7. **Click the Edit button.**

The Connection Properties dialog box opens (see Figure 22-3).

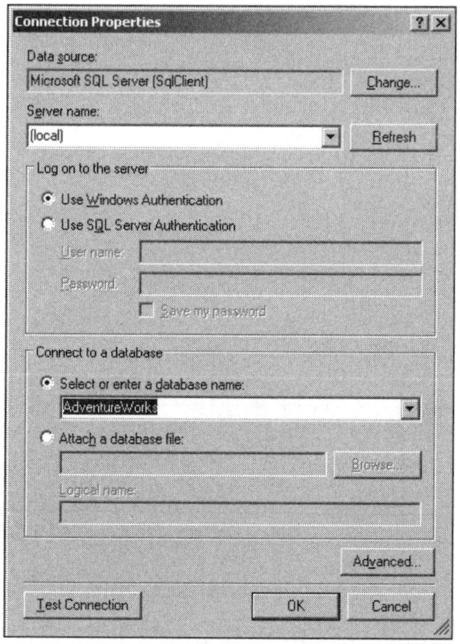

**Figure 22-3:**
The
Connection
Properties
dialog box.

8. **Type** (local) **(including the parentheses) in the Server Name drop-down menu. If you're connecting remotely to an instance of SQL Server, replace** (local) **with the server name (for a default instance) or** *serverName\instanceName* **for a named instance. In the Select or Type a Server Name drop-down menu, select the Adventureworks option.**

9. **Click the Test Connection button. When the connection succeeds, click OK to dismiss the message telling you that you connected successfully.**

10. **Click OK to return to the Select the Data Source screen.**

   It looks like Figure 22-4.

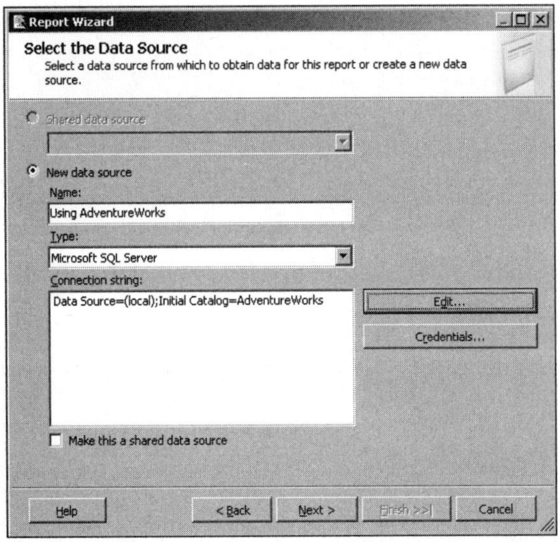

**Figure 22-4:** The Select the Data Source screen.

11. **Click Next.**

   The Design the Query screen displays, as shown in Figure 22-5.

   You have two options:

   Write or paste a T-SQL query in the Query String text box: Click Next and skip to Step 24.

   Design a query visually: Continue with Step 12.

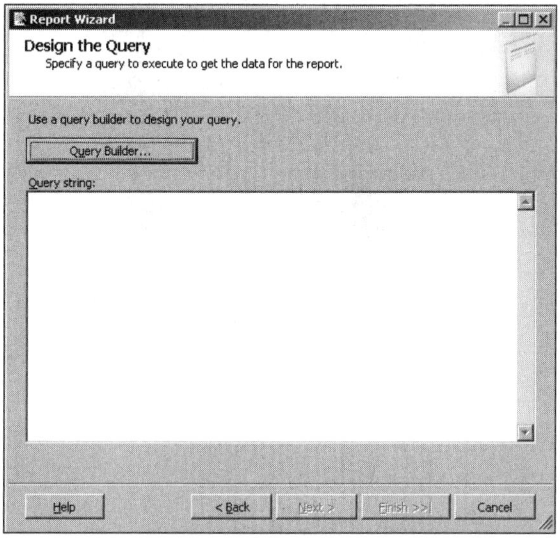

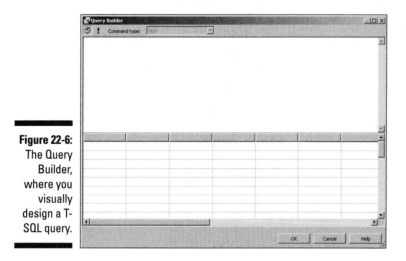

**Figure 22-5:**
The Design
the Query
screen.

12. **Click the Query Builder button to design a query visually.**

    The Query Builder opens, as shown in Figure 22-6.

**Figure 22-6:**
The Query
Builder,
where you
visually
design a T-
SQL query.

13. **Click the button to the left of the exclamation mark in the top-left corner of the Query Builder.**

    The visual design tools appear, as shown in Figure 22-7.

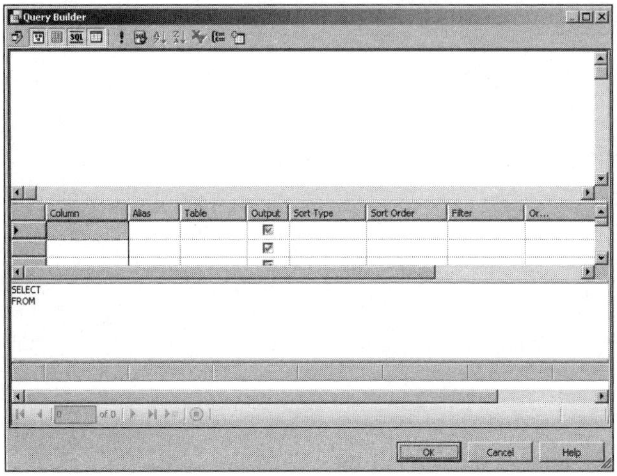

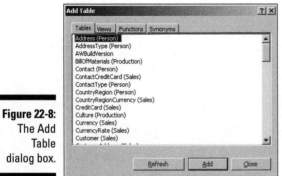

**Figure 22-7:** The Query Builder with visual design tools visible.

14. **Maximize the Query Builder so that you can get a good view of all the tools.**

15. **In the top blank area, right-click and select Add Table from the context menu.**

    The Add Table dialog box opens, as shown in Figure 22-8.

**Figure 22-8:** The Add Table dialog box.

16. **Select each of these tables and click Add. After you add all tables, click Close in the Add Tables dialog box.**

- Customer
- SalesTerritory
- CustomerAddress
- SalesOrderHeader
- Address
- StateProvince

17. In the `Customer` table, select the following check boxes: `CustomerID` and `TerritoryID`.

18. In the `SalesTerritory` table, select the following check boxes: `TerritoryID`, `Name`, `Group`, `SalesYTD`, and `CostYTD`.

19. In the `CustomerAddress` table, select the following check boxes: `CustomerID` and `AddressID`.

20. In the `SalesOrderHeader` table, select the following check boxes: `SalesOrderID`, `OrderDate`, `TerritoryID`, `CustomerID`, and `TotalDue`.

21. In the `Address` table, select the following check boxes: `AddressID`, `StateProvinceID`, and `City`.

22. In the `StateProvince` table, select the following check boxes: `StateProvinceID` and `Name`.

The appearance is similar to Figure 22-9. I repositioned the shapes representing the tables to help you see the relationships among the tables. Notice that a T-SQL statement is created automatically from the tables and columns you selected.

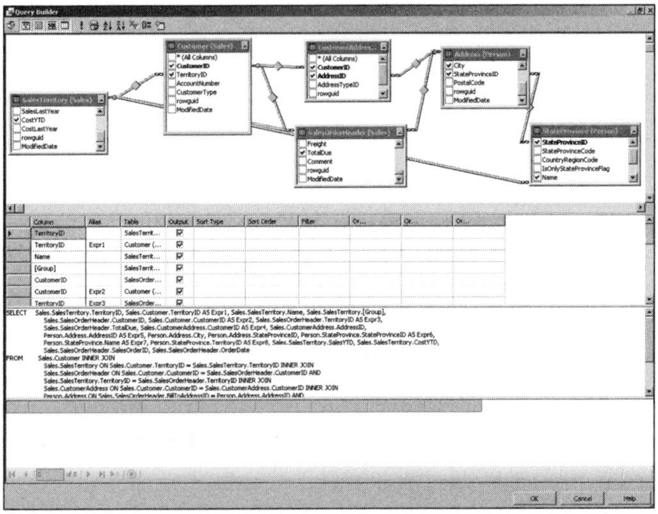

**Figure 22-9:**
The Query Builder after creating a query.

23. **Click OK; when you return to the Design the Query screen, click Next.**

24. **On the Select the Report Type screen, select Tabular and click Next.**

25. **On the Design the Table screen, select Group and click the Page button. Select Name (it's territory name) and click the Group button. Select City, CustomerID, SalesYTD, and CostYTD and click Details.**

26. **Click Next.**

27. **On the Choose Table Layout screen, select Stepped and click Next.**

28. **On the Choose the Table Style screen, select Corporate. Click Next.**

29. **On the Completing the Wizard screen, name the report** Chapter 22 Sample Report. **Check the Display Preview check box. Click Finish.**

    After a delay, you see an appearance similar to Figure 22-10. The windows may not be similarly laid out depending on your Business Intelligence Development Studio preferences.

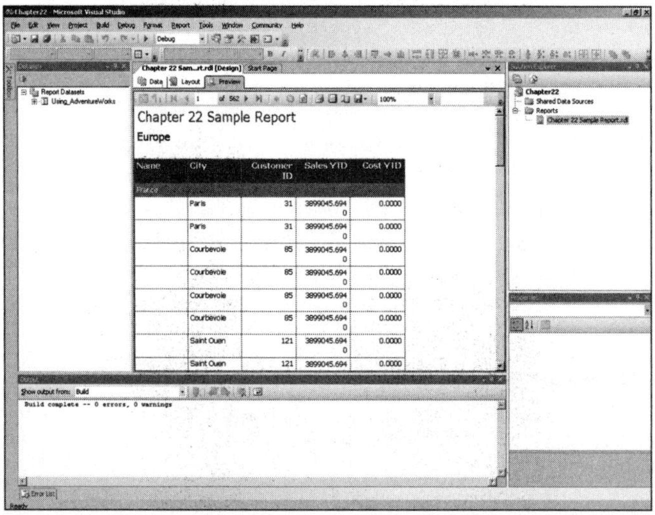

**Figure 22-10:** Previewing a report created with the Report Wizard.

You can see that the `SalesYTD` and `CostYTD` columns have too many decimal places.

30. **Click the Layout tab.**

    The Layout tab displays.

31. **Select the cell below `SalesYTD` and `CostYTD` by clicking the first and Ctrl+clicking to select the second. In the Properties pane, find the `Format` property and give it a value of `c` to indicate currency.**

32. **Drag the right edge of the design surface a little to the right to allow you to increase column width.**

33. **Click above `CostYTD` and drag the column edge slightly to the right.**

    The column width increases.

34. **Click above `SalesYTD` and drag the column edge slightly to the right.**

    The column width increases.

35. **Click the Preview tab and the appearance is similar to Figure 22-11.**

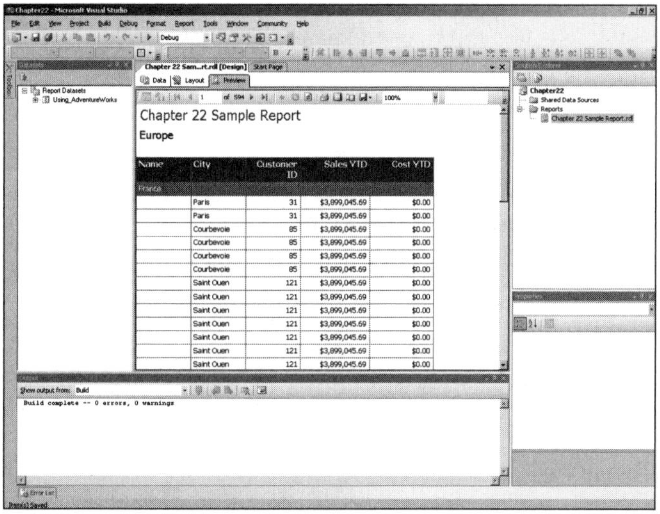

**Figure 22-11:**
Sales
shown as
currency
and column
widths
increased.

36. **To save your report, choose File⇨Save All.**

On the Layout tab, you can alter the appearance of text, reposition items on the page, and so on. This example is simply to give you an indication of how you might use the Report Wizard.

After you design a report to give you an appearance that you're satisfied with, you deploy the report. To deploy a report, you need to specify where it is going to be deployed and then deploy it.

To specify where a project is going to be deployed, follow these steps:

1. **In the Solution Explorer, right-click the Chapter 22 at the top (not the Chapter 22 Sample Report.rdl node) and select Properties.**

    The Chapter22 Property Pages dialog box opens, as shown in Figure 22-12.

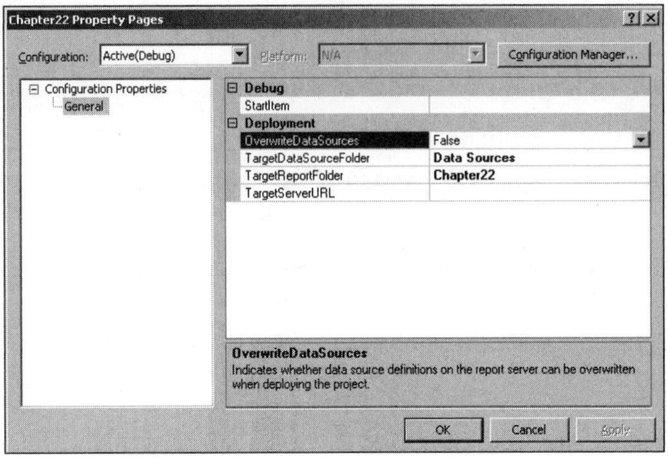

**Figure 22-12:**
The
Property
Pages
dialog box.

2. **If you're deploying locally, enter** http://localhost/ReportServer **as the value of the `TargetServerURL` property.**

3. **Click OK to confirm the changes in deployment properties.**

To deploy the report, right-click Chapter 22 in the Solution Explorer and choose Deploy from the context menu that appears. In the Output window, you see a message indicating that deployment has started and then completed successfully.

# Viewing Reports

After you create some reports, you can view them by using the Report Manager. To open Report Manager, follow these steps:

1. **Open Internet Explorer.**

2. **Type the following URL in the address bar: http://localhost/Reports. If you're attempting to access a remote Reporting Services server, substitute the server name for localhost in the URL.**

3. **Press the Enter key.**

   The Report Manager opens after a delay and displays a list of reports deployed on the server (see Figure 22-13).

**Figure 22-13:**
The Report
Manager.

# Managing Reports

SQL Server 2005 Reporting Services offers you two tools to manage reports:
through Report Manager and SQL Server Management Studio.

## Managing in Report Manager

Report Manager is a browser-based tool that displays reports according to
the permissions granted to a user. If you are an administrator, you can see all
reports on a report server and adjust their properties.

You can grant appropriate properties to individual users or groups of users.
For example, a group called Developers may have access to a Test Reports
folder, which end users cannot see.

## Managing in SQL Server Management Studio

In the Registered Servers pane of SQL Server Management Studio, you can register Reporting Services instances. You can view and manage any registered Reporting Services instance in the Object Explorer.

## Distributing reports to those who need them

You can use Reporting Services to distribute reports in several ways. A subscription to a report (or group of reports) consists of the following parts:

- ✔ A report that can run unattended. Typically, a report server stores the credentials.
- ✔ A delivery method or location such as e-mail or a file share.
- ✔ A rendering extension to produce the report in the desired output format.
- ✔ Conditions for processing the report — for example, a scheduled time or a specified event.
- ✔ Parameters to use when the report runs.

### Scheduled reports

Scheduled reports are distributed at scheduled times. Scheduled reports on a Reporting Services report server use the SQL Server Agent service. If you plan to use scheduled reports, be careful to ensure that SQL Server Agent is set to start automatically. If you don't do that and the Reporting Services restarts, you can expect that the SQL Server Agent service won't start and your users won't receive any scheduled reports.

### E-mailing reports

You can use e-mail in two ways. You can send reports to users. Or you can e-mail users a URL to access a desired version of the report.

## Report Definition Language

The Report Designer in Business Intelligence Development Studio gives you a design surface to specify data sources and create the visual appearance of reports. Behind the scenes, a Report Definition Language (RDL) file is created.

When you deploy a report from Business Intelligence Development Studio, an RDL file is deployed to the Reporting Services server. The RDL file contains information about the data source(s) for the report, together with layout information.

The version of RDL for SQL Server 2005 is different from the version of RDL used in Reporting Services 2000. A Reporting Services 2000 server is unable to run the RDL for SQL Server 2005.

# Report Builder

Report Builder is a tool new in SQL Server 2005. Report Builder allows information workers to create Reporting Services reports by using a graphical interface that is significantly simpler than the Business Intelligence Development Studio.

Before an information worker can create a report in Report Builder, a developer — you — must create a *report model* in Business Intelligence Development Studio.

You create a report model in Business Intelligence Development Studio.

To create a Report Model project, follow these steps:

1. **Open Business Intelligence Development Studio.**

2. **Choose File➪New➪Project.**

   The New Project dialog box opens.

3. **Select Business Intelligence Projects in the left pane.**

4. **Select Report Model Project in the right pane (see Figure 22-14).**

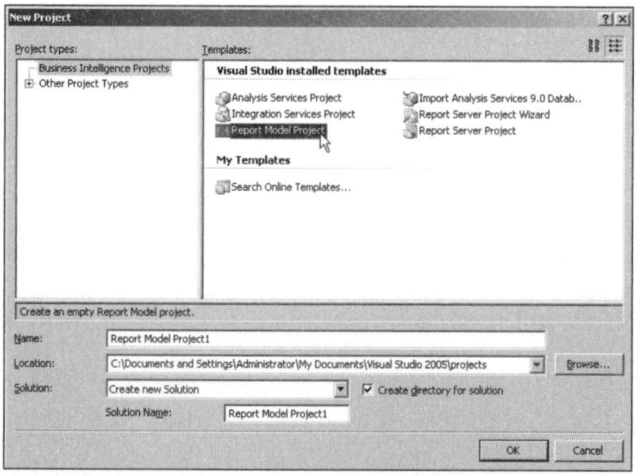

**Figure 22-14:** Selecting the Report Model Project template in BIDS.

You then go on to select business data that the end user needs to design a report. The Visual Studio solution that you create is deployed to a Reporting Service server. Space constraints prevent me showing a fully worked example.

Users use Report Manager to access the Report Server. From Report Manager, the user clicks to download, install, and run Report Builder (see Figure 22-15). In Report Builder, the information worker then manipulates a user-friendly representation of the report model to create table, matrix, or chart reports.

When you choose from the available report models, the Report Builder displays a design surface. You can drag items from the Explorer to the design surface to specify an *ad hoc* report (see Figure 22-16). To view the report, click the Run Report button and the report is displayed.

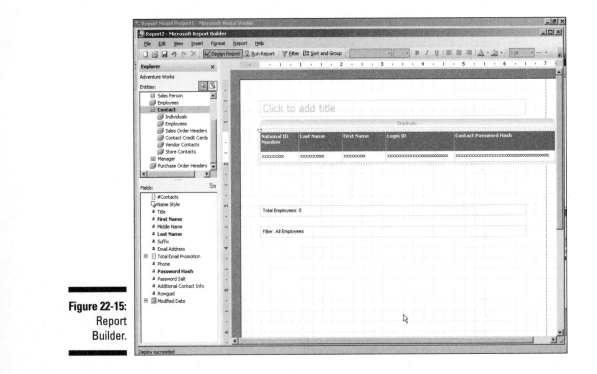

**Figure 22-15:**
Report
Builder.

# Report Viewer Controls

In the previous sections, I described server-based reporting functionality. Microsoft has added, in Visual Studio 2005, reporting functionality based on the client. You don't need a connection to a Reporting Services server to view a report.

The ReportViewer Controls are provided if you have Visual Studio 2005. You use the ReportViewer controls in a Visual Studio Windows Forms solution. These controls are not included with Business Intelligence Development Studio.

# Part VII
# The Part of Tens

The 5th Wave     By Rich Tennant

"We're here to clean the code."

# In this part . . .

*I*n the confines of this book, I can cover only so much of what you might want to know about SQL Server 2005. So in this part, I show you resources where you can find more information (Chapter 23) and third-party tools that you can use with SQL Server 2005 (Chapter 24).

# Chapter 23

# Ten Sources of Information on SQL Server 2005

. . . . . . . . . . . . . . . . . . . . . . . . . . . . . . . . . . . . . . . . . . . . . . . .

*O*ne of the biggest problems in getting fully to grips with SQL Server 2005 is the sheer size of the suite of programs. To say SQL Server is enormous doesn't do it justice. SQL Server 2005 consists of several components — the database engine, Integration Services, and Analysis Services to name a few — that are enormous by themselves.

In this chapter, I describe some of the many sources where you can find additional information about SQL Server 2005.

## Books Online

Books Online is the official Microsoft documentation for SQL Server 2005. It is often affectionately referred to as *BOL*. Despite its name, you'll likely use it offline.

If you are used to SQL Server 2000 Books Online, you will notice huge changes in Books Online for SQL Server 2005. The interface has been completely redesigned. At first, this can make finding information difficult.

You can install Books Online separately from the rest of SQL Server 2005. It's located at `www.microsoft.com/technet/prodtechnol/sql/2005/ downloads/books.msp`. If it's not there, do a Google search for **SQL Server 2005 Books Online site:microsoft.com** and you have a good chance of finding it.

In the Index pane and Contents pane of BOL, you can filter content by major topics such as Integration Services and Reporting Services. Filtering allows you to find the information you want.

The Search functionality has been redesigned. The toolbar has a Search button. You can filter searches by technology and content type.

If you also install Visual Studio 2005 and MSDN, you find all BOL content is added to MSDN. Using the filters is a huge help if you want to reduce the chance of being overwhelmed with information.

# The Public Newsgroups

SQL Server newsgroups are a great place to get help with specific problems.

SQL Server has a broad range of public newsgroups where you can get support from Microsoft MVPs, Microsoft staff, and other users of SQL Server.

The news server is `msnews.microsoft.com`. Use a newsreader such as Outlook Express, Thunderbird, or Agent to access the SQL Server newsgroups. The SQL Server newsgroups are at microsoft.public.sqlserver.*.

# Microsoft Forums

Microsoft, shortly before this book was finalized, created several forums that allow users to ask questions about SQL Server 2005.

At the time of writing, the forums are in beta. To access them, go to `forums.microsoft.com/msdn/default.aspx?ForumGroupID=19`.

If the link has changed by the time you read this, try `forums.microsoft.com/msdn/default.aspx` or `http://forums.microsoft.com`. You can likely find a link to the SQL Server forums.

# The SQL Server 2005 Web Site

Microsoft's main Web site for information about SQL Server 2005 is at `www.microsoft.com/sql/2005/default.mspx`. This provides overview information with links to many sources of more detailed information including technical white papers.

If the preceding URL doesn't work by the time you read this, try
`www.microsoft.com/sql/`. You should be able to find SQL Server 2005
information from there.

# The SQL Server Developer Center

The SQL Server Developer Center at `msdn.microsoft.com/sql/` contains
a lot of useful information for anyone carrying out development tasks on SQL
Server 2005.

# The Business Intelligence Site

A dedicated SQL Server 2005 Business Intelligence Web site is at
`www.microsoft.com/sql/bi/default.mspx`. You can find useful information about SQL Server Integration Services, SQL Server Analysis Services,
and SQL Server Reporting Services.

# The Integration Services Developer Center

As I mention earlier, SQL Server Integration Services is an extensive program. It
has its own Developer Center at `msdn.microsoft.com/SQL/sqlwarehouse/`
`SSIS/default.aspx`. You can find technical white papers, information
about Webcasts, blogs, and a host of other information to help you with
Integration Services development.

# The Reporting Services Web Site

The Reporting Services Web site has information about SQL Server 2000 and
SQL Server 2005 Reporting Services. It's at `www.microsoft.com/sql/`
`reporting/default.mspx`.

You can find downloads of sample reports, service packs, white papers, and a
range of other relevant information.

# Channel 9

Channel 9, `channel9.msdn.com`, has a host of interesting information on a range of Microsoft products. There are a few videos that include interviews with SQL Server 2005 team members.

Finding content on Channel 9 can be difficult. Often the best way to find specific topics is to use the Google site search feature.

# Other Web Sites

A huge number of Web sites are available on SQL Server 2005. I could attempt to list some here. Instead I'm recommending one of the best tools for finding additional information about SQL Server 2005: Google.com.

If you want to find information on any SQL Server 2005 topic, a Google search of the form **SQL Server 2005 *topic words* site:microsoft.com** is often the quickest and most effective way to find any information about SQL Server 2005 on the Microsoft site.

Of course a simple **SQL Server 2005 Integration Services** search term in Google can turn up some very interesting material.

If you are not familiar with Google syntax for searches, use the Advanced Search option.

Remember that you can search Usenet newsgroups by clicking the Groups link on the Google home page.

# Chapter 24

# Products that Work with SQL Server 2005

● ● ● ● ● ● ● ● ● ● ● ● ● ● ● ● ● ● ● ● ● ● ● ● ● ● ● ● ● ● ● ● ● ● ● ● ● ● ● ● ● ● ● ● ● ●

*A*t the time I am writing this chapter, SQL Server 2005 has not yet been released. Therefore I can mention useful products only in a preliminary way. Many products intended to work with SQL Server 2005 won't be released in final versions until after SQL Server 2005 is released. So, check with third-party Web sites for the situation that is current at the time you read this.

Other useful products will be made available as third-party developers see the potential for synergy with the SQL Server 2005 platform. Some of these are likely to be described on the SQL Server 2005 Web sites I mention in Chapter 23.

## Visual Studio 2005

Visual Studio 2005 and Business Intelligence Development Studio use the same shell. If you install Visual Studio 2005 on the same machine that you install Business Intelligence Development Studio, you will find that business intelligence project templates are seamlessly added to Visual Studio.

If you want to create Windows or Web solutions that contain the new Report Viewer controls, you need Visual Studio 2005. Similarly, to use SQL Server Management Objects, Replication Management Objects, and other new APIs (Application Programming Interface) in SQL Server 2005 you create projects (often Windows Forms projects) in Visual Studio 2005.

# Microsoft Office InfoPath 2003

InfoPath is new in Office 2003 Professional Enterprise Edition. It is a forms design and completion tool. Its benefits include submitting data as XML. Data sources and destinations include SQL Server and Microsoft Access.

You can find further information on InfoPath 2003 at `www.microsoft.com/office/infopath/prodinfo/default.mspx`.

# Red-Gate Tools

Red-Gate (at `www.red-gate.com/`) is well known as a manufacturer of products for SQL Server 2000. Versions of the following software for SQL Server 2005 are expected to be available by the time this book is in print:

✔ **SQL Compare:** Automates the comparison and synchronization of SQL Server database schemas.

✔ **SQL Data Compare:** Automates the comparison and synchronization of data in SQL Server databases.

✔ **SQL Packager:** Assists in deploying SQL Server databases, including as part of a .NET application.

✔ **SQL Backup:** Creates compressed and encrypted SQL Server backups.

✔ **DTS Compare:** Compares DTS (Data Transformation Services) 2000 on SQL Server instances. An updated version for Integration Services is expected.

# Quest Software

Quest Software (at `www.quest.com/sql%5Fserver/`) produces tools that assist with performance, availability, and code quality and optimization for SQL Server. Updates for SQL Server 2005 of the following products are expected:

✔ **TOAD for SQL Server:** Provides a development environment for creating and debugging T-SQL code.

✔ **Benchmark Factory:** Allows you to load test SQL Server.

✔ **DataFactory:** Produces test data for use with SQL Server.

  ✔ **Quest Central for SQL Server:** A data management workbench for DBAs (database administrators).

  ✔ **Spotlight on SQL Server:** Diagnoses SQL Server problems in real time.

  ✔ **LiteSpeed for SQL Server:** Backup and recovery software for SQL Server.

# PromptSQL

The Query pane in SQL Server Management Studio does not provide Intellisense. PromptSQL (`www.promptsql.com/`) provides Intellisense for T-SQL code. Intellisense suggests context-sensitive completion for code statements. A version of PromptSQL has been available for SQL Server 2000 Query Analyzer for some time. I expect a version for SQL Server 2005 to by available by the time you read this.

# Index

# Notes

# Notes

## USINESS, CAREERS & PERSONAL FINANCE

**Grant Writing For Dummies**
0-7645-5307-0

**Home Buying For Dummies** (2nd Edition)
0-7645-5331-3 *†

**Also available:**

- Accounting For Dummies †
  0-7645-5314-3
- Business Plans Kit For Dummies †
  0-7645-5365-8
- Cover Letters For Dummies
  0-7645-5224-4
- Frugal Living For Dummies
  0-7645-5403-4
- Leadership For Dummies
  0-7645-5176-0
- Managing For Dummies
  0-7645-1771-6

- Marketing For Dummies
  0-7645-5600-2
- Personal Finance For Dummies *
  0-7645-2590-5
- Project Management For Dummies
  0-7645-5283-X
- Resumes For Dummies †
  0-7645-5471-9
- Selling For Dummies
  0-7645-5363-1
- Small Business Kit For Dummies *†
  0-7645-5093-4

## OME & BUSINESS COMPUTER BASICS

**Windows XP For Dummies**
0-7645-4074-2

**Excel 2003 All-in-One Desk Reference For Dummies**
0-7645-3758-X

**Also available:**

- ACT! 6 For Dummies
  0-7645-2645-6
- iLife '04 All-in-One Desk Reference
  For Dummies
  0-7645-7347-0
- iPAQ For Dummies
  0-7645-6769-1
- Mac OS X Panther Timesaving
  Techniques For Dummies
  0-7645-5812-9
- Macs For Dummies
  0-7645-5656-8

- Microsoft Money 2004 For Dummies
  0-7645-4195-1
- Office 2003 All-in-One Desk Reference
  For Dummies
  0-7645-3883-7
- Outlook 2003 For Dummies
  0-7645-3759-8
- PCs For Dummies
  0-7645-4074-2
- TiVo For Dummies
  0-7645-6923-6
- Upgrading and Fixing PCs For Dummies
  0-7645-1665-5
- Windows XP Timesaving Techniques
  For Dummies
  0-7645-3748-2

## OOD, HOME, GARDEN, HOBBIES, MUSIC & PETS

**Feng Shui For Dummies**
0-7645-5295-3

**Poker For Dummies**
0-7645-5232-5

**Also available:**

- Bass Guitar For Dummies
  0-7645-2487-9
- Diabetes Cookbook For Dummies
  0-7645-5230-9
- Gardening For Dummies *
  0-7645-5130-2
- Guitar For Dummies
  0-7645-5106-X
- Holiday Decorating For Dummies
  0-7645-2570-0
- Home Improvement All-in-One
  For Dummies
  0-7645-5680-0

- Knitting For Dummies
  0-7645-5395-X
- Piano For Dummies
  0-7645-5105-1
- Puppies For Dummies
  0-7645-5255-4
- Scrapbooking For Dummies
  0-7645-7208-3
- Senior Dogs For Dummies
  0-7645-5818-8
- Singing For Dummies
  0-7645-2475-5
- 30-Minute Meals For Dummies
  0-7645-2589-1

## NTERNET & DIGITAL MEDIA

**Digital Photography For Dummies**
0-7645-1664-7

**Starting an eBay Business For Dummies**
0-7645-6924-4

**Also available:**

- 2005 Online Shopping Directory
  For Dummies
  0-7645-7495-7
- CD & DVD Recording For Dummies
  0-7645-5956-7
- eBay For Dummies
  0-7645-5654-1
- Fighting Spam For Dummies
  0-7645-5965-6
- Genealogy Online For Dummies
  0-7645-5964-8
- Google For Dummies
  0-7645-4420-9

- Home Recording For Musicians
  For Dummies
  0-7645-1634-5
- The Internet For Dummies
  0-7645-4173-0
- iPod & iTunes For Dummies
  0-7645-7772-7
- Preventing Identity Theft For Dummies
  0-7645-7336-5
- Pro Tools All-in-One Desk Reference
  For Dummies
  0-7645-5714-9
- Roxio Easy Media Creator For Dummies
  0-7645-7131-1

* Separate Canadian edition also available
† Separate U.K. edition also available

Available wherever books are sold. For more information or to order direct: U.S. customers visit www.dummies.com or call 1-877-762-2974.
U.K. customers visit www.wileyeurope.com or call 0800 243407. Canadian customers visit www.wiley.ca or call 1-800-567-4797.

**WILEY**

## SPORTS, FITNESS, PARENTING, RELIGION & SPIRITUALITY

0-7645-5146-9

0-7645-5418-2

**Also available:**
- Adoption For Dummies
  0-7645-5488-3
- Basketball For Dummies
  0-7645-5248-1
- The Bible For Dummies
  0-7645-5296-1
- Buddhism For Dummies
  0-7645-5359-3
- Catholicism For Dummies
  0-7645-5391-7
- Hockey For Dummies
  0-7645-5228-7

- Judaism For Dummies
  0-7645-5299-6
- Martial Arts For Dummies
  0-7645-5358-5
- Pilates For Dummies
  0-7645-5397-6
- Religion For Dummies
  0-7645-5264-3
- Teaching Kids to Read For Dummies
  0-7645-4043-2
- Weight Training For Dummies
  0-7645-5168-X
- Yoga For Dummies
  0-7645-5117-5

## TRAVEL

0-7645-5438-7

0-7645-5453-0

**Also available:**
- Alaska For Dummies
  0-7645-1761-9
- Arizona For Dummies
  0-7645-6938-4
- Cancún and the Yucatán For Dummies
  0-7645-2437-2
- Cruise Vacations For Dummies
  0-7645-6941-4
- Europe For Dummies
  0-7645-5456-5
- Ireland For Dummies
  0-7645-5455-7

- Las Vegas For Dummies
  0-7645-5448-4
- London For Dummies
  0-7645-4277-X
- New York City For Dummies
  0-7645-6945-7
- Paris For Dummies
  0-7645-5494-8
- RV Vacations For Dummies
  0-7645-5443-3
- Walt Disney World & Orlando For Dummi
  0-7645-6943-0

## GRAPHICS, DESIGN & WEB DEVELOPMENT

0-7645-4345-8

0-7645-5589-8

**Also available:**
- Adobe Acrobat 6 PDF For Dummies
  0-7645-3760-1
- Building a Web Site For Dummies
  0-7645-7144-3
- Dreamweaver MX 2004 For Dummies
  0-7645-4342-3
- FrontPage 2003 For Dummies
  0-7645-3882-9
- HTML 4 For Dummies
  0-7645-1995-6
- Illustrator CS For Dummies
  0-7645-4084-X

- Macromedia Flash MX 2004 For Dummi
  0-7645-4358-X
- Photoshop 7 All-in-One Desk Reference For Dummies
  0-7645-1667-1
- Photoshop CS Timesaving Technique For Dummies
  0-7645-6782-9
- PHP 5 For Dummies
  0-7645-4166-8
- PowerPoint 2003 For Dummies
  0-7645-3908-6
- QuarkXPress 6 For Dummies
  0-7645-2593-X

## NETWORKING, SECURITY, PROGRAMMING & DATABASES

0-7645-6852-3

0-7645-5784-X

**Also available:**
- A+ Certification For Dummies
  0-7645-4187-0
- Access 2003 All-in-One Desk Reference For Dummies
  0-7645-3988-4
- Beginning Programming For Dummies
  0-7645-4997-9
- C For Dummies
  0-7645-7068-4
- Firewalls For Dummies
  0-7645-4048-3
- Home Networking For Dummies
  0-7645-42796

- Network Security For Dummies
  0-7645-1679-5
- Networking For Dummies
  0-7645-1677-9
- TCP/IP For Dummies
  0-7645-1760-0
- VBA For Dummies
  0-7645-3989-2
- Wireless All In-One Desk Reference For Dummies
  0-7645-7496-5
- Wireless Home Networking For Dummi
  0-7645-3910-8

## ALTH & SELF-HELP

0-7645-6820-5 *†        0-7645-2566-2

**Also available:**

- Alzheimer's For Dummies
  0-7645-3899-3
- Asthma For Dummies
  0-7645-4233-8
- Controlling Cholesterol For Dummies
  0-7645-5440-9
- Depression For Dummies
  0-7645-3900-0
- Dieting For Dummies
  0-7645-4149-8
- Fertility For Dummies
  0-7645-2549-2

- Fibromyalgia For Dummies
  0-7645-5441-7
- Improving Your Memory For Dummies
  0-7645-5435-2
- Pregnancy For Dummies †
  0-7645-4483-7
- Quitting Smoking For Dummies
  0-7645-2629-4
- Relationships For Dummies
  0-7645-5384-4
- Thyroid For Dummies
  0-7645-5385-2

## UCATION, HISTORY, REFERENCE & TEST PREPARATION

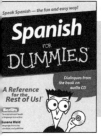 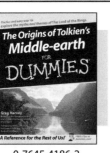

0-7645-5194-9        0-7645-4186-2

**Also available:**

- Algebra For Dummies
  0-7645-5325-9
- British History For Dummies
  0-7645-7021-8
- Calculus For Dummies
  0-7645-2498-4
- English Grammar For Dummies
  0-7645-5322-4
- Forensics For Dummies
  0-7645-5580-4
- The GMAT For Dummies
  0-7645-5251-1
- Inglés Para Dummies
  0-7645-5427-1

- Italian For Dummies
  0-7645-5196-5
- Latin For Dummies
  0-7645-5431-X
- Lewis & Clark For Dummies
  0-7645-2545-X
- Research Papers For Dummies
  0-7645-5426-3
- The SAT I For Dummies
  0-7645-7193-1
- Science Fair Projects For Dummies
  0-7645-5460-3
- U.S. History For Dummies
  0-7645-5249-X

---

# Get smart @ dummies.com®

- **Find a full list of Dummies titles**
- **Look into loads of FREE on-site articles**
- **Sign up for FREE eTips e-mailed to you weekly**
- **See what other products carry the Dummies name**
- **Shop directly from the Dummies bookstore**
- **Enter to win new prizes every month!**